Misfire

The Tragic Failure of the M16 in Vietnam

BOB ORKAND
and
LYMAN DURYEA

STACKPOLE
BOOKS

Guilford, Connecticut

Published by Stackpole Books
An imprint of The Rowman & Littlefield Publishing Group, Inc.
4501 Forbes Blvd., Ste. 200
Lanham, MD 20706
www.rowman.com

Distributed by NATIONAL BOOK NETWORK
800-462-6420

British Library Cataloguing in Publication Information available

Library of Congress Cataloging-in-Publication Data available

Names: Orkand, Bob, author. | Duryea, Lyman, author.
Title: Misfire : the tragic failure of the M16 in Vietnam / Bob Orkand and
    Lyman Duryea.
Other titles: Tragic failure of the M16 in Vietnam
Description: Guilford, Connecticut : Stackpole Books, an imprint of The
    Rowman & Littlefield Publishing Group, Inc., [2019] | Includes
    bibliographical references and index.
Identifiers: LCCN 2019001930| ISBN 9780811737968 (cloth : alk. paper) | ISBN
    9780811767958 (electronic)
Subjects: LCSH: M-16 rifle—History. | Vietnam War, 1961-1975—Equipment and
    supplies.
Classification: LCC UD395.M2 O74 2019 | DDC 623.4/425—dc23 LC record
    available at https://lccn.loc.gov/2019001930

♾ ™ The paper used in this publication meets the minimum requirements of American
National Standard for Information Sciences—Permanence of Paper for Printed Library
Materials, ANSI/NISO Z39.48–1992.

Printed in the United States of America

In Memory of Lyman "Chan" Duryea
Colonel, United States Army, Infantry (Retired)
May 25, 1938–April 17, 2019

CONTENTS

INTRODUCTION

Bob Orkand and Lyman "Chan" Duryea

To a large extent, the flawed decision-making that accompanied the introduction of the M16 rifle into combat operations by U.S. Army and
Marine units in South Vietnam, beginning in 1965, was symptomatic of similar
questionable decision-making that became the tragedy of the war in Vietnam,
in terms of its ultimately disappointing outcome.

The authors of this book—both combat infantry officers in Vietnam with
the 1st Cavalry Division (Airmobile)—had first hand experience leading men
in battle armed with the troubled M16 rifle. Lyman (Chan) Duryea, a West
Point graduate with a doctor of philosophy degree in military history from
Temple University, commanded a rifle company of the 2nd Battalion (Airmobile), 7th Cavalry in 1966–1967. "My first casualty in Vietnam," he recalls,
"was one of my men being killed by return fire at night when his M16 jammed
after firing one round at a group of approaching NVA (North Vietnamese
Army) soldiers."

On a second tour in Vietnam, Duryea served as the district senior advisor
of Phong Dien District in Can Tho Province, in the Mekong Delta.

Bob Orkand, drafted into the Army during his senior year at Columbia
University, served simultaneously in 1967–1968 as executive officer and operations officer of the 1st Battalion (Airmobile), 7th Cavalry, holding down both
positions because of casualties.

On an earlier assignment in Vietnam, Orkand was spokesman for the
Saigon-based U.S. Army Headquarters Area Command, which had responsibility for defending against all acts of terrorism in the South Vietnamese capital
through its 716th Military Police Battalion.

1

The 1st Cav, as the division was commonly called, was the Army's first airmobile division, arriving in Vietnam in August 1965. Because of its unprecedented helicopter-borne mobility, the division was capable of being shifted rapidly to newly arisen battlefield hotspots, in the process sustaining more casualties—5,444 of its soldiers killed in action, 26,592 wounded in action—than any other Army division.

As a newly promoted captain, Duryea was assigned from 1964 until his first posting to Vietnam in 1966 to the U.S. Army Infantry Board at Fort Benning, Georgia, home of the Infantry School and Center. As a test officer, he helped evaluate the performance of the then-experimental XM16E1 rifle under combat conditions (including night parachute jumps), compared with the Army's then-standard rifle, the M14.

Duryea's reports analyzing test results and the Infantry Board's conclusions are discussed in depth in Chapter 4.

As deputy director of the Infantry School's Weapons Department in 1971, Orkand headed a task force dispatched to Fort Lewis, Washington, to investigate why soldiers who had undergone advanced infantry training at that post were shooting poorly in Vietnam with their M16 rifles, compared with trainees from other basic training centers. The team's findings (faulty and inadequate training) led to immediate revisions in marksmanship training procedures at all Army training installations.

As the co-authors of this book began researching the litany of errors at virtually every level of command—both civilian and military—that led to the flawed introduction of the M16 rifle into the Vietnam War, it soon became apparent that the garbled decision-making with respect to the XM16E1/M16 rifle ran parallel to the multitude of similar judgmental errors that the chain of command—from the Oval Office of the White House, through the Pentagon, to headquarters of the Military Assistance Command Vietnam in Saigon—subsequently at Tan Son Nhut Airbase outside Saigon—had made with respect to the overall conduct of the Vietnam War.

In other words, the misfires that involved the M16 rifle in Vietnam were often symptomatic of other high-level judgmental errors that characterized many of the strategic and tactical decisions that doomed the Vietnam War effort to its eventual unfortunate—albeit avoidable—conclusion.

Thus, the narrative of the flawed introduction of the M16 rifle into combat operations in Vietnam is equally the tale of a well-intentioned but nevertheless misguided campaign by a global superpower, resulting in the loss of more than 58,300 American lives in the rice paddies and jungles of Southeast Asia.

And so our account of the tragedy of Vietnam and the misfiring M16 rifle commences on a cold, snowy, blustery Friday morning in Washington, D.C. It's January 20, 1961, as the curtain rises.

So to begin . . .

1

FOR WANT OF A NAIL

Let every nation know, whether it wishes us well or ill, that we shall pay any price, bear any burden, meet any hardship, support any friend, oppose any foe, in order to assure the survival and the success of liberty.

—John F. Kennedy, inaugural address, January 20, 1961

Eight inches of thick, densely packed snow had blanketed the nation's capital the night of Thursday, January 19, 1961, jeopardizing the inaugural ceremonies and parade scheduled to begin at noon the following day.

At those ceremonies, Senator John F. Kennedy of Massachusetts would take the oath of office as our nation's 35th chief executive, becoming —at age forty-three—America's youngest elected president and first to be born in the 20th century, replacing Dwight D. Eisenhower who—at age seventy—was at that time the oldest ever to lead the United States.

In the 1960s and well into the '70s, the District of Columbia's snow-removal plan was described by a long-time resident as "Wait until August and it will melt." The district's snow-removal equipment was woefully inadequate, as was the case with many of the city's services, so emergency messages went out the night of January 19 to help clear the inaugural parade's route along Pennsylvania Avenue and all streets leading to Capitol Hill, where Kennedy's inauguration would take place.

The eight inches of snow that had fallen overnight would result in Washington's "most crippling traffic jam (for its time)," according to the National Weather Service. "Hundreds of cars were marooned and thousands of cars were abandoned," the Weather Service reported.

At noontime January 20, as inaugural ceremonies were scheduled to commence, the official temperature was twenty-two degrees Fahrenheit, with a nineteen-mile-per-hour wind blowing from the northwest, "making it feel like the temperature was 7 degrees above zero," according to the Weather Service.

Airline passengers returning to Washington from the Panama Canal Zone the night of January 19 were met at Miami International Airport by Eastern Airlines personnel and were told that they would have to remain in Miami overnight because Washington National Airport (later to be re-designated as Ronald Reagan Washington National Airport, or Reagan National) had been shut down. Its runways couldn't be cleared, the airline agents explained, because all available snow-removal equipment was being used to clear the inaugural parade route and remove abandoned cars from the line of march.

At Fort Belvoir, Virginia—about twenty miles south of Washington—the Army Engineer School marshalled its graders, snowplows, and anything that might move tons of thick, wet snow to the sides of Pennsylvania Avenue, and began a late-night convoy into the very heart of our nation's capital. It was a snow-clearing mission probably never anticipated by previous commandants of the Engineer School (among them Col. Robert E. Lee of Virginia, who had led the school until six years before the onset of the Civil War).

With WNA shut down, former President Herbert Hoover (eighty-five), who had left office in 1933, was unable to fly to the capital from New York City, where he resided at the Waldorf Towers. But outgoing President Dwight Eisenhower was present, as was Ike's vice president, Richard Nixon, whom Kennedy had defeated by the narrowest of margins—112,827 ballots nationwide in the popular vote, eighty-four in the Electoral College—in the November 1960 presidential election. Nixon's supporters, including Eisenhower, had urged him to challenge perceived voting irregularities in Texas and Illinois. In the latter case, some claimed without corroboration that Chicago Mayor Richard J. Daley's political machine had caused "dead voters" to rise from their graves and proceed to polling places to vote for Kennedy.

Texas, home state to Kennedy's newly elected vice president, Lyndon B. Johnson, had awarded its twenty-four Electoral College votes to the Democratic candidate, who carried the state by only 46,000 votes out of 2.3 million cast, amid suspicions of voter fraud in the state, where Johnson wielded huge political sway.

Ironically, just over one thousand days would elapse before Lyndon Johnson would himself take the presidential oath of office, becoming America's 36th president in an impromptu swearing-in aboard Air Force One—a Boeing 707—as it sat on the tarmac at Dallas's Love Field, with the coffin of the assassinated young president, John F. Kennedy, just inside the airplane's rear door.

Inaugural ceremonies began belatedly on January 20 to allow last-minute snow clearing. The newly elected president, coatless and hatless despite the twenty-two-degree weather, was anxious to demonstrate the vigor and youthfulness with which his new administration would conduct its affairs of state.

After an invocation and prayers, Marian Anderson—the supremely gifted African American contralto opera singer who in 1939 had been denied a singing performance at nearby Constitution Hall because of her race—opened the ceremonies with a rendition of "The Star-Spangled Banner" that thrilled the bundled-up spectators seated at the recently renovated East Front of the U.S. Capitol. Millions more tuned in at home in front of the black-and-white television sets still prevalent in 97 percent of American homes in the early 1960s.

Kennedy's inauguration address—largely crafted by thirty-three-year-old chief speechwriter Ted Sorensen—was a masterpiece of oratory. Its soaring rhetoric still resonates with us more than half a century later: "Let the word go forth from this time and place, to friend and foe alike, that the torch has been passed to a new generation of Americans. . . ." "To those peoples in the huts and villages across the globe struggling to break the bonds of mass misery, we pledge our best efforts to help them help themselves, for whatever period is required. . . . Let every nation know, whether it wishes us well or ill, that we shall pay any price, bear any burden, meet any hardship, support any friend, oppose any foe, in order to assure the survival and the success of liberty."

Thereupon, the new president, determined to put his mark upon a world and nation very much unsettled by the ever-present threat of a nuclear encounter with the Soviet Union, assembled a team of advisors and confidantes drawn largely from industry and academia who were correctly assessed by Pulitzer Prize–winning journalist David Halberstam as "The Best and the Brightest," in a 1972 summary of the origins of America's involvement in the Vietnam War.

From this group of advisors—described as "Dramatis Personae" (the characters or actors in a drama) in an accompanying listing of significant players in "The Tragedy of Viet-Nam"—decisions emerged that helped preordain America's intervention in the war involving the Republic of Vietnam, resulting in its ultimate tragic denouement in 1975.

The Tragedy of Viet-Nam
(A Drama in Five Acts)
Dramatis Personae

John Fitzgerald Kennedy .... 35th President of the United States of America
Lyndon Baines Johnson .... Vice President, later 36th President
of the United States
Robert Strange McNamara ... Secretary of Defense under Kennedy and Johnson
General Maxwell Davenport Taylor .... Chairman, Joint Chiefs of Staff,
later ambassador to South Vietnam
General Earle Gilmore Wheeler .... Army chief of staff, later chairman,
Joint Chiefs of Staff
General William Childs Westmoreland ...... Commander, U.S. Forces Vietnam,
1964–68, later Army chief of staff
General Creighton Williams Abrams Jr. ...... Commander, U.S. Forces Vietnam,
1968–72, later Army chief of staff
Dr. Alain C. Enthoven .... Assistant Secretary of Defense for Systems Analysis
Dr. Charles C. Hitch .... Assistant Secretary of Defense (Comptroller)
Walt Whitman Rostow .... Special Assistant for National Security Affairs
to Kennedy and Johnson
David Dean Rusk .... Secretary of State under Kennedy and Johnson
McGeorge Bundy .... Special Assistant for National Security
to Kennedy and Johnson
Supporting Cast .... 2.7 million U.S. soldiers, Marines, airmen,
and sailors who served in Vietnam

The Five Acts of The Tragedy of Viet-Nam
Act I: Bear Any Burden
Act II: Light at the End of the Tunnel
Act III: Mired in Stalemate
Act IV: If I've Lost Cronkite, I've Lost Middle America
Act V: When Will They Ever Learn?

Robert S. McNamara, Kennedy's choice as secretary of defense, thereby became a key player in decision-making related to the Vietnam War, not only in terms of overall strategic considerations, but equally in the flawed decisions concerning the introduction of the militarized version of the AR15 rifle into ground combat operations.

McNamara, a highly regarded U.S. Army Air Forces lieutenant colonel in World War II with degrees from the University of California at Berkeley and Harvard Business School, had been hired by Henry Ford II upon mustering out of the military to work for Ford Motor Company at its Dearborn, Michigan, headquarters. Along with McNamara, Ford assembled a group of other bright former USAAF officers to join its postwar team of fresh, new management executives. Working under McNamara, this group of nine other statistically oriented executives, all under thirty, instituted relatively new concepts they'd practiced and perfected in the military, such as systems analysis; updated planning and organizational techniques; and management-control systems for logistics, personnel, and time-charting.

McNamara's team, dubbed "whiz kids" because of their skills and acumen (together perhaps with considerable intellectual snobbism), did much to revitalize postwar prospects at Ford Motor Company, resulting in McNamara's ascendancy in 1960 to the company's presidency. As such, he became the first leader of the company with no Ford family ties.

McNamara was only forty-four years old, a year older than Kennedy, when the new American president asked him to leave Ford's presidency after only seven weeks on the job to become our nation's eighth secretary of defense. McNamara reportedly joked, according to *The New York Times*, that he "could barely tell a nuclear warhead from a station wagon when he arrived in Washington."

"Mr. President, it's absurd; I'm not qualified," the *Times* reported in its obituary when McNamara died in 2009 at age 93. Kennedy's response? "Look, Bob, I don't think there's any school for presidents, either."

And so McNamara took the helm of the Pentagon immediately after Kennedy's inauguration, serving Kennedy and his successor, Lyndon Johnson, for the next seven years until 1968.

Almost from the outset, blunders in foreign policy beset the new administration. Kennedy authorized an Eisenhower administration plan for Cuban exiles to invade their homeland in mid-April 1961 at the Bay of Pigs but withdrew promised air support at the last minute, resulting in more than one hundred deaths among the invaders, with another 1,200 imprisoned by the Castro regime.

Two months later, Kennedy met at a two-day summit in Vienna with Soviet Premier Nikita Khrushchev and was made to look like a babe in the woods by the Politburo veteran. "I never met a man like this," the chagrined Kennedy told *Time* magazine's White House correspondent. "I talked about how a nuclear exchange would kill 70 million people in 10 minutes, and he just looked at me as if to say, 'So what?'"

Another two months later, on August 13, 1961, the German Democratic Republic (East Germany), acting at Khrushchev's behest and with the Kremlin leader's confidence that he could outpoint the inexperienced American president, began construction of a wall isolating West Berlin from East Berlin and East Germany. The Berlin Wall would remain as a principal Cold War symbol for the next twenty-eight years.

Another two months passed and saw the Berlin Brigade's M48 tanks go almost muzzle to muzzle with Soviet T55 tanks in an armored standoff at Checkpoint Charlie in Berlin on October 22, in a dispute over border-access procedures. Had an officer or NCO of Company F, 40th Armor panicked and given an order to fire, no one can predict what consequences might have ensued.

A year later, after Khrushchev had clandestinely deployed intermediate- and medium-range ballistic missiles, along with Ilyushin light bombers and perhaps one hundred tactical nuclear weapons to Cuba—ninety miles from the continental United States—Kennedy and our nation lived through the Cuban Missile Crisis, the thirteen days in October 1962 when the world came perilously close to war between its two nuclear-equipped superpowers.

Although Kennedy and his advisors were generally accorded high marks for their successful handling of the Soviet missile threat in Cuba, on the other side of the world yet another crisis was building. Back in 1954, when Kennedy was then a junior senator from Massachusetts, his predecessor in the White House, Dwight D. Eisenhower, held a significant press conference on April 7, intended to rally public support for French efforts in Vietnam against nationalist forces under Ho Chi Minh.

"You have a row of dominoes set up," Eisenhower explained in his occasionally fractured syntax. "You knock over the first one, and what will happen to the last one is a certainty that it will go over very quickly." Thus, Ike added, disintegration in Southeast Asia would ensue, with the "loss of Indochina, of Burma, of Thailand, of the Peninsula, and Indonesia following." Even Japan might be in danger, he pointed out.

Exactly one month after Eisenhower outlined his Domino Theory, the 3,000-man French garrison at Dien Bien Phu was overrun on May 7, 1954, by 25,000 communist Viet Minh soldiers under Gen. Vo Nguyen Giap. And so the situation in Southeast Asia worsened appreciably.

One day before Eisenhower's press conference, John F. Kennedy, the junior senator from Massachusetts with just over a year in office, had stood on the floor of the United States Senate and argued forcibly against U.S. involvement in Vietnam: "I am frankly of the belief that no amount of American military assistance in Indochina can conquer an enemy which is everywhere and at the same time nowhere, 'an enemy of the people' which has the sympathy and covert support of the people."

Kennedy was speaking then about the folly of providing military and logistic aid to a French nation fighting desperately for the maintenance of its colonial sovereignty in Indochina. But that was 1954, and he was a freshman senator. Seven years later, he had assumed duties and responsibilities as president of the United States, leader of the Free World, and had pledged at his inauguration to "pay any price, bear any burden, meet any hardship, support any friend, oppose any foe, in order to assure the survival and the success of liberty."

As president, Kennedy inherited the Southeast Asia Treaty Organization (SEATO), signed in Manila on September 8, 1954, four months after the fall of Dien Bien Phu. Although the majority of the eight signatory nations lay outside Southeast Asia (Thailand and the Philippines were the only signatories directly impacted), the intent of the SEATO Treaty was to provide for a common defense of the region, similar to what NATO was accomplishing in Europe.

The nations comprising the former Indochina—Vietnam, Cambodia, and Laos—were prohibited by Geneva agreements signed in July 1954 from participating in any military alliances. But the SEATO Treaty provided the Eisenhower administration with sufficient rationale to intervene militarily in those nations if attacked, particularly the Republic of South Vietnam. A protocol, or codicil, to the SEATO agreement provided military protection to these three countries, if required.

And so the youthful American president, fresh off one foreign-policy disaster after another in the early months of his administration, was being obligated to take a stance vis-à-vis South Vietnam that he had strongly opposed as a senator in 1954, when reinforcing the French presence in Indochina was being evaluated by the Congress.

Ten months into his presidency, Kennedy paid a visit in mid-October 1961 to Fort Bragg, North Carolina, home of the Army's Special Warfare Center and the Special Forces. Accompanied by Brig. Gen. William P. Yarborough, the center's commander, Kennedy was fascinated by a series of demonstrations conducted by the elite Special Forces personnel. These included a stealthy raid across a lake using a rubber boat, along with a free-falling parachute jump by four men with smoke grenades attached to their ankles involving a mid-air exchange of an item that turned out to be a baton engraved with the president's name and date of his visit to Fort Bragg.

Visibly impressed, the commander in chief said, "This demonstration is the finest example of our Special Forces soldiers. This unit needs a mark of distinction and a badge of excellence to depict its abilities." Whereupon General Yarbrough unbuttoned his khaki shirt and brought forth a green beret, which Kennedy approved five months later as "a symbol of excellence, a badge of courage, a mark of distinction in the fight for freedom."

A handful of Special Forces personnel had begun operating in Laos—another country carved out of the former French Indochina—in the early fall of 1959, as Dwight Eisenhower was nearing the end of his eight-year presidency. Twelve mobile training teams, under command of legendary special-operations warrior Lt. Col. (later Colonel) Arthur "Bull" Simons, took up the task of training elements of the Royal Laotian Army in their fight against the army of the communist Pathet Lao.

The 7th Special Forces Group at Fort Bragg, North Carolina, deployed a number of these advisors, among them Capt. Walter H. Moon, an advisor to the 6th Battalion of Lao infantry, who was captured in April 1961 and executed (shot in the head by his Pathet Lao captors) on or about July 22, 1961, following several escape attempts. Captain Moon (posthumously promoted to major by President Kennedy and awarded the Silver Star Medal for gallantry in action) was the fourteenth U.S. service member killed in Southeast Asia and is the fourteenth name engraved on the Vietnam Veterans Memorial Wall in Washington, out of more than 58,300 names on the memorial.

Even before Kennedy had become impressed with Special Forces capabilities during his October 1961 visit to their center at Fort Bragg, he had begun dispatching Special Forces advisory teams to train South Vietnamese military units and village-defense militia in counterinsurgency warfare. In his first year as president, Kennedy increased total Special Forces strength from approximately 1,500 to 9,000 men authorized to wear the Green Beret.

In May 1961—just four months into his presidency—Kennedy dispatched 400 "special advisors" to South Vietnam to commence the training process of ARVN (Army of the Republic of Vietnam) troops. As 1962 ended, the president had sent 11,000 advisors in-country. By the time of his death in November 1963, Kennedy had committed more than 16,000 American advisory personnel to the struggle for South Vietnam, together with helicopter units used to transport ARVN soldiers as the tactical situation required. Thus, the stage had been set for U.S. intervention in the Vietnam conflict, although no U.S. ground combat units were as yet directly involved.

As president, Lyndon Johnson was the first to commit American combat brigades and divisions into the war, beginning in March 1965 when nearly 5,000 Marines of the 9th Marine Expeditionary Brigade—carrying their M14 rifles—flew from Okinawa to Da Nang to secure the U.S. airbase there. Two months later, the Okinawa-based 173rd Airborne Brigade—issued the new rifles (still in an experimental stage and officially designated as "Rifle, 5.56mm, XM16E1") at the last minute and with limited training on the weapon—deployed to South Vietnam as the first U.S. Army ground combat unit sent into the war.

The newly formed 1st Cavalry Division (Airmobile) began arriving in-country from Fort Benning, Georgia, in August 1965, equipped with the XM16E1. But infantrymen of follow-on Army divisions—the 1st Infantry Division ("Big Red One"), the 25th ("Tropic Lightning"), and the 4th ("Ivy") still toted their M14 rifles, soon to be replaced by XM16E1s. As an instance of the combat-preparation and supply-chain confusion, the 196th Light Infantry Brigade was rushed, in July 1966, from Fort Devens, Massachusetts, to Tay Ninh Province on the Cambodian border, following training on the M14 rifle, only to have the older weapons replaced with XM16E1s as its soldiers were boarding ships bound for Vietnam.

The need to dispatch American combat forces to the struggle for South Vietnam tore at Johnson's heart. He had committed his presidency—first as Kennedy's successor in 1963 and later as an elected president in his own right—to the creation of what he termed a "Great Society," in which domestic programs could be employed to overcome poverty and racial injustice at home. A major war in Southeast Asia would therefore become a conflict not only with communist forces, but also with Johnson's goals and priorities for America. A prolonged struggle would drain precious resources such as financial appropriations, infrastructure, and key personnel, along with the American public's notoriously short-lived attention span that would be diverted from the Great Society's ambitious goals.

The escalating war in Vietnam was even exerting major pressures on our forces opposing the Soviet Bloc in Europe. In 1966, for example, major draw-downs of Army infantry, artillery, and armor officers took place throughout U.S. combat units in Europe, as these officers were reassigned either directly to Vietnam or to replenish the expanding training base in the Continental United States.

A possibly apocryphal tale being passed around by personnel of the Berlin Brigade in 1966 had LBJ telling four-star General Andrew P. O'Meara, com-mander of U.S. Army forces in Europe, "General, whatever you do, don't rock the boat with the (expletive) Russians in Berlin. I've got a war a-building on the other side of the world, and I haven't got the troops to fight another one with the (expletive) Russians."

Initially—and for several years—the American public was for the most part supportive of the Vietnam War effort. Thus, when Army Staff Sgt. Barry Sadler wrote and recorded "The Ballad of the Green Berets" about Vietnam in 1966, it reached No. 1 nationally for five consecutive weeks on the "Bill-board Hot 100" chart. And John Wayne's 1968 film *The Green Berets*—in which "The Duke" portrays a fictional Special Forces colonel who leads a mission into North Vietnam to kidnap a key North Vietnamese general—proved to be popular, even as it was universally (and deservedly) panned as being nothing more than a warmed-over Eastern western. Critic Roger Ebert awarded it zero stars, said it suffered from extensive use of clichés, and that it depicted the Vietnam War in terms of "cowboys and Indians"—all valid cri-tiques. But the public paid good money to see it and the movie made a ton of money, appearing on Variety's list of "Big Rental Films of 1968."

The American public, it seems, hadn't yet turned decisively against the war in Vietnam. That would take place in the weeks and months following the enemy's Tet Offensive in the opening months of 1968.

Robert S. McNamara—sworn into office as Kennedy's secretary of defense exactly one day after Kennedy's inauguration—surrounded himself in the Pen-tagon with many talented young analysts, much as he had done in 1948 at Ford Motor Company. A number of these analysts were recruited by McNa-mara from the Santa Monica, California-based RAND Corporation.

RAND (an acronym for Research and Development) had been spun off in May 1948 from the Douglas Aircraft Company as an independent, private nonprofit company. In other words, it evolved into a highly sophisticated think tank with expertise in "a wide range of fields, including mathematics, engineering, aerodynamics, physics, chemistry, economics, and psychology."

According to the RAND website, the corporation "developed the planning, programming, and budgeting system that Secretary of Defense Robert McNamara's 'Whiz Kids' promoted throughout the federal government in the early 1960s and that was mandated as the federal standard by President Lyndon Johnson in 1965."

Among McNamara's proselytes to the Pentagon from RAND was thirty-one-year-old Dr. Alain C. Enthoven (doctorate in economics from MIT), who had been at RAND since 1956, focusing on U.S. and NATO defense strategies against forces of the Soviet-led Warsaw Pact. Enthoven became McNamara's assistant secretary of defense for systems analysis, oftentimes displaying arrogance and impatience with high-ranking military officers who he felt were resistant to the new order of things that Team McNamara was imposing on Pentagon decision-making.

At one point in fact, the youthful Enthoven reportedly was quarreling with an Air Force general who had questioned one of the assistant defense secretary's analyses. "General," Enthoven is reported to have said, "I've fought as many nuclear wars as you have."

In another Pentagon exchange, this time with an Army general, one of Enthoven's staffers argued that the standard eleven-man Army rifle squad was basically unchanged since days of the Roman legions. How could it be—the whiz kid reportedly challenged the general with unconcealed disdain—that in two thousand years a more effective infantry squad hadn't been developed by the U.S. Army? Could money be saved by reducing the rifle squad from eleven to ten men? (It's worth noting, perhaps, that the operations research/systems analysis–trained staffer neglected to ask the obvious parallel question of whether the addition of a twelfth rifleman, machine gunner, or grenadier might help make the rifle squad even more combat effective.) In 1959, however, the report of testing conducted at the Combat Developments Experimentation Center at Fort Ord, California, concluded that a smaller squad of five to seven men armed with the AR15 could deliver more firepower than the eleven-man squad armed with the M14 with, presumably, two of the eleven, the automatic riflemen, armed with the M14E2. McNamara was certainly aware of these results. He directed that another study of the AR15 be conducted in Vietnam. The results of this evaluation, published in 1962, further confirmed the suitability of the AR15 for Vietnamese soldiers. The problem created by his young and somewhat arrogant assistants was that they disregarded the advice of more knowledgeable military weapons specialists that more time and attention was needed to address design and functional issues along with ammunition compatibility.

In adapting to the new world of McNamara-directed system analysis, the Army lagged well behind its counterparts in the Air Force, which was supported by the RAND Corporation (which Air Force General Curtis LeMay had helped found back in 1948) and the Navy, backed up by the Center for Naval Analysis, a federally funded nonprofit research and development center. Thus, in the above-cited squad-manning discussion, the Pentagon whiz kid was opining that the somewhat troglodytic Army had no rational justification for its manpower requirements other than past practices.

Lacking analytical justification, the whiz kids reasoned, there was undoubtedly presumptive evidence that Army manpower requirements were being overstated and that cost-efficient reductions should be considered. To give them their just due, they encountered continuing resistance from the Chief of Ordnance, who defended his M14 and M14E2 until his office was disestablished in 1962. By defending the 7.62mm family of weapons he was in effect defending the eleven-man rifle squad.

Kennedy's defense secretary, backed by his bright youthful team, quickly asserted himself to impose order on what was correctly perceived as a host of inefficiencies, duplication, and waste in Pentagon procurement procedures. McNamara borrowed an analytical system he had used at Ford—Planning, Programming and Budgeting System (PPBS)—and relocated it to the Pentagon.

And so it came to pass in 1966 that Enthoven's Office of Systems Analysis was formally put in charge of evaluating progress (or lack thereof) in the Vietnam War. In a conflict in which holding and seizing terrain carried a relatively low priority in General William C. Westmoreland's fallible playbook, Enthoven and his staff concluded that quantifying the count of slain enemy soldiers— together with statistics on the number of South Vietnamese villages either resettled or pacified—would become reliable indicators of progress being made.

Unfortunately, Enthoven and his staffers failed to take into account the fact that casualties among the North Vietnamese and Viet Cong soldiers fighting in the South simply weren't a credible, important statistic as far as Ho Chi Minh and General Vo Nguyen Giap were concerned. The expenditure of fighting men, the two North Vietnamese leaders believed, was a tolerable price to be paid if all of Vietnam was to be freed from foreign oppression.

On the other hand, American infantry commanders in too many instances were pressured by higher headquarters to inflate the number of enemy bodies actually recovered after an engagement. This unfortunate situation came about when enemy dead were dragged away by their comrades for religious reasons and to deny us the ability to accurately determine the effectiveness of any given operation. Beyond religious or humanitarian concerns, this is a standard military security practice. The entire American military chain of command in Vietnam—down to rifle company commanders—was being pressured by McNamara's whiz kids through Westmoreland's MACV (Military Assistance Command, Vietnam) headquarters to show progress in the war, supposedly reflected by ever-increasing body counts of dead enemy combatants.

After all, careers were on the line in Vietnam for many U.S. military officers. Success in their normal six-month command time of a brigade, battalion, or rifle company was clearly a prerequisite for higher-level advancement. Unit leaders who failed to measure up in combat or who unnecessarily endangered their men were replaced on the spot, given what was facetiously termed a vaudevillian "midnight hook," as in being lifted away in darkness by a CH-47 banana-shaped Chinook helicopter.

Successful leadership of a unit in combat is considered perhaps the most salient indicator of an officer's fitness for career advancement and because higher headquarters insisted upon a body count, commanders generally complied with a conscientious estimation. Since the enemy evacuated their dead and wounded whenever possible, the body count was often just a best guess.

As one example, after an Arc Light bombing mission flown by Guam-based B-52 bombers in November 1967 had dropped their 500-pound bombs, obliterating a large fortified underground enemy bunker complex—hospital, armory, storage rooms, communications center, etc.—the operations officer of a 5,000-man brigade of the 1st Air Cavalry Division pressured his counterpart at battalion level for a body count. As was customary, however, combatants of the elite 2nd NVA (North Vietnamese Army) Division had removed virtually all their dead from the debris, leaving behind charred web gear, destroyed weapons, and other equipment. But it was essential for the brigade headquarters to fully justify the long-distance mission and expensive commitment of the Air Force bombers.

Accordingly, the body-count fixation caused the battalion operations officer to negotiate with his superiors at brigade before arriving at an estimated total of one hundred enemy dead, which was duly reported through the chain of command and was probably mentioned the following day in Saigon at the daily press briefing at the Rex Hotel in downtown Saigon—facetiously dubbed by the media as "Five O'clock Follies" because so much of what was being spun to them on a daily basis presented an overly optimistic picture of steady progress in the war effort.

It wasn't, though, that the body count of "one hundred" was pure fabrication. The correct figure may have been twenty or perhaps as high as two hundred. But constant efforts by McNamara and Enthoven to quantify the unquantifiable resulted in a false, unrealistic picture of what was actually taking place—developments that were good and bad alike as measures of progress—in Vietnam.

In effect, McNamara's whiz kids were diligently analyzing and ineffectually counting on their Pentagon computers the number of waves breaking on a seashore, while on the not-too-distant horizon a tsunami-like tidal wave was bearing down on them, such as was destined to happen during the Tet Offensive in early 1968.

The saga of the M16—the "black rifle" as it was termed by friend and foe alike because its black polymer gunstock replaced standard wooden stocks found on most other military weapons—represents a case study in flawed, haste-makes-waste decision making. This unseemly, unscientific process was imposed by SecDef Robert McNamara and his Pentagon staffers in a concerted effort to convince what they regarded, with some justification, as a hidebound U.S. Army, that its old-style full-automatic 7.62mm M14E2 rifle (which had been standardized just a few years earlier in 1963) was obsolescent for use in a jungle-warfare environment. It proved to be no match for the Soviet bloc AK47 being used in Vietnam by communist soldiers. The XM16E1 was rushed into production but hadn't been subjected to important developmental considerations standard for military rifles.

The AK47, or Avtomat Kalashnikova, named for its inventor, Soviet Lt. Gen. Mikhail Kalashnikov, debuted in 1947, two years after the end of World War II, and was therefore sixteen years and a weapons generation older than the American M14E2 rifle. And yet the AK47, to McNamara's frustration, was outperforming the M1 Garands and M2 carbines issued in Vietnam to ARVN soldiers who were in contact with the enemy in the days prior to the 1965 arrival of the first U.S. combat units in Vietnam.

It was time for McNamara's systems-analysis techniques to be brought to bear on the problem. The SecDef, in a secret October 1962 memo to Secretary of the Army Cyrus Vance, directed that tests be conducted involving three infantry weapons: the M14E2, the AK47, and the newly developed AR15, forerunner of the XM16E1.

McNamara had made no secret of his antipathy to the M14E2 or to the stubborn persistence of the Army brass, which kept insisting that the M14E2—formulated along traditional U.S. military weaponry guidelines—was the weapon of choice for American infantry units that would sooner or later be deployed to Vietnam. The fact that the M14E2 had been fashioned and had evolved from longstanding U.S. Army weapons-development protocols may have accounted in part for McNamara's implicit bias against the weapon. Having been developed in a traditional way, the M14E2 ran counter to the Mc-Namara/Enthoven predilection for change, even if there was failure to differentiate between useful and destructive change. In this case the change was needed but the standard developmental protocols had been bypassed.

They contended, with some justification, that the U.S. military leadership was irretrievably mired in the past and that the military's resistance to change was consequently misguided. Some of the early comparisons seemed to have been prejudiced in favor of the 7.62mm family of weapons, and this undermined the Army's arguments in favor of retaining the M14E2.

Among McNamara's recruits from the RAND Corporation was a brilliant economist named Dr. Charles J. Hitch, whom he installed as assistant secretary of defense (comptroller), overseeing the management of the vast Pentagon budget. Hitch, a Rhodes Scholar with a doctorate in economics from Harvard who would later serve as president of the University of California, was fifty-one years old when he joined McNamara's team in 1961, older by far than many of the SecDef's whiz kids, and an early proponent of operations research to help guide and shape strategic thinking.

Tasked by McNamara to develop a long-range program-oriented budget designed to reduce the Defense Department's considerable waste and duplication of efforts, Hitch implemented the sophisticated planning and budgeting system that became known as PPBS.

In late 1961, coincident with President Kennedy's enthusiasm for Special Forces and unconventional combat operations, McNamara had approved the purchase by DoD (Department of Defense) of 1,000 AR15s for use by American military advisors (many of them Green Berets) and their ARVN counterparts. The Star Wars-like appearance of the new rifle resonated with the White House; Kennedy's military aide even provided a sample AR15 for the commander in chief to pose with for a photo op.

(The sleek, ultramodern AR15/XM16E1, with its black finish and light weight of 6.37 pounds unloaded, caused many American soldiers and Marines armed with the weapon in Vietnam to term it "the Mattel" or "the Mattel rifle" because it seemingly resembled a toy gun made by Mattel Inc., the El Segundo, California-based maker of Barbie dolls and Hot Wheels. Some soldiers even claimed to have seen the toy company's logo on the handgrip of their rifles and complained about it. These rumors, some as late as 1969, were all refuted; Mattel has never had a role in the rifle's manufacture, although it did market numerous plastic toy replicas of classic firearms in the 1950s and 1960s.)

Hitch, like his boss in the Pentagon, had no love for the M14 and the M14E2 or for the Army's seemingly stubborn insistence on retaining the older weapons as its primary infantry rifle and automatic rifle. The Army was looking ahead to a new rifle, the Special Purpose Individual Weapon, or SPIW, that was expected to come on line in the not-too-distant future and replace the 7.62mm standard weapons. The expectation of a significantly more effective rifle further discouraged acceptance of what was believed by many to provide just a marginal improvement in firepower. Hitch and his systems analysts were suitably impressed in 1962 when early battlefield reports from ARVN units, through their U.S. advisors, spoke approvingly about the AR15's effectiveness in the close-combat jungle environments found in much of South Vietnam. The AR15's .223 caliber 5.56mm round (considerably smaller and lighter than the 7.62mm NATO cartridge used with the M14E2) was demonstrating surprisingly effective stopping power in skirmishes between the ARVN and Viet Cong, three years before American combat units—equipped with the XM16E1—would begin arriving in-country.

The AR15's lighter weight (6.37 pounds unloaded versus 9.2 pounds for a comparably unloaded M14E2) certainly favored the average ARVN special operations combatant, who stood perhaps five foot six or five foot seven inches tall (Vietnamese have the lowest average height among the peoples of Southeast Asia, according to a 2013 study) and who weighed about 112 pounds. However, it would be several years and far too long into what had deteriorated into an unpopular war at home before General Westmoreland and his MACV staffers would ultimately conclude that equipping the bulk of regular ARVN forces with the now mostly upgraded XM16E1, by now re-designated as the M16A1, was necessary. The official designation of the rifle had changed, but the improvements were implemented one by one as they checked out, and many of the M16A1s did not have all of the upgrades.

But by then it was too late to reverse the war's course or to rekindle American public support for the war. Westmoreland's deputy at MACV, General Creighton W. Abrams Jr., who took over when Westmoreland rotated home in June 1968 to become the Army's chief of staff, had perceived for a long time the shortfalls in Westmoreland's strategy and undertook a concerted effort to "Vietnamize" the war. But by then, of course, the war had been lost back home in America's newsrooms, living rooms, and television dens.

Westmoreland's misplaced priorities of employing American military forces in the major combat role against the North Vietnamese and Viet Cong—instead of prioritizing the training and equipping of ARVN Infantry divisions—would lead ultimately to the failure of America's efforts in South Vietnam. Historian Lewis Sorley (PhD from Johns Hopkins), a West Point graduate who served in Vietnam in 1966–67 as executive officer of a tank battalion, subtitled his 2011 biography of Westmoreland *The General Who Lost Vietnam.*

By late 1962, Hitch had completed his analyses of the military's small-arms programs, concluding that the compact, lightweight AR15, with its smaller 5.56mm ammunition, was best suited to become the standard rifle for the U.S. military. In this, he acquired an unlikely ally in the new Air Force chief of staff, General Curtis LeMay, who had been assiduously courted by the Colt's Manufacturing Company (later re-designated Colt), manufacturer of the AR15.

As recounted by Pulitzer Prize-winning *New York Times* writer C. J. Chivers in his seminal 2010 book about the AK47, *The Gun*, Colt's sales team invited LeMay—at that time Air Force vice chief of staff—to the sixtieth birthday party of Richard S. Boutelle, president of Fairchild Corporation, which in 1954 had acquired ArmaLite—developer of the AR15 rifle. Boutelle, an avid big-game hunter, had maintained a "long-standing friendship" with LeMay, a fellow gun fancier who would rise to the sky service's top post on June 30, 1961, five months after Kennedy had assumed the presidency.

Chivers, a Marine infantry captain in the First Gulf War and a graduate of the Army's Ranger School at Fort Benning, tells how LeMay in mid-1960 was invited to a combination Fourth of July and birthday party at Boutelle's "gentlemen's farm in Maryland," much of which had been converted into recreational shooting ranges. Given a sample AR15 to fire at three target watermelons, LeMay—never a big fan of the Springfield Armory-developed M14 rifle—blasted the first two melons into red pulp before deciding to spare the third one for consumption at the party.

So Colt Firearms, which in 1959 had acquired production rights to the AR15, "for the price of three watermelons and Independence Day cocktails, had a high-level convert" in LeMay, according to Chivers. With LeMay as its top gun, the Air Force in May 1962 contracted with Colt to buy 8,500 AR15s, causing Chivers to comment, "This was a small order. But just like that, the AR-15 formally entered the American military arms system, via a side door."

McNamara, as noted earlier, had approved the acquisition in late 1961 of 1,000 AR15s for use by ARVN special operations teams and their U.S. advisors. But LeMay's purchase was intended for use by U.S. Air Force personnel and represented a figurative Rubicon crossing as far as U.S. infantry small arms was concerned.

Small order or not, LeMay had made a de facto commitment by the U.S. Air Force and its 883,300 servicemen and women in 1962 that the AR15 was the weapon of choice for America's air arm. Even though McNamara, Hitch, and Enthoven had shown prejudices against the old-style M14E2 and were tilting inevitably in favor of the AR15/XM16E1, LeMay had one-upped them by jumping ahead with procurement orders for the "black rifle."

Even as comparison weapons testing of the M14E2, AK47, and AR15/XM16E1 would continue until mid-November 1965, combat units (9th Marine Expeditionary Brigade, 173rd Airborne Brigade, 1st Air Cavalry Division, 1st Infantry Division, elements of the 25th Infantry Division, and 101st Airborne Division, etc.) were already battling the Viet Cong and North Vietnamese that year, by now equipped with the XM16E1. Those units that had arrived with the semi-automatic M14 and full automatic M14E2 rifles, with only two men in a rifle squad of eleven men armed with the M14E2, had been at a serious firepower disadvantage compared to their North Vietnamese counterparts. By the end of 1965, an estimated 184,300 American combat troops were positioned in South Vietnam. The decision had been made to arm all U.S. forces in Vietnam with the XM16E1. It's worth noting that an unknown number of American "grunts" in Vietnam traded in their troubled XM16E1s for captured enemy AK47s after experiencing problems with their issued rifle.

(In the tumultuous 1968 presidential election, LeMay—retired from the Air Force—ran unsuccessfully for vice president of the United States on the third-party American Independent Party ticket. Former Alabama governor George Wallace, a segregationist, headed the ticket, which carried only five states—all in the Deep South—with a miniscule total of forty-six electoral votes. After a dispirited Lyndon Johnson announced on March 31, 1968, that he wouldn't run for reelection, Americans that year elected Richard M. Nixon as president and Maryland governor Spiro Agnew as vice president, both of whom were subsequently forced to resign their offices in disgrace during their second terms. Nixon's resignation in August 1974 created what some called "the greatest constitutional crisis since the Civil War." As heads fell in 1974 and other governmental leaders quit their posts in protest, one macabre bit of humor making the rounds of the Pentagon's corridors went: "If my boss calls, get his name.")

Given McNamara's distaste for the older M14E2 and Hitch's analyses of the AR15's successes with the ARVN in Vietnam in tests dubbed Project AGILE, it was perhaps inevitable that a militarized version of the AR15 would prevail, although additional comparison testing was still taking place by the U.S. Army Infantry Board at Fort Benning as late as mid-November 1965 (Chapter 4), while American combat units were arriving in Vietnam, relatively untrained on the new weapon and with inadequate cleaning gear and lack of training on proper weapons maintenance for the XM16E1.

In December 1963, the Defense Department purchased a total of 104,000 XM16E1 rifles: 85,000 for the Army; 19,000 for the Air Force. With some exceptions for special operations forces, the 7.62mm family of weapons continued to be standard for Army and Marine forces based in Europe and other deployment locations.

The SecDef, in a rush to judgment, directed that the XM16E1 be adopted as an experimental model of the AR15, and that it be issued to troops, even though a number of problems hadn't yet been resolved. Many design modifications were still under consideration, the most significant bearing directly on reliability. Two versions of the rifle were authorized: the XM16E1 with a forward assist for the Army and Marines, and the M16 without the forward assist for the Air Force.

And—perhaps more significant than anyone thought possible at the time—there wasn't enough 5.56mm ammunition available in 1965 and 1966 for distribution to American divisions and brigades increasingly being committed to combat. Compromises and substitutions (described in later chapters) would unfortunately be authorized, jeopardizing the lives of American soldiers and Marines when their XM16E1s failed to extract spent cartridge cases on all-too-many occasions, reducing the effectiveness of the supposedly high-tech XM16E1 to roughly that of a muzzle loader of Revolutionary War vintage.

As misfires with the XM16E1 persisted in Vietnam in 1965 and 1966, the Army Weapons Command, along with tech reps from Colt, sent representatives in the fall of 1966 to look into the problem. They concluded, rather self-servingly, that "weapons were in an unbelievable condition of rust, filth, and lack of repair," and conveniently used this as cover for the deficiencies of the rifle/ammunition combination that was primarily responsible for the failure to extract. Neither Colt nor the Army inspectors were ready to concede the possibility of problems with the rifle's design, manufacture, or ammunition substitutions. They also noted that "there was a shortage of technical manuals, cleaning equipment and repair parts as well as a shortage of officers and NCOs who knew anything about the maintenance of the rifle."

A 1967 Department of the Army study of more than 1,500 troops who had served in Vietnam up to that point concluded that 80 percent had experienced some form of stoppage with their XM16E1 rifles while engaged with the enemy. In an unforgivable lack of planning, proper cleaning supplies (bore brushes, cleaning rods, and lubricants) hadn't been procured or shipped to Vietnam. An Army field manual with illustrated maintenance instructions wasn't published until 1968, three years after the first U.S. combat units arrived in-country.

Benjamin Franklin, in his 1758 essay "The Way to Wealth," offered a version of a proverb dating back to the 13th or 14th century. It goes like this:

> *For want of a nail the shoe was lost,*
> *For want of a shoe the horse was lost,*
> *and for want of a horse the rider was lost,*
> *being overtaken and slain by the enemy,*
> *all for want of care about a horse-shoe nail.*

How did the world's most technologically advanced nation allow itself in the middle years of the 20th century to become embroiled in a conflict in Southeast Asia that it wasn't sure it wanted to win, even though its leader had promised to "bear any burden"?

How did the most prestigious decision makers of their generation commit so many decision-making blunders?

How were 2,709,918 American men of all ages, races, religions, and ethnicities who served in uniform in Vietnam and elsewhere in Southeast Asia from roughly 1959 to 1973 committed into combat without a commensurate commitment from their leaders and the American public that they would be backed by the same determination and willpower that had sustained our fighting forces in World War II and Korea?

How did so many of America's "best and brightest" come together in Washington, D.C., in the early and mid-1960s only to generate so many unwise, muddle-headed decisions with respect to developments in nations overseas?

And how did the XM16E1 rifle and the incompatible ammunition that accompanied it to Vietnam get rushed into acceptance and production before its engineering shortcomings were resolved and its logistical tail was accurately and satisfactorily developed—before the "black rifle" was ready to be fully committed to combat?

How, one wonders?

What misfired?

2

WHY REPLACE THE M14?

The M14 was the standard rifle for soldiers and Marines as American engagement in Vietnam accelerated in 1965. The XM16E1 was already in service with Army Special Forces. They indicated that this was the weapon needed to effectively counter an enemy armed with the AK47. The side that could bring the most firepower to bear in the sharp close encounter type of firefight common in Vietnam would win the day. The M14E2 was a version of the M14 designed to fill the role of the automatic rifle, a replacement for the Browning Automatic Rifle (BAR). It was unwieldy and hard to hold on target when firing in the fully automatic mode. Even with this shortcoming, only two of eleven men in a rifle squad would have this version of the M14. The remainder would be limited to firing in the semi-automatic mode. They would be at a disadvantage in any engagement with an enemy armed with an individual weapon capable of fully automatic fire. In recognition of this, airborne and airmobile units were armed with the XM16E1. Other units were issued XM16E1s as soon as they became available, often with little or no training. Unfortunately, the XM16E1 was subject to frequent malfunctions, exacerbated by hard use in a humid climate.

In July 1965 Specialist 4 Robert Towles was issued his XM16E1 at Fort Benning, Georgia. He wasn't issued cleaning supplies for his rifle because he, and others who were issued the XM16E1 at that time, were told "*the gunpowder would burn so hot that the weapon would be practically self-cleaning.*" Towles moved with the 1st Cavalry Division (Airmobile) to Vietnam in September, assigned as a gunner in the Anti-Tank Platoon of Delta Company, 2nd Battalion, 7th Cavalry. His first chance to test his XM16E1 came one morning in early October in Happy Valley (Vinh Thanh Valley). The men were told they could burn off a magazine on auto at whatever target had bothered them during the night. He fired a full magazine of twenty rounds in one long burst. For the next month he fired only single shots and had no problems. However, on November 17, Delta Company was on its way to Landing Zone (LZ) Albany after the tremendous fight at LZ X-Ray. On the way to Albany, the 2nd of the 7th was ambushed by a much larger force of North Vietnamese soldiers. As Towles describes it:

> *I was sitting with my back resting against a tree when a single shot rang out, then another—two, three, multiple. Auto kicked in, followed by machinegun and topped off with mortar fire. This all took place within a matter of seconds. As I peered into the undergrowth in the direction of the firing, rounds started coming from my right, followed by machinegun and mortar fire. As I turned in the direction of this new danger, I saw the wall of vegetation explode as dozens of PAVN[1] burst through firing at the run. I settled and fired a round at the closest target and hit him in the chest. He continued to charge and I hit him again and again. As he closed on me I flipped the auto on and fired a burst. He went down. I turned to the next target and squeezed the trigger. Nothing happened. I squeezed again, nothing. I jerked the trigger, nothing. The fear I had turned to panic. I turned my rifle over and saw brass sticking out of the breech. I ejected the casing and hit the forward assist to make sure the new round seated itself and began firing again. Success, two down. Turning to a third target I squeezed and nothing happened. Looking, I saw another casing sticking out of the breech. I ejected again and slammed the forward assist. From that point onward, I didn't think about it, I just automatically ejected a round following each burst and slammed the forward assist. However, this action eventually caused pain and blood from the wound it opened in the heel of my hand. Still this maneuver worked until I was wounded in the right arm. My hand froze to the pistol grip, making it impossible to do it anymore. Luckily my trigger finger still worked, but after my wounding I only fired single shots and so did not have the jamming problem anymore. During the battlefield clean-up (at LZ X-Ray), to the right front of the landing zone, Alpha Company, 1st Platoon, 1st Squad, squad leader, Sergeant Thomas James' body was discovered with an AK (AK47) in his hands, having discarded his M16 for a more reliable weapon. A sweep of the area on the far side of the landing zone found Sergeant Palmer Miles, a squad leader in Delta Company's Recon Platoon, with a bullet hole in his forehead, and a jammed casing in the breech of his M16.[2]*

The hills and mountains of Vietnam are majestic and graceful. Sunset seen from high on Hon Cong Mountain above An Khe is a visual treat. The Central Highlands, an area of high rolling hills interspersed with rice-growing areas, often covered with thickets of nearly impenetrable brush and vegetation, offer a wide variety of terrain. The rice-producing lowlands are fertile and productive. The climate is hot and muggy. Rice is the major crop throughout Vietnam. North of the Mekong Delta, the paddies are mostly in lowland areas, usually near the coast. In the Delta, they are the dominant feature. Even in the rice-growing areas there are stands of dense vegetation.

There are nearly impenetrable bamboo thickets, particularly in the hill country, and bamboo is present just about everywhere. It is an interesting and challenging military landscape with open views from some of its higher points, and a tangle of vegetation, some so thick that a military unit has to cut through it with machetes or Bowie knives, rotating the point man periodically as exhaustion sets in. In many places, this terrain easily conceals a waiting enemy.

The mountainous area of the Mang Yang Pass, one major terrain feature to the west of the An Khe Pass, is nearly in the center of the highlands. It was from this area in 1954, while withdrawing from the pass, that French *Groupement Mobile 100* was ambushed, suffering very heavy casualties. The elevation is high enough to be refreshing to tired men accustomed to dealing with the usual Vietnamese warm and humid climate. Further to the west, the mountains rise to nearly 5,000 feet along the Cambodian and Laotian borders. When not drenched in rain, the climate here is pleasant, but cold at night. The triple-canopy jungle is shady and mountain rivers are fast-running and clear.

The Vietnamese culture combines elements of the traditional and progressive. The people are hardworking and decent. When well led, they become fine and courageous soldiers. As our allies, the South Vietnamese paid a very high price. Their war did not end after a single year or multiple tours of duty. The best of them were killed sooner or later during long years of conflict. The North Vietnamese too were courageous and competent warriors. They were doing what their leaders required of them, and paid a high price. Vietnam was a land with a long history of war. Its traditional foe was China.

Charlie Company, 2nd Battalion, 7th Cavalry, 1st Cavalry Division (Airmobile) was bloodied early in the war in Vietnam. It arrived in-country in Vietnam with the main elements of the division in mid-September 1965. The division debarked at Qui Nhon, a coastal city on the South China Sea a little more than halfway up the coast of South Vietnam. It established a base camp, Camp Radcliff, near the village of An Khê in the Central Highlands. A large 1st Cavalry Division patch painted onto the rocky mountainside of Hon Cong Mountain was visible from the base camp.

North Vietnamese Army soldiers (NVA) had established themselves prominently in many parts of the extensive operational area of the division. This area of operations (AO) extended from the lowland rice-growing areas near the coast, through the Central Highlands and westward into the higher mountainous region reaching the Cambodian and Laotian borders.

The division initiated aggressive operations in search of North Vietnamese main force units almost immediately. In November 1965 the 3rd Brigade—the Garry Owen Brigade—launched a major operation against a known enemy presence near the Chu Pong Massif in the mountainous part of its area of operations near the Cambodian border. This was the Ia Drang Valley campaign. On November 17, following the first phase of this engagement, the tremendous and brutal fighting at LZ X-Ray, the 2nd Battalion of the 7th Cavalry Regiment was airlifted into LZ X-Ray following the battle at X-Ray involving the 1/7 Cav. It was moving tactically through the densely covered mountain terrain on its way to LZ Albany when it was attacked by a much larger force of North Vietnamese regulars. During a vicious fight for survival and ultimately the upper hand, the battalion sustained very heavy casualties. Beginning the operation with a field strength of over 100, less than a squad (generally eleven men) of Charlie Company's soldiers walked out of this fight unscathed.

The whole idea of "heavy casualties" took on new significance. Personnel losses that in earlier conflicts would have called for a substantial period of reforming a badly mauled unit became simply brief periods of respite while the unit awaited replacements. On occasion, there was no break in operations whatsoever. Unit commanders made do with the men still able to carry on, with platoons executing company missions. Following the action at Ia Drang, those not wounded seriously enough for stateside evacuation returned to their unit as soon as they were released from medical care. Most of them would have it no other way. They were anxious to rejoin their comrades. This loyalty to unit and comrades characterizes the sentiment and fellowship of fighting organizations.

Following the Ia Drang battles, Charlie Company now consisted of those who had survived LZ Albany, along with new replacements and those returning from various medical facilities. On January 28, 1966, Charlie Company again engaged a major North Vietnamese force in Operation Masher/Whitewing near the village of Bong Son. The company assaulted into LZ 4, a landing zone in a graveyard. The North Vietnamese had the landing zone covered by fire and were waiting for the air assault. There was another vicious firefight. When the dust settled, the company had endured over forty casualties. The company now consisted mainly of replacements, returned wounded, and a handful of men who had come in-country with the division in September, some four and a half months earlier. In this short period, Charlie Company had lost more than 160 men from the company rolls, many of them killed in action.

By early April 1966, after the earlier heavy fighting, Charlie Company consisted mostly of replacements and a few men who had arrived with the division in 1965. We were usually short of platoon leaders; two of the platoons were led by very competent noncommissioned officers. Well over half of the men in the company at that time had been wounded and returned to duty. Several had been wounded more than once. In the field, several of the men had armed themselves with the Chinese-manufactured AK47, the Soviet-designed assault rifle the Chinese provided for use by the North Vietnamese. On Vietnamese battlefields there was always a variety of captured weapons from which to choose. Captured weapons in addition to the AK47 included the Soviet-designed and Chinese-manufactured SKS rifle, some older American rifles and submachine guns, and a few weapons of other origin that had worked their way into the Viet Cong and North Vietnamese inventory. The AK47 was considered the best for appropriation and employment. Additionally, the company obtained a few 12-gauge shotguns through supply channels. Other Army and Marine units also used captured AK47s in preference to malfunctioning XM16E1s.[3]

Throughout all our engagements during my year with the 1st Cavalry Division, we were armed with the XM16E1 rifle firing a 5.56mm cartridge with a 55-grain bullet, an individual weapon capable of both semi-automatic and full-automatic fire. The nomenclature of American military weapons follows some logic but wanders into the arbitrary from time to time. In the case of the XM16E1 rifle, "X" means the model is still in the development phase, "M" is for model, and the "16" is a model number that followed the designation of the ArmaLite AR15 as "15," an apparently appropriate sequential designation within a series of related ArmaLite arms. The "E" means experimental and the "1" refers to the first experimental modification: the bolt-assist device, considered superfluous by the Air Force, unnecessary but acceptable by the Navy and Marines if it didn't otherwise affect performance, but essential by the Army. This device satisfied the standard requirement of providing the rifleman a means of assuring that a cartridge was fully in place in the chamber.

Other "standard" military rifle specifications, notably among them a chromed bore and chamber, weren't incorporated into the civilian-designed weapon, the latter a requirement in military rifle specifications for many years. This was America's contribution to the category of individual military weapons known as assault rifles. Most contact with the enemy occurred within a range of 100 or less meters. This was the case in Vietnam. There are still advocates for a higher-caliber cartridge. There are still those who disapprove of arming all the riflemen in a squad with a weapon capable of full automatic fire.[4]

The selection of an appropriate individual weapon for the man on the ground usually looks backward to the experience of the last war. Experience is important and should permit the avoidance of mistakes learned from hard lessons. It's a positive factor if combined with an open mind. Often innovative ideas and improvements in weapons design encounter overly conservative thinking. Traditional dedication to particular weapons systems, a personal or professional stake in current standard armaments, bureaucratic lethargy, short-sightedness, and sometimes self-interest all contribute to poor decision making.

Major decisions regarding weapon design and procurement, like just about everything else, are affected by political and economic considerations. Some poor decisions arise from ignorance, some border on negligence. Major advances in weapons technology and the influence they have on tactics sometimes go unrecognized for long periods. Militaries that are slow to recognize change suffer higher casualties and sometimes defeat until reality takes hold and they too adjust to change.

Warriors at one time furnished their own arms and equipment. This was always expensive and became more so as changing tactics and technology favored new and improved means of engaging an enemy. Combat evolved using everything from spears and lances, various types of edged weapons, long-bows and crossbows, and varieties of muskets: smooth-bore and rifled, flintlock and caplock, breech loading and muzzle loading. Muzzle-loading rifles gave way to breech-loading rifles: bolt-action; clip-, magazine-, and drum-fed; semi-automatic and fully automatic; and of small caliber and large caliber. These and other weapons and combinations of weapons, ammunition, and armor all competed at one point or another for supremacy in combat. They have become increasingly expensive; movement from a traditional weapon system to what appears to be an improved system is expensive.

Economic, political, and personal factors enter the decision-making equation. Military power has come to rely increasingly on an economic base that furnishes arms and other logistical support. Research and development are major components of logistical support. Tradition, cost, and politics all play a role in getting the right weapons to the right people when needed.

If we use the American Revolution as an arbitrary historical starting point, we observe that many colonists were accustomed to using firearms. Hunting and defense along the frontier were very basic preparations for military service. Americans resisted discipline but used their skill with firearms to advantage. We refined the tradition of accurate shooting and coupled it with muskets that rewarded shooting skills. The first standard infantry weapon of the American Army, a flintlock smoothbore musket adopted in 1795, was a near duplication of a French musket brought twenty years earlier from France by the Marquis de Lafayette. It was produced by Springfield Armory and continued as the standard infantry weapon until 1841 with the adoption of a caplock rifle, although the British had armed one regiment with a flintlock rifle as early as 1800. The idea of making each shot count and of being able to reach out and touch the enemy before he was able to respond was alive and well during the Revolutionary War.

In the American Civil War, the Union Army resisted the introduction of many breech loading and even some repeating rifles, considering them unreliable. Finally, the Army adopted a .45-caliber single-shot breechloader, the Springfield Model 1873, thirty-two years after the Prussian Army had first adopted a breechloader and European armies were rearming with repeaters.[5] The Civil War was one in which accuracy, rapid loading, as well as lethality and extended range were important, reinforcing the idea of accurate shooting employing weapons with a range that took account of shooting skills. Men fought from behind prepared positions as well as in very personal combat where, if one side didn't break, the bayonet came into play. Still, America was behind the times in developing and standardizing available technology in our individual military rifles. We had entered into the era of rifled muskets and early lever-action rifles. The American military was traditional and slow to modernize.

"*At various times in their history, the Army bureaus responsible for small-arms development have gone by different names, including . . . the Army Materiel Command and the Ordnance Department. The ordnance corps had overseen small-arms development for the Army for more than a hundred years* [from the perspective of 1981]. *In questions of technology, it emphasized the outlook of the 'gravel-bellies'—the sharpshooters and marksmen who measured a weapon by how well it helped them hit a target 400, 500, 600 yards away in peacetime rifle competition.*"[6] This tradition of long-range accuracy went a long way back. It was reinforced by the American tradition of personal firearms use and ownership.

In 1892 the Army adopted the Krag-Jorgensen rifle in caliber .30–40 Krag. This weapon was manufactured by Springfield Armory and—along with the Springfield trapdoor rifle—was employed by American troops during the Spanish-American War. It was a Norwegian design that won out in a comparative evaluation with American rifles. This marked the beginning of the "not-invented-here" reaction to sometimes better foreign weapons. Both rifles, the Krag and Springfield, weren't as easy to load as the Spanish model of the German-designed Mauser Model 1893. This led to the U.S. development of the Springfield rifle M1903. This was a fine weapon used by American soldiers and Marines in the First World War.

The design was modeled on the German Mauser. The United States paid Mauser $200,000 for the manufacturing rights, but it was manufactured at home and avoided the stigma of "not invented here." In the First World War, small arms supporting fire was provided by models of the .30 caliber Browning machine gun as well as the M1918 Browning Automatic Rifle, the BAR, which came into service during the war and served into the 1970s. America developed a fixation on the .30 caliber weapon. It served us well. Here again we see the tradition of accurate shooting with a caliber where a rifleman who shot well could reach out to an effective range of nearly 1,000 yards and take out his target. Sergeant Alvin York epitomizes this tradition, although his extraordinary heroism involved shooting at much lesser ranges.

The .30–06 cartridge worked well in the bolt-action 1903 Springfield rifle, but the long cartridge functioned less efficiently in weapons firing in the semi-automatic and automatic fire modes. In 1928 the War Department appointed a board of officers to select an appropriate caliber for a future shoulder-fired automatic weapon. This board was called the "Pig Board." It conducted ballistic wound testing at Aberdeen Proving Ground, Maryland, in July 1929, using different calibers: .30, .276, and .256 and live pigs as targets. The board concluded that if the future rifle employed the standard .30–06 cartridge, it would be as heavy or heavier than the 1903 Springfield, as indeed the BAR had proved to be. The board also concluded that small-caliber, higher-velocity bullets were more lethal than the .30–06 round within the normal effective range of infantry combat. This was the first of several tests suggesting that a caliber smaller than the long-standard .30 caliber might be more suitable for use in an infantry weapon. In 1929 the Ballistics Research Laboratory also recommended that small-caliber, high-velocity cartridges be evaluated for effectiveness. There was no suggestion that every man in a rifle squad should be armed with a rifle capable of fully automatic fire.

Controversy still exists about what should be considered a normal combat range. For many years that range was pegged at 500 yards, and this was the case back in 1929. The 500-yard measure was still standard when the XM16E1 was so designated and produced for use in Vietnam. By then, several studies had concluded that most enemy targets engaged by Marines and soldiers are within a range of 300 yards. Three hundred yards was the maximum range claimed for the XM16E1 rifle and its ammunition by its developer. The Army, however, was insistent on 500 yards. The effectiveness of the XM16E1 at 500 yards is questionable, but at 300 it will do the job. There remains a great deal of controversy over what should be considered an essential effective range; some advocates of a more powerful cartridge still contend that that range should be at least 500 yards. They contend that the residual energy of the bullet at that range should ensure a kill, something claimed for the XM16E1 but not at all certain.

By this time (the early 1930s) Garand rifles were available to test against rifles in .276 caliber. The Army resisted adopting a different caliber, citing cost and supply issues. The existing inventory of .30 caliber weapons would become obsolete as well as ammunition on hand and machine tools used in weapon manufacture. In 1932, Army chief of staff General Douglas MacArthur resolved the issue with a decision that any future weapon should use the standard .30–06 cartridge. This confirmed the military fixation on a .30 caliber round.

Another consideration was the continued emphasis on bayonet training, using a rifle sufficiently stout to be employed in individual hand-to-hand combat. The rifle itself was a weapon. Thus, although there was an early recognition that a smaller, lighter automatic rifle with a lower-caliber high-velocity cartridge and adequate lethality was feasible, that awareness met with an older tradition of a .30 caliber weapon with greater range, as well as weight and strength that enhanced its utility for close-in bayonet combat. The operative concept was still that of selectively arming designated individuals as automatic riflemen with a special weapon of the same caliber designed for full-automatic fire. The idea of an assault rifle issued as the basic infantry weapon didn't exist. The term itself lacked a concept. The military would go on to develop small, light .45 caliber fully automatic weapons, but these were thought of more as special-purpose arms, convenient for carry in vehicles or aircraft, useful for local security, effective for clearing out trenches, and for clearing buildings in urban fighting. They weren't intended to be employed as principal infantry weapons.

Although the U.S. military was a little slow on the uptake, there was nevertheless awareness that weapons of less than .30 caliber might have the potential to reduce the weight of the rifle and ammunition, while still meeting range and lethality criteria. As noted, in 1929 the Ballistics Research Laboratory had recommended that small-caliber, high-velocity cartridges, such as .276 and .25 caliber, be evaluated for effectiveness. They would save weight and possibly increase lethality. The Army opted instead for the proven .30 caliber cartridge and set about developing an automatic rifle to accommodate it. Such an automatic rifle would employ the same ammunition as the Browning Automatic Rifle and the then-standard machine guns. The semi-automatic M1 Garand was the result of this decision.

In 1936 the military standardized the M1 rifle, firing the .30–06 cartridge, as the standard U.S. service rifle. It continued the tradition of a rifle capable of successfully engaging an enemy at extended ranges, accurate and lethal at 1,000 or more yards. In 1940 the Garand was tested against another .30 caliber contender, the Johnson semi-automatic rifle. The Johnson came out second-best and the Garand was already in production.

Our military continued to follow and believe in the tradition of accurately aimed and effective fire by soldiers familiar with firearms. We trained men to shoot accurately, although by now fewer men came from a rural background with a presumed familiarity with firearms. The M1 remained the standard rifle until 1959 and was the rifle issued to American soldiers and Marines in World War II and Korea. It had an eight-round, easy-to-load clip. The Army and Marines also employed different models of the Browning machine gun: the M1917A1, a water-cooled model, and the M1919. The BAR filled the recognized need for a greater automatic fire capability in the infantry squad.

These were all .30 caliber weapons. Excluding handguns, other infantry weapons included the M1 carbine, in service from 1942 through 1973, and the M2 carbine, capable of full automatic fire, in service from 1943 through 1973. Both were smaller and lighter than the Garand, firing a smaller .30 caliber carbine cartridge. They were issued to airborne soldiers, officers, NCOs, ammunition bearers and forward observers. The M2 carbine was in use by the U.S. Air Force for security personnel until it was upgraded in 1964 with the M16, a version of the AR15 minus the bolt-assist. Also in service were two .45 caliber submachine guns, the Thompson, invented in 1918 and used by notorious criminals, and in military service from 1938 through 1971. The second was known to troops as the "grease gun" due to its resemblance to the similarly named mechanic's tool. It was designated the Submachine Gun, caliber .45, M3 and was simpler and lighter than the Thompson.

The M3 served from December 1942 through 1992. The M2 carbine and grease gun were both on hand for use by advisors in Vietnam. These were light and convenient for vehicle carry, self-defense, or local guard duty. They were useful for close-in urban combat or self-defense at close quarters, but had insufficient range, penetration ability, and lethality to be acceptable for standard infantry use in combat. Submachine guns fire a handgun cartridge of one type or another. They weren't forerunners of the assault rifle but special purpose weapons of limited issue. At the time, the U.S. Army hadn't considered employing either a rifle configured as an assault rifle or arming every rifleman with such a weapon, whether it fired a .30 caliber cartridge or one of lesser caliber. It would be up to the German army to develop the concept in World War II.

The Army defines assault rifles as short, compact, selective-fire weapons that fire a cartridge intermediate in power between submachine gun and rifle cartridges. They look different. Because they are shorter, they are less likely to hang up on vegetation, they can be brought quickly to bear on a suddenly appearing enemy and are easier to employ when negotiating corners in rooms or moving from one place to another inside buildings. A major factor distinguishing them from submachine guns is that the cartridge they employ has a higher velocity and greater target penetration and lethality than a handgun cartridge. It may or may not qualify as what we would call today "high velocity," something on the order of over 3,000 feet per second. Assault rifles are capable of selective fire. Selective fire gives the shooter the choice of firing a single round with a single pull of the trigger, or of continuous fire until the magazine is emptied if the trigger is held back.

With the realization that short bursts, optimally three-round bursts, are more accurate and more effective than long bursts of automatic fire, the ability to fire in three-round bursts has been incorporated into many assault rifles. The various modes of fire are controlled by a selector switch usually within reach of the firer's thumb for a right-handed shooter. Other characteristics of an assault rifle include a detachable box or drum magazine capable of holding anywhere from twenty rounds (the usual minimum in a box magazine) and up to fifty rounds or more in a drum magazine. It should have an effective range of at least 300 meters.

One of the principal advantages of an assault rifle is that the intermediate caliber ammunition with its reduced recoil makes it easier to hold the weapon on target when firing in the fully automatic and controlled-burst modes. This was one of the reasons for its initial development. Another characteristic of many assault rifles is that, by employing a stamped-steel design, they are easier and less expensive to produce than standard rifles. This less-expensive manufacturing method is an option, not a required characteristic. It is very possible to design a rifle in the assault-rifle configuration firing the 7.62mm NATO cartridge or some other 7.62mm cartridge such as that employed in the AK47. The downside here is weight.

In 1941 the Soviets developed the PPSh41, a recoil or blow-back automatic rifle firing a 7.62x25mm pistol cartridge. They developed this weapon for the Winter War in Finland to counter the Finns, who were using their own submachine gun. Properly speaking, the PPSh41 was a submachine gun because it fired a pistol cartridge, the 7.62x25mm Tokarev. It had many of the handling characteristics of an assault rifle. Production began in late 1941 and came on line in 1942. The caliber was analogous to the .45 caliber pistol cartridge used by the Thompson submachine gun and the grease gun. In configuration it was an early "assault rifle" and was employed as such. It had a box magazine that could be loaded with thirty-five rounds and a drum magazine that held seventy-one at full load. It was commonly called a "burp gun" by Americans who confronted this weapon in the hands of North Korean and Chinese soldiers in the Korean War.

The Soviet PPSh41 prompted the Germans to design their own assault rifle, the Sturmgewehr 44, but they upgraded the caliber. This was the first true "assault rifle," firing a 7.92x33mm intermediate powered cartridge. It was inexpensively produced, using the stamped-steel design, and came on line in 1944, late in World War II. Having originated the idea of employing a fully automatic weapon in the form of an assault rifle as the standard infantry weapon, the Soviets followed this up with the AK47.

The AK47 is a gas-operated automatic rifle employing a rotating bolt system firing the standard Soviet-Warsaw Pact 7.62x39mm cartridge. Its estimated effective range is 200 to 250 meters, considered by the Soviets to be adequate for war in Europe. It was adopted as a standard Soviet weapon in early 1949. The Russians accepted the reduced range in exchange for a high volume of fire with adequate lethality for close-in fighting. It was sufficiently accurate and lethal at ranges out to 300 meters. The Chinese manufactured it for use by the North Vietnamese. The AK47 was a principal infantry weapon rather than a lightweight submachine gun for vehicular- or tank-crew use.

The first glimmer of change in the basic armament of the infantry soldier was evident by the conclusion of the Second World War. By the end of fighting in Korea, the move to arming the fighting Marine and soldier with a fully automatic weapon should have been clear. This was more than just recognition of the potential for rifles firing an intermediate caliber cartridge, high velocity or not, to replace rifles firing the standard .30 caliber cartridge. It was a new direction in weapons development. The principle was becoming clear. A rifle squad had to be able to dominate the battlefield with automatic fire. To be competitive with a similarly armed enemy, with the possible exception of officers and men armed with machine guns—or other specialized weapons such as grenade launchers—every infantryman would have to be armed with a rifle capable of fully automatic fire. The logistical means of supporting the increased need for ammunition would have to be developed.

The point is made that riflemen tend to waste ammunition with a rifle that fires on full automatic, and that there is a tendency to fire away madly at an unseen enemy. But the enemy is usually unseen, even when we are receiving effective fire. Returning automatic fire will suppress some of the enemy's fire. When the enemy attacks, which he will do when he senses a significant advantage, then a full-automatic capability is even more important. Such engagements take place at very close quarters. The same is true when the enemy is suddenly confronted while on the move or when entering an enclosed space. The full-automatic capability, properly employed by a trained warrior, will determine who survives.

If an effective intermediate cartridge and a lighter rifle could be developed, so much the better. At the same time and as part of this evolution, the configuration of the rifle would change. As well as being lighter, it would likely be shorter. The rifle bore would be more in line with the stock rather than offset, as with the traditional rifle. The rifle would be just as accurate, but more dependence would be put on both suppressive fire and dominating the immediate area with fire when first contact occurred. This domination with suppressive fire in close contact with the enemy is a principal characteristic of the assault rifle, essential for basic survival in the close-in type of contact common to both jungle fighting and urban warfare. Overwhelming suppressive fire would facilitate both fire and movement and fire and maneuver. The accuracy of the weapon should assure engaging an enemy with lethal fire out to at least 300 meters, with a somewhat greater range capability being desirable. Beyond the effective rifle range, the 7.62mm machine guns and supporting fires would take over.

Accurate fire was still important, and every army trained highly skilled snipers, but the average infantryman wasn't that proficient with a rifle. Increasingly, success depends on superior firepower, measured by rounds on target and suppressive fire in the vicinity of a target. This permits movement and an opportunity to close on an enemy position. Up close, automatic fire is more effective than semi-automatic fire. The same is true in the defense, particularly when confronted by large numbers of an advancing enemy. There are two downsides. First, the rifle is less useful in hand-to-hand combat and bayonet fighting. Second, special training is necessary to develop an instinct for accurate pointed fire, that is, the immediate accurate engagement of a suddenly appearing enemy. This training is easy to accomplish. Good fire control also responds to discipline and good training.

For many years, the western powers continued to focus on .30 caliber rifles and automatic rifles, attempting with limited success to improve the capabilities of individual weapons in that caliber. The soldiers of most foreign armies didn't come from countries where young men grew up with firearms, so the militaries of such countries were more open to innovation. The American Army and Marine Corps were still thinking accuracy and lethality at longer ranges. The Army's rifle squad had two men armed with the Browning Automatic Rifle very effectively employing the .30–06 cartridge. The BAR, however, couldn't match the burp gun in the volume of fire it generated. When confronted with close and advancing superior numbers of an enemy armed predominantly with the PPSh41 in Korea, a squad armed with the M1 and BARs was outgunned. The gap was filled with the light machine gun, but that still left the infantry squad at a disadvantage and dependent upon suppressive fire from crew-served weapons. The United States, however, was slow to recognize the advantage of arming the individual rifleman with a weapon capable of fully automatic fire and exerted a strong influence on its European allies to follow our lead.

Work on the next rifle began with prototypes in 1945 to meet a requirement for a lightweight automatic rifle. In the late 1950s, the search for a cartridge that was more suitable for automatic fire resumed. This was the 7.62x51mm NATO cartridge, adopted officially in 1957. This was still a .30 caliber round but was shorter and functioned more efficiently in the semi-automatic and automatic modes of fire. The new powder, ball powder, standardized as the powder for military rifles in 1942—although loaded into a slightly smaller NATO standard cartridge case than the .30–06 round—delivered the same velocity and energy characteristics. The fixation on .30 caliber or 7.62mm was still in effect. This was the cartridge, now a standard NATO round, that the then-prototype of the future M14 fired in competition against the Belgian *Fusil Automatique Léger*, or FAL, candidate rifle. The "not-invented-here" attitude favored the M14 prototype, so the competition was biased in its favor. The U.S.-produced weapon ultimately proved to be better.

The U.S. military was still contemplating an automatic rifle capable of being selectively fired in the full automatic mode, a follow-on to replace the BAR, but not an assault rifle. The M14 was produced to meet this requirement. Although the M14 was designed to be capable of selective fire, it was believed at that time that issuing a rifle capable of fully automatic fire to every rifleman would waste too much ammunition. Those issued to other than the squad's automatic riflemen weren't equipped with the selector switch enabling fully automatic fire. This was thinking in the past and is a further indication that the assault rifle concept hadn't found a home in U.S. military thinking.

Production of the M14 began in 1959, and the rifle was standardized in 1961. The modified version—the M14E2—intended as a replacement for the

BAR—was standardized in 1963. But there was a problem. The fully automatic variant of the M14 wasn't suitable as a shoulder-fired automatic rifle. When shoulder fired, it was too heavy and hard to hold on target when firing in the fully automatic mode. It was too light for accurate sustained automatic fire when employed with its bipod and wasn't suitable as a replacement for the BAR. Although an effective rifle, it lacked the easy handling characteristics of the assault rifle configuration.

In sum, the M14E2 version wasn't an adequate automatic rifle. A version of the M14, the M15, with a heavier barrel, bipod and shoulder rest had been standardized but proved no better in the automatic rifle role than the M14E2[7] and would have incurred additional expense. It was never produced. The M14 and M14E2 were simply an out-of-date weapon combination. The caliber exceeded the need for a lethal round at combat ranges.

For greater ranges, the M60 machine gun met the need. An assault rifle could employ a lighter cartridge and the individual could carry significantly more ammunition. The rifleman would be less hesitant to expend it when he believed it to be advantageous. The military recognized the desirability of a lighter, more efficient weapon and had devised a prototype that was called the Special Purpose Individual Weapon, or SPIW. This weapon employed a .22 caliber discarding sabot round containing several darts fired at a very high velocity. It also incorporated a grenade launcher. It was unwieldy, and the darts proved to have an insufficient penetration capability, being easily deflected by brush and foliage. This was to be the military's answer to the shortcomings of the M14. It required some imagination to think such a weapon might morph into a satisfactory primary infantry arm. It did not.

Expecting a SPIW to come on line and be the next individual weapon development kept attention focused on the M14 when the AR15 first came to the military's attention in 1957. The Army was waiting for a major advance in effectiveness, and while many recognized the advantages of the AR15, others still aggressively defended the 7.62mm cartridge and the M14 family. The Army anticipated a significantly greater gain in effectiveness from the never-to-be-acceptable SPIW. They intended its timely arrival as a replacement for the M14. More significantly, the planners were thinking in the past. We were already in the assault rifle era and didn't realize it.

There were no candidates for an assault rifle. The concept wasn't appreciated by traditionally minded military personnel. For them, there were rifles, automatic rifles, and machine guns, along with handguns and a few weapons of lower caliber unsuitable for employment as principal infantry weapons. The idea of an assault rifle firing an intermediate caliber cartridge, lethal at the expected ranges of engagement out to 300 yards, was simply outside-the-box thinking. As we shall see, the specified effective range for the AR15 was arbitrarily extended to 500 yards with unintended negative consequences for the XM16E1. The concept of an assault rifle would have to await a clear need and overcome the prejudice that favored .30 caliber weapons. Further, the concept of arming all members of a rifle squad with a fully automatic capable individual weapon hadn't yet come of age.

It might have been possible to design a satisfactory assault rifle firing the standard NATO round and intended for general issue and use. The cartridge itself was suitable for use in the fully automatic mode of fire. It would have been fairly heavy, but the troops would have accepted it uncomplainingly if it was reliable. Inured to carrying mortar base-plates, mortar ammunition, radios, and an extra basic load, they would have packed a 7.62mm assault rifle with little difficulty. The basic load of ammunition would have had to be somewhat less, and men would have had to be more careful with ammunition expenditures.

By insisting on .30 caliber as the standard cartridge size, whether .30–06 or 7.62mm NATO, the concept of developing a truly lightweight automatic rifle proved totally impractical. The idea of a lightweight rifle firing a smaller cartridge was still alive, but the concept and design of an automatic rifle in the assault rifle configuration would await the development of the ArmaLite AR15 by imaginative people unassociated with the military. Civilian development would lead to serious complications, however, as we shall see.

Early in 1958, the Army had renewed its interest in a lightweight rifle. In that year, the U.S. Army Infantry Board at Fort Benning, Georgia, conducted tests of the AR15 and found it to be a satisfactory weapon. Shortly thereafter, also in 1958, as General Willard G. Wyman, commanding the Continental Army Command (CONARC) at Fort Monroe, Virginia, readied for retirement, he established a program to review the Army's rifle development program and attempted to resolve the issue of which caliber was best for the individual infantryman. This was the Powell Board, led by General Herbert B. Powell, General Wyman's deputy at CONARC. The board recommended that no further consideration be given to the .223 caliber round and that the M14 rifle (M14E2) be retained for the automatic rifle role. It recommended that an AR15 type of weapon be expedited to replace the M14 in the rifle role and that its caliber should be a .258 round. This recommendation was a sound one and if followed might have produced a weapon whose range and lethality characteristics would have been less open to challenge.

But coming on the heels of the AR15, it rather muddied the waters. In late 1958, CONARC headquarters directed that a study be conducted to compare the performance of different calibers of infantry rifles. More testing was conducted with the AR15 in 1959 at the Combat Developments Experimentation Center at Fort Ord, California. The ArmaLite AR15, initially in .222 caliber, was available for testing, along with a Winchester lightweight military rifle. These rifles were compared with the M14. The AR15 came out on top, with reliability comparable to the M14.

This was the evaluation that concluded that a lightweight, smaller-caliber rifle was more effective in terms of volume of fire and target hits than the M14. A smaller squad of five to seven men armed with the lighter rifle could deliver more firepower than an eleven-man squad armed with the M14 with, presumably, two men armed with its automatic version, the M14E2. This conclusion proved to be the heart of the matter. Riflemen should be armed with an infantry rifle capable of fully automatic fire. More testing by the Arctic Test Board in Alaska arrived at the same conclusion as the Infantry Board in 1959, that the AR15 was a satisfactory weapon.

Throughout this early testing phase, the ArmaLite AR15 functioned reliably. It employed ammunition charged with Improved Military Rifle (IMR) propellant, a tubular nitrocellulose type of powder that the rifle had been designed to accommodate. This combination of rifle and ammunition functioned reliably.

But the U.S. military was irrevocably committed to the NATO 7.62mm round. Cost and supply factors were a continuing consideration, along with the fact that the 7.62mm cartridge had been standardized in 1957. These were deciding factors. For these reasons, along with (we suspect) a military prejudice for the now-standard .30 caliber weapon-ammunition combinations, the Army chief of staff, General Maxwell Taylor, in January 1959 determined to stick with the NATO 7.62mm ammunition and associated arms. This was confirmed by the next chief of staff, General Earle Wheeler, in September of the same year. Since the United States was committed to the NATO cartridge, and had leaned heavily and successfully on our allies to continue to employ a .30 caliber round, there was understandable resistance to coming up with a rifle firing a different, smaller-caliber cartridge.

The various test results favoring a lighter automatic rifle firing a smaller caliber was something the military had to acknowledge. It was a long-appreciated fact by our potential enemies and came to be employed by them in Vietnam. We were behind the curve on this one. However, the military hadn't developed specifications for such an individual assault rifle. The Army chief of staff had opted for the NATO standard caliber. There were no military specifications for an individual automatic rifle using a cartridge other than 7.62mm. The Ordnance Department had long-established specific standards for military rifles, and these weren't included in the development of rifles by ArmaLite. The military had devised no specifications whatsoever for what might be considered an assault rifle, and neither the M14E2 nor the never-to-be-practical SPIW was such a weapon. The fixation on .30 caliber had stymied individual rifle development for many years. It was time to replace the M14, but the Army was not yet on board.

A rifle in the assault rifle configuration, while less suitable for use with a bayonet, is easier to handle and manage in full automatic fire. It requires some additional training for accurate pointed fire. This training requirement is largely compensated for by fully automatic fire, particularly when the rifle has a design that minimizes muzzle climb, as is the case with the M16 family of individual weapons. The concept of an assault rifle would have to await a clear need and overcome the prejudice that favored .30 caliber weapons. Further, the concept of arming all the members of the rifle squad with a fully automatic-capable individual weapon had not come of age. Military decision makers were thinking in the past. We were already in the assault rifle era and did not see it. As one 101st Airborne Division (Airmobile) veteran of the Vietnam War, a Long Range Patrol Team leader confirms: "In all my training—everything from day one, but especially in the line outfit—it was always fire superiority that mattered."[8]

There was no candidate for an assault rifle. The concept was not appreciated by traditionally minded military personnel. There was thus no plan to develop such a rifle firing either the standard caliber cartridge, effective out to 1,000 yards, or a lighter rifle firing an intermediate caliber cartridge lethal at the lesser expected ranges of engagement. Five hundred yards was still the standard when the XM16E1, still in a developmental stage, was produced for use in Vietnam. By then, several studies had concluded that most enemy targets engaged by the Marine and soldier are within a range of 300 yards, and that was the maximum effective range claimed for the rifle and its ammunition by the developer. When the military began to look at the AR15, the effective range was arbitrarily extended to 500 yards in anticipation of the objections any lesser effective range might raise. This had unintended negative consequences for the XM16E1. At 500 yards the effectiveness of a 5.56mm cartridge is less than that of a 7.62mm cartridge but still adequate.

Some advocates of a more powerful cartridge continue to contend that that range should be at least 500 yards and that the residual energy of the bullet at that range should ensure a certain kill. The 7.62mm NATO 144 grain bullet can punch through wooden structures, brush, other heavy vegetation, and personal armor more consistently than the now-standard 5.56mm NATO cartridge with a 62-grain bullet.

Because of deficiencies in the Army procurement process and the ever-present influence of politics in the Department of Defense, American fighting men soon learned that the newest infantry rifle, the XM16E1, was plagued with known deficiencies when it was introduced into combat in Vietnam. These deficiencies were unrelated to lethality. The XM16E1 would frequently jam in a firefight, and the most frequent malfunction, failure to extract, could not be cleared by immediate action.

In the following chapter we'll examine the developmental history of the M16 family of weapons.

3

THE M16 AND ITS DEVELOPMENT

Lt. Gen. Mikhail Kalashnikov (1919–2013): I was in the hospital, and a soldier in the bed beside me asked, "Why do our soldiers have only one rifle for two or three of our men, when the Germans have automatics?" So I designed one. I was a soldier, and I created a machine gun for a soldier. It was called an Avtomat Kalashnikova, the automatic weapon of Kalashnikov—AK—and it carried the date of its first manufacture, 1947.[1]

David Southall, an experienced competitive shooter, both small bore and high power, describes his experience with the XM16E1. Entering the military in 1966, he was trained with the XM16E1 during advanced individual training at Fort Polk, Louisiana, and had very few problems with it there. He was assigned to the 1st Infantry Division and in December, in Vietnam, was issued an XM16E1. He first used it on Operation Cedar Falls in early January 1967.

He describes what happened:

We began to have extraction problems almost immediately. Not every round would fail to extract [but] regardless of whether the rifle was clean or not, one of the cartridges would have its rim torn off leaving the case in the chamber. Sometimes after 10 or more shots, sometimes on the first shot. One thing I noticed was that when we shot up "old ammo" for practice we nearly never had failures to extract. The problem initially was only with "fresh ammo." After May of '67 there was no "old stock" ammo in First Division stores so that all of the ammo gave problems. . . . This was less of a problem once our Battalion went "mechanized" . . . and our squad tactics changed somewhat due to the unreliability of the M16. We began to rely more on the M60 and squad sizes went from 12 to 6 or 8. This may have been caused by the slowness with which replacements got to the front lines, but the net result was more M60s and M79s and less reliance on the M16 at the squad level. . . . Those who carried the M16 always had an assembled 3-piece cleaning rod attached to the side of his rifle with "blousing rubbers." That facilitated getting the fired case out of the chamber as quickly as possible. Those cases popped right out with the slightest tap from the cleaning rod, so they were not "stuck" due to corrosion or dirty or rough chambers. At the time it was really insulting to claim that we soldiers were not maintaining our weapons properly. Our guns were certainly clean enough to function properly. We tried all the rumored "fixes" like oiling the rounds, only loading magazines with 12 or 13 rounds. At least to me, the problem was caused by either the cartridge's rim being too soft or the action attempting to extract the fired case while the chamber pressure was too high.[2]

He goes on to state that no one was interested in his opinion at the time.

The M14E2 was difficult to control in automatic fire, with excessive muzzle climb. Additionally, soldiers couldn't carry sufficient ammunition. American soldiers and Marines armed with the M14 and M14E2 were outgunned by an enemy armed with the AK47. This should have been foreseen, but the Army failed to fully consider earlier test results showing the advantage of equipping all riflemen in a rifle squad with weapons capable of well-controlled fully automatic fire. The history of arming just two men in a rifle squad with an automatic rifle of the standard .30 caliber or 7.62mm cartridge was well established. Contributing to this lack of vision, the Army consistently downplayed the quality of the AK47, alleging it to be a crude and poor-quality weapon. It was a wake-up call when the South Vietnamese and their American advisors found themselves at a firepower disadvantage.

The main consideration in the choice of an infantry rifle is effective firepower. Weight is also a factor. The 7.62mm NATO ammunition and the M14 rifle together were heavier than the AK47-ammo combination. Military planners were thinking about the combined weapon-ammunition weight and were concerned with how much additional ammunition might be carried in the basic load. A soldier or Marine armed with an XM16E1 could carry two and a half times as much ammunition for the same weight load as he could have when armed with an M14. That said, the U.S. military loads its soldiers and Marines down with load-carrying gear and other equipment. Our Army's gear is notably heavier as well as more durable than that of most other armies. At the same time, it's more burdensome and reduces foot mobility, a significant factor for the Marine and soldier when seeking an elusive and fast-moving foot-mobile enemy. The heavy weight of U.S. military load-bearing gear, weapons, and other equipment is significant because it places an upper limit on the amount of ammunition the soldier or Marine can carry. They load up on ammunition, usually more than the basic load, and leave unneeded gear behind when they are on operations.

The military first showed an interest in the small-caliber, high-velocity (SCHV) concept in the years following World War II and Korea. In 1952, Donald L. Hall, an engineer at Aberdeen's Ballistics Research Laboratories, prepared a report based on theoretical calculations that concluded that an appropriate smaller-caliber cartridge (i.e., smaller than .30 caliber), matched with an appropriate weapon, would be more effective than the M1 rifle firing the Army standard .30 caliber round. Hall acknowledged the fact that this finding was contrary to accepted doctrine when he submitted his report.[3]

A study prepared by Norman A. Hitchman of the Operational Research Office at Baltimore's Johns Hopkins University appeared very soon after the Hall study. This report confirmed Hall's findings and suggested that automatic fire was more effective than semi-automatic fire. The Army, however, remained firmly committed to a .30 caliber military cartridge and to selectively arming only two men in a rifle squad with rifles capable of fully automatic fire. However, the Hitchman report led to a long-term study, Project Salvo, that extended from its inception in 1953 through 1960. This project led off in two directions. The first and most innovative conceptualized the Special Purpose Individual Weapon, or SPIW, that came to naught, as well as investigating duplex and other special cartridges, the former showing promise.[4] The second opened the way to further consideration of smaller-caliber military weapons, leading ultimately to the M16.

These men and others, civilian and military, were thinking ahead of the military's commitment to .30 caliber individual weapons. They contended that a lower-power cartridge, intermediate between .30 caliber and handgun calibers, already demonstrated to be effective at normal combat ranges, that is somewhere between 200 and 300 yards, would improve the effectiveness of the rifle squad. This would enable the rifleman to carry more ammunition in his basic load. Some authorities were considering the advisability of making the basic infantry weapon capable of full automatic fire.

This concept would come to fruition in later testing conducted at Fort Ord, California, and Hunter Liggett Military Reservation in Monterey County, California, in 1958 and 1959. The results of these tests showed that a smaller infantry squad of five to seven men armed with rifles firing a smaller-caliber cartridge but capable of fully automatic fire were significantly more effective than a standard eleven-man squad armed with M14s.[5] Our Army had long been focused on improving our standard .30 caliber weapons and avoiding the introduction of an additional ammunition requirement into the field which effectively slowed to a crawl any serious Army support for an intermediate-caliber rifle in the 1950s.

Earlier, in 1953, the beginning of an American automatic rifle in an assault rifle configuration was taking shape, thanks to the imagination and energy of several people. These individuals were still thinking in terms of a .30 caliber rifle, but one capable of fully automatic fire and of employment as the basic infantry rifle. They were thinking in terms of the weapon, not on the concept of an "assault rifle" and its implications for infantry combat. This would come later. George Sullivan, an aeronautical engineer and patent counsel for Lockheed Aircraft Corporation in Burbank, California, was an early proponent of a better automatic rifle utilizing lighter materials. He teamed up with another firearms buff, Jacques Michault, an arms salesman, and the two of them came up with plans that were completely different from those used to produce standard rifles, both military and civilian. Sullivan then met Paul S. Cleveland, the secretary of the Fairchild Engine and Airplane Corporation, at an aviation industry luncheon where they discussed weapons design and innovative manufacturing techniques to produce a lighter rifle. At this time, there was no consideration of an "intermediate cartridge." Cleveland subsequently reported this conversation to Richard Boutelle, at that time president of Fairchild Engine and Airplane Corporation. As it happened Boutelle, a former major in the Army Air Corps and big-game hunter, was also intrigued by the idea. Boutelle and Sullivan formed the ArmaLite Division of Fairchild Engine and Airplane Corporation and incorporated it on October 1, 1954. Charles Dorchester was plant manager of the ArmaLite Division. They soon hired Eugene Stoner as their senior design engineer. Stoner had served in the Marines and had a background in aviation ordnance.[6]

Eugene Stoner (1922–1997) was one of those very interesting and competent people who became one of the world's small arms experts and developer of an entirely different type of automatic rifle that eventually became the standard for U.S. armed forces. With no formal engineering training, he had the foresight, imagination, and engineering skills to incorporate new materials and designs into firearms that conformed, at the right time, to changing military perceptions of firepower needs. Stoner attended high school in Long Beach, California. With no funds to go to college, he started out working for the Vega Aircraft Company installing armament. During World War II, he enlisted in the Marines and served in aviation ordnance in the South Pacific and northern China. According to an April 1997 *New York Times* article, his interest in developing a new individual automatic rifle for the military came from a belief that many soldiers in World War II and Korea failed to fire their weapons.[7] This well-known story originated with reports by Brig. Gen. S. L. A. ("SLAM") Marshall, a World War II and Korean War historian, that in combat nearly four-fifths of soldiers didn't fire their weapons, presumably because they seldom saw the enemy directly and thought it not worth their while to fire random single shots at an unseen enemy.

Men armed with the Browning Automatic Rifle, on the contrary, could hose down an area with automatic fire with some hope of hitting an enemy if they had a general idea of his location, and at least providing suppressive fire. Soldiers close by tended to fire more frequently the closer they were to the BAR man. Marshall was also writing actively during the Vietnam conflict.[8] One Marine officer, the late Major Dick Culver, thinks that men not firing their weapons in combat ". . . is a sorry indictment of our military leadership." He also maintained that the squad automatic rifles were the most important weapons in the rifle squad and the job of each fire team was to keep them in business.[9] He contends that focusing on the automatic riflemen promoted squad cohesion. This would seem to infer that having only one man in a fire team armed with a fully automatic rifle may be better than having all men so armed. This, however, is probably not what he intended to imply. Squad cohesion depends on leadership, not on the weapons of individual squad members. Marshall's observation may apply to the circumstances of earlier wars, but some of his writing was later challenged. His contention that most soldiers didn't fire their rifles in combat is questionable. In one book about Vietnam, *Vietnam: Three Battles*, he wrote about the fight at Tuy Hoi in June 1966. I was there as a company commander, and his description of people and events in that battle is contrived and inaccurate.[10]

The likelihood that soldiers and Marines hesitated to use their rifles effectively in World War II and Korea doesn't conform to the experience of those who served in Vietnam. In any event, Stoner set about developing an automatic rifle that would be easier to employ and fire than the BAR. In the early development of an infantry automatic weapon, Stoner was interested in .30 caliber systems. A major component of Stoner's concept was a rifle configuration that would optimize the ability to hold a rifle on target while firing in the automatic mode by designing the weapon to minimize muzzle climb.

James Sullivan is another major player in the ArmaLite story, another firearms buff and a skilled engineer. He studied engineering for two years at the University of Washington and subsequently enlisted in the Army, serving from 1953 to 1955. He wanted to be an Army diver, so he attended the Sparling School of Deep Sea Diving in Long Beach, California. The Army trained him as a signals technician but eventually relented and sent him as a military diver to Korea in 1954. Out of the Army, he returned to the University of Washington for a while but dropped out again to work for Boeing. After reading an article about ArmaLite, he applied for a job and was hired in 1957 as a draftsman in the ArmaLite Division of Fairchild. After a year on the job, he was promoted to design engineer, reporting directly to Stoner.[11]

ArmaLite itself was a very small operation, interested in developing rifle designs that could be marketed to major weapons manufacturers. As design engineer at ArmaLite, Stoner designed several rifles that had potential for sale, among them the AR1 Parasniper. Note the designation of this rifle as AR1. Sequential numerical designations would follow for other weapon designs and prototypes. The AR1 included some new design ideas but didn't sell. Stoner, as chief design engineer, then introduced many new rifle concepts. One of these was the AR5 chambered in .22 Hornet, an early .22 caliber high-velocity hunting cartridge. The Air Force adopted the AR5 in 1956 as a survival rifle with the military designation MA1. ArmaLite then developed a civilian semi-automatic version dubbed AR7 and chambered for .22 long rifle. Both fire-arms could be disassembled, with components stored in the buttstock. The AR7 would even float.

Although the military now grudgingly acknowledged the advantages of a lighter weapon firing a less-than-.30 caliber cartridge, the Army's Ordnance Department had devised no specifications for a rifle in .22 caliber, nor any other intermediate caliber cartridge. This, even though testing in 1929 at Aberdeen had suggested the suitability of intermediate caliber cartridges between .22 caliber and .30 caliber. There was no thought or planning about what might be considered an assault rifle. The automatic rifle role was to be fulfilled by the M14E2. The next upgrade was to be the never-to-be-practical SPIW. Neither of these individual weapons (SPIW or M14E2) could be considered an assault rifle.

ArmaLite wasn't making a great deal of money with these innovations. But in 1955, with the military's search to replace the Garand, ArmaLite was invited to compete for the next infantry rifle. There were two basic competitors: the T44, a conventional model firing the 7.62 NATO cartridge, which won the competition after a bit of special attention. It was an in-house Spring-field Armory design and entered production as the M14. The second competitor was the T48, a version of the Belgian *Fusil Automatique Léger* or FAL. The FAL went on to European production and success but lost out to the M14 in the United States.

Eugene Stoner's ArmaLite candidate, the AR10, also chambered the NATO cartridge but was hastily and incompletely readied for testing. It had been tested shortly before at Springfield Armory, and the barrel failed a torture test. However, its lightweight (6.85 pounds empty) had been noted and there had been several favorable comments. It too lost out to the M14 in the 1955 U.S. military rifle evaluations and competition, which extended into 1956. The AR10 featured most of the innovative design characteristics of the not-yet-developed AR15. The barrel was in a straight line with a stock that reduced muzzle climb in full automatic fire. It had elevated sights and a flash suppressor that also reduced recoil. It was constructed with a forged aluminum alloy receiver and used a new composite stock that was light, wouldn't warp under extended adverse conditions, and was about one and a quarter pounds lighter than the T44. After losing the U.S. competition, the deficiencies were corrected and Fairchild-ArmaLite sold a five-year manufacturing license to a Dutch arms manufacturer, *Atillerie Inrichtingen*. The rifle was employed by several foreign militaries.

Within the Office of the Chief of Ordnance (OCO) in 1955, there was a decided prejudice in favor of the Springfield Arsenal-developed T44, which in 1957 would be designated the M14. Production began in 1959 and official standardization followed in 1961. The M14 was an in-house weapon, designed by engineers at Springfield Armory. In 1955 William C. Davis, an engineer at Aberdeen who had participated in the early testing of the Small Caliber, High Velocity (SCHV) concept, wrote the chief of ordnance, requesting funds for further evaluation and testing. The request was denied by Dr. Frederick H. Carten, the chief of small arms development in the Ordnance Department, later known as the Father of the M14.[12] Dr. Carten did everything that his authority and position allowed to protect the yet-to-be officially adopted M14 from competition. He thereafter consistently discouraged consideration of any competing rifles. This prejudice continued to be reflected in other tests conducted during the period that the AR15 was under consideration for standardization. Proponents of 7.62mm and 5.56mm systems defended their positions. The Ordnance Department was in the 7.62mm camp, and so there were no specifications for a 5.56mm weapon. The stage was set for problems when civilian-designed and developed prototypes became available for testing.

Dr. Carten had been the civilian executive for Colonel René R. Studler, the chief of ordnance, and a distinguished small arms expert. Colonel Studler was a pilot, flight instructor, and in 1921, commander of the 258th Heavy Bombardment Squadron stationed at Aberdeen Proving Ground. Proficient in five languages, he spent several years leading up to World War II in Europe gathering technical intelligence. He was recalled in 1940 to the United States to serve as chief of ordnance during the war years and until he retired in 1953.

At that time, his protégé, Dr. Carten, steadfastly continued Studler's views and prejudices and carried on the fight to protect the .30 caliber weapons tradition. He was technically competent but intransigent and actively discouraged innovation. The M14 was his special project.

It is largely due to the stubbornness and inflexible thinking of Dr. Carten and other like-minded traditionalists that the U.S. military failed to conceptualize and develop standards for small-caliber, high-velocity weapons following the Korean War. The groundwork hadn't been done. This closed-minded approach to weapons development was equally responsible for the failure to appreciate the coming domination of the assault rifle. The two concepts go hand in hand.

There were standards for military weapons, but no study of their application to rifles of calibers not considered for military use or for their ammunition. The AR15 came on the scene with no input from military technicians, without the benefit of specifications that might have established some baselines generated by years of experience. The military tampered with the AR15, sometimes usefully, but not having done the design work from the beginning, the patchwork fixed some problems and introduced others.

Pursuing the SCHV concept had been consistently vetoed by the military's insistence on a standard .30 caliber cartridge. By 1956, however, there was a forward-thinking group looking for a military rifle that would take advantage of the concept. This group finally had a senior officer interested in its possibilities. General Willard G. Wyman of the Continental Army Command arranged a meeting with Stoner and asked him to design a version of the AR10 to handle a .22 caliber round. The selection of a .22 caliber cartridge at this juncture has been debated ever since. Selecting a slightly more powerful cartridge of 6 or 6.5mm would have calmed the worries of traditionalists regarding what many considered to be a "varmint" round. There would have been less controversy over lethality, while a combat-effective range of 500 meters would have been easier to achieve.

ArmaLite agreed to the proposal and went to work. The company was well ahead of any planning by a U.S. arsenal and took advantage of the opening. Eugene Stoner, working with Jim Sullivan and another ArmaLite weapons design engineer, Robert Fremont, went to work and downsized the AR10 to 5.56mm. This rifle incorporated the design features of the AR10. The coaxial barrel/buttstock design allowed the recoil forces to drive straight to the rear. The recoil spring is in the stock directly behind the action. It serves as both operating spring and recoil buffer. This configuration offers the same advantage as in the AR10: reduced muzzle rise when firing, particularly in the automatic mode. High pressure gas drives the bolt carrier and bolt directly rather than with an intermediate piston/rod; a direct impingement rather than a mechanical system. This meant fewer parts and lighter weight but directly introduced gas from the propellant into the bolt carrier, bolt, and receiver. This creates a serious problem if the powder doesn't ignite cleanly.

In 1957, Boutelle accompanied General Curtis LeMay, then the Strategic Air Command commander, on an African safari. Just how this came about is unclear, but Boutelle surely made a pitch for the AR15 to LeMay as the perfect opportunity presented itself. Shortly thereafter, in May, Stoner demonstrated the AR15 at the U.S. Army Infantry School at Fort Benning. The M14 had just been adopted by the Army as a replacement for the M1, so the SCHV concept had been overtaken by events, but the idea and the need persisted. The Army now was obliged to reconsider Wyman's 1957 request. As commander of the U.S. Continental Army Command (CONARC), General Wyman wanted the Army to develop a lightweight rifle capable of fully automatic fire that employed a .223 caliber or 5.56mm cartridge. This would be a rifle that took advantage of the SCHV concept that earlier testing had proven to be more effective with respect to weight, hit probability, and lethality at combat ranges than the standard .30 caliber cartridges. It exceeded the lethality of the .30 caliber cartridge used in the M1 and M2 carbines. Initially, the Infantry Board had determined that accuracy and lethality out to 300 yards would be sufficient. General Wyman had wanted an effective range of 300 yards, so in 1957 the Infantry Board, in response to his recommendation, submitted a formal request for the development of a SCHV weapon that would meet this requirement. The USAIB agreed in principle with the 300-yard effective range but was worried that it wouldn't be acceptable to CONARC. They upped the range to 400 yards. CONARC decided to up the range another 100 yards, believing that an effective range of 500 yards would be more acceptable to the Pentagon.[13] Now the Army wanted a round capable of penetrating a helmet at 500 yards. This was an arbitrary requirement that would necessitate redesign of the bullet and tighten the propellant tolerances to assure an adequate muzzle velocity without exceeding allowable chamber pressure. This ultimately led to the production of ammunition that was incompatible with the AR15 and the XM16E1, and the root cause of the failure to extract malfunction. Arbitrary assumptions and decisions may, and in this case did, lead to unintended consequences.

To further complicate matters for Dr. Carten, Springfield Armory had entered its own rifle for consideration, the Caliber .224 Springfield Infantry Rifle, which reached its evolutionary dead end in mid-1957. Dr. Carten, already leery of General Wyman's end run around the Ordnance Department, ordered the Armory ". . . to terminate its .224 rifle project and refrain from any further SCHV development work."[14]

In March 1958 Aberdeen conducted an initial trial of the AR15. Dr. Carten, ever protective of his M14, still in an early stage of development, omitted the favorable results from the conclusions and recommendations of the Aberdeen report.[15] An additional test, a rain-in-the-bore test with the AR15, was conducted at Aberdeen in early 1958. The small diameter bore of the ArmaLite weapon tended to retain water when immersed. This resulted in a burst barrel when the weapon was fired. In fact, infantrymen keep water from the bore, or carefully drained it, with rifles of all calibers. It was with the XM16E1, as well as earlier vintage rifles, a common practice to protect the bore with a condom when immersion was anticipated or likely. This susceptibility of the 5.56mm bore to retain water was one additional factor that the Office of the Chief of Ordnance employed to discourage the SCHV rifle program.

In 1958, CONARC directed the Infantry Board and Aberdeen Proving Ground to compare and test the M14, the .224 caliber Winchester Lightweight Military Rifle (LMR), and the AR15. The CONARC final SCHV report following these tests concluded that "The ArmaLite and Winchester rifles have demonstrated sufficient potential to justify continued development but are not acceptable for Army use at this time."[16] The report recommended that "both developers be encouraged to modify their weapon to correct all deficiencies enumerated . . . as a result of Ordnance testing."[17]

As noted in the previous chapter, before he retired in 1958, then-CONARC commander General Wyman, still a strong supporter of the AR15, convened a new board to evaluate the SCHV concept. It was called the Powell Board after his deputy, General Herbert B. Powell. This board looked at both the AR15 and the Winchester lightweight automatic rifle, now firing the similar but not identical .223 caliber cartridge. The board, apparently in response to constant pressure from the Chief of Ordnance's office (OCO), and despite the favorable reports from the Infantry Board, recommended that neither the ArmaLite AR15 nor the LMR was acceptable at that time. However, the board recommended further evaluation of the AR15 and the purchase of 750 rifles for further testing.

In December 1958, the ArmaLite AR15 was tested by the Arctic Test Board at Fort Greely, Alaska. The OCO was still working to protect the now-standardized M14. Stoner had been told earlier that he would be present for the tests, as he had been during the testing at Fort Benning. However, the cold-weather testing began without him. With the tests already under way, he finally received an invitation. He discovered that some of the weapons had been abused by what appeared to be inappropriate tampering with their front sights, as well as having been maintained with improper spare parts that could have affected the AR15's performance.[18] The results of the cold-weather testing were reported to the Powell Board while Stoner was still in Alaska, and so he lacked an opportunity to comment on the findings. To meet Army environmental standards, a weapon and its ammunition had to perform equally well at sixty-five degrees below zero and 125 degrees above. The AR15s tested in Alaska fell short in this department. In cold weather, their accuracy decreased. The OCO was able to use this in its efforts to detract from the otherwise favorable reports on the rifle.[19]

At this point, in February 1959, General Maxwell Taylor, chief of staff of the Army, made his decision. It was based on several factors: available ammunition, the fact that the hard fight for a standardized 7.62mm round for NATO had been fought and won, the availability of spare parts, existing production tooling, as well as a probable affinity for the standard .30 caliber tradition. Taylor proceeded to veto any further purchases of .223 caliber weapons. The contract for 750 ArmaLite rifles never materialized.

Following production of .45 caliber pistols and water-cooled machine guns in World War II, production came to a halt at Colt's Patent Fire Arms Manufacturing Company in Hartford, Connecticut. During the heyday of its production for the war effort, Colt had grown careless with its new affluence. Those workers and engineers who could, retired. By 1955 the company faced bankruptcy. In that year, it merged with another company called Penn-Texas. Penn-Texas had acquired Pratt & Whitney Machine Tool Company the same year. Colt had become Colt Industries.

In February 1959, ArmaLite, unable to produce either the AR10 or the AR15 in quantities sufficient to meet the limited demand for further evaluation, licensed both designs to Colt. With the acquisition of production rights for the AR15, Colt had a new lease on life. It also continued production of its single-action revolvers and other classic handguns. Colt paid ArmaLite $75,000 and a four and a half percent royalty on AR15 production, which must have seemed like a pretty good bet to the small, cash-starved division of Fairchild. But it was, in retrospect, a financial mistake for ArmaLite. Without governmental recognition or standardization of a design, the rifles couldn't be marketed under the Foreign Military Sales program. A large contract was essential if ArmaLite were to be able to gear up and organize to produce weapons in a marketable quantity. Even with no prospect of doing the manufacturing, ArmaLite didn't grasp the potential of its design. In the same year, ArmaLite moved all its facilities—administrative and engineering—to Costa Mesa, California. In 1962 Fairchild dissolved its association with ArmaLite.

In July 1960, General LeMay was invited to a demonstration of the AR15 at his friend Richard Boutelle's farm. He was impressed. The Air Force conducted tests with the rifle and, based on the results of these tests, validated a requirement to procure more for use and further testing.

At about this time Colt, encouraged by renewed interest in the AR15, made some unusual and, later to prove damaging, claims about its reliability. Of course, they were speaking of the rifle/ammunition combination that was used in all the testing: ammunition loaded with Improved Military Rifle (IMR) powder. Their assertions were as follows:

> *Disassembly, assembly, cleaning and minor repairs may be undertaken by anybody. . . . An occasional simple cleaning will keep the weapon functioning indefinitely. Working parts can be cleaned by wiping with a cloth. The simplicity of field cleaning makes it possible to quickly and easily train a recruit in minimum time.*
>
> *Corrosion resistant materials facilitate the assembly and interchangeability of parts and reduce the service and maintenance of the Colt AR-15 to an absolute minimum. Firing of the Colt AR-15 with complete absence of lubricants in a chemically cleaned condition has in every country where this test has taken place resulted in a performance far exceeding any requirements.*
>
> *The Colt AR-15 will fire longer without cleaning or oiling than any other known rifle.*[20]

Whatever prompted knowledgeable military personnel and firearms specialists to accept this propaganda, at least until reports from the field began to accumulate, is difficult to understand.

With the inauguration of President John F. Kennedy in January 1961, a new era was afoot in the Department of Defense. The new secretary of defense, Robert S. McNamara, a former Army Air Forces lieutenant colonel, had little respect for ordnance professionals. His staff, young PhDs with no firearms expertise, was similarly inclined. These DoD decision makers took the bait. Colt claimed the rifle was ready to go and needed very little maintenance. That was good enough for them and the secretary went along, although he had military experience and shouldn't have been fooled. Subsequently, the Defense Department's stubbornness and arrogance, coupled with pressure to move rapidly into production, led to, among other planning shortcomings, the failure to chrome-plate the rifle chamber. One of McNamara's staffers asserted that if Stoner had thought the M16 chamber needed to be chromed, he would have designed it that way.

In the summer of 1961, General LeMay was promoted to Air Force chief of staff. In 1961 Stoner moved to Colt as a consultant. One of the results of the Fairchild Whitney takeover of Fairchild was a general reshuffling of personnel. Boutelle was fired. In December of that year, because of the increasing pressure arising from incipient American involvement in Vietnam, McNamara approved the acquisition of 1,000 AR15s for evaluation in Vietnam by the Advanced Research Projects Agency. Colt, now a part of the Fairchild Whitney conglomerate, received an order for 1,000 AR15s. An Air Force plan to buy 8,500 Colt AR15s was disapproved by a congressional subcommittee on DoD appropriations.

The first shipment of AR15s arrived in Vietnam in January 1962. The object was to evaluate the use of the weapon by the small-statured Vietnamese, its suitability for combat conditions in Vietnam, and to compare its suitability with the M2 carbine for use by selected Vietnamese units. The M2 carbine is a fine weapon, capable of full automatic fire. However, it was never designed to be a principal arm for the infantryman. It fell more into the category of a supporting weapon, much like the submachine gun. It was underpowered and outclassed by the AK47. The testing concluded that the AR15 was the right weapon for Vietnam. The reasons listed were: ease of training, suitable physical characteristics, ease of maintenance, ruggedness and durability, lower logistical burden, best weapon tactically, as good as the M1 for semi-automatic fire, better than the BAR for automatic fire, and preferable for Vietnamese troops, according to U.S. advisors.[21]

The problem with these results is that they depended on the rifle/ammunition combination that had been employed for all the earlier testing and evaluation. The rifle had been designed around a specific ammunition. Every firearm is designed for one or more types of ammunition. Considerations of propellant, case hardness, pressure of combustion, bullet configuration, and composition are all basic ammunition characteristics. They must be matched with specific rifle design characteristics: parts design specifications, chamber dimension tolerances, cyclic rate of fire in automatic weapons, material used, as well as other considerations. Attention to these considerations is essential when one deals with firearms likely to be subjected to unusually challenging conditions and hard use.

Moreover, when the weapon is designed for sustained fire in the fully automatic mode, these considerations take on added importance. In a small-caliber, 5.56mm weapon and ammunition combination intended for employment under adverse environmental conditions, the tolerances become even more critical. A change in any single element of the several developmental and engineering considerations will have some effect on performance. It may be slight, it may be inconsequential, or it may be serious, even disastrous.

Ultimately, Secretary McNamara decided in favor of the M16, although his lack of small-arms expertise and that of his staff had tragic consequences. They pushed acceptance of the rifle as tested despite advice from Stoner, as well as from experienced technical military experts, that the rifle needed additional evaluation and possibly modifications before being accepted and produced as a standard weapon.

In May 1962, General LeMay's purchase was finally approved. Because events in Vietnam were escalating, rifles for the Air Force became part of a larger package. More than 20,000 AR15s were approved, with the larger part destined for Navy SEAL teams and some special South Vietnamese Army units and their U.S. advisors.[22] In January 1962 the Air Force classified the AR15 as standard in its inventory. This was the Colt Model 601 with 1:14 inch rifling. In the same year, 1,000 more went to U.S. Army Special Forces personnel in Vietnam. American advisors were lavish in their praise of its stopping power and pressed for its adoption. In these evaluations the ammunition employed was essentially the same as that used in its development, a type of so-called Improved Military Rifle (IMR) propellant. Soon after these tests in Vietnam, the Air Force officially adopted the rifle, followed by the Navy. The model 601 AR15s used in the evaluations had twenty-inch barrels with four grooves of rifling. With the right-hand rifling twist and one turn in fourteen inches, it was the same rifling used in sporting rifles. It provided good accuracy but proved to cause the 5.56mm 55grain M193 round to yaw in flight.

Continued testing by the Air Force in 1963 found that in dense arctic air, this model of the M16 didn't group well. The bullet did more than yaw, it wobbled. The rifling was subsequently changed to one turn in twelve inches. This was the model 602. This gave the bullet greater stability but—because it was less likely to tumble when it hit its target—the lethality was reduced. Tumbling bullets create larger wound channels, increase the probability of striking a critical organ or artery, and tend to expend more kinetic energy in its human target with lower probability of a pass-through wound. Both models 601 and 602 were virtually identical models of the AR15 except for the rifling. Years later, in 1980, when the cartridge was standardized by NATO and its weight increased, the rifling twist was further changed to one in seven inches.

Dr. Carten's continued intentional failure to recognize the advantages of the SCHV concept and the M16 were his undoing. He had ignored the favorable reports of his own experts. His authority was weakened and finally, the Office of the Chief of Ordnance was discontinued in 1962.[23]

Traditionalists were still worried about the lethality of the lighter 5.56mm cartridge, which prompted more lethality testing in 1962. Tested were the 5.56mm cartridge, the now-standard 7.62mm NATO cartridge, and the 7.62x39mm cartridge used in the AK47. This testing began on October 26 and was conducted on outdoor ranges at Aberdeen Proving Ground in Maryland. It involved goats and human heads, the latter imported from India. The testing was in response to the task given the Army chief of staff, General Earle Wheeler, to compare the AK47 with the M14 and AR15. The tests were close hold, and because of the macabre use of human heads as targets, it proved to be a source of embarrassment. The results simply confirmed the more-than-adequate lethality of all the cartridges at combat ranges.[24]

More testing of the same weapons was done later in 1962 in response to Wheeler's order and was intended to settle the matter of the suitability of SCHV weapons for military use. The testing was conducted at Aberdeen and was completed in January 1963. It produced the final report of Wheeler's evaluation. The results of this phase of evaluation for the AR15 weren't good. It had a malfunction rate eight times that of the M14.

Now, for the first time, the question of ammunition came into play. It appeared that the fault lay primarily with ammunition, which had been produced hurriedly and not subjected to adequate quality control. Some of the AR15s used in the tests also appeared to have escaped adequate quality inspection. The AR15 survived the results of these tests and received the benefit of the doubt. The malfunctions attributable to both the rifle and the ammunition were assumed to be "readily correctible." However, the earlier tactical tests that had demonstrated the superiority of a smaller squad armed with the AR15 over an eleven-man traditional squad armed with the M14 were incongruously characterized as inconclusive. As for the AK47, it got short shrift: "the tests had shown it to be 'clearly inferior' within U.S. tactical applications to both American weapons." After all, it was "not invented here," or in plain speak, "NIH." It was characterized as crude and unsophisticated, the product of poor manufacturing techniques, cheaply made and unsuitable for Americans.[25] It didn't come up to our standards, although it turned out to be more reliable than the XM16E1 and just as deadly. The mediocre reliability results for the AR15 were unusual but were attributed to correctible problems.

Unknown at the time was that a subsequent and unanticipated change of propellant would raise again—and in a more serious context—the issue of reliability. There would also be serious questions regarding quality control at Colt as demand forced an increased rate of production. The quality control by both Colt and the Army was not only inadequate but was intentionally and negligently lax to enable the logistical chain to meet the Army's needs.[26]

Deputy Secretary of Defense Cyrus Vance proposed what was essentially a compromise. Starting in fiscal year 1964 the Army would procure enough modified M14s—the M14E2—to provide an automatic rifle capability for all infantry squads. The Army would also procure between 50,000 and 100,000 selective-fire AR15s commercially from Colt for issue to U.S. Army air assault, airborne, and Special Forces units. Production of standard M14s in the existing procurement program would be reduced accordingly. Continuing the SPIW program with a reaffirmed schedule was expected to produce a truly advanced follow-on basic infantry rifle to replace the M14 and M14E2 by the end of fiscal year 1965.[27]

The cat was out of the bag. In anticipation of the SPIW, the Army accepted the AR15. The M14 contract would expire and wouldn't be renewed. There would never be an acceptable SPIW. The XM16E1 would come to be the Army and Marine Corps standard infantry weapon.

There were eleven more preproduction modifications made to the M16. The stock, handguard, and pistol grip were to be black rather than brown and the dimensions of the chamber were adjusted to conform more precisely to those of the M193 ball cartridge. (One may wonder how any such problem might still exist at this late stage of development.) The charging handle was redesigned. The front sling swivel was modified with a plastic coating so as to make less noise. A new firing pin was developed to eliminate a slamfire problem. There were two aspects to this problem: (1) The original firing pin had sufficient mass and inertia to occasionally cause a round to fire when it stripped the round from the magazine and forced it into the chamber. The rifle would fire unexpectedly with whatever consequences that entailed. (2) Sometimes the firing pin would fire the cartridge before the bolt closed and locked. This could occur if the chamber was sufficiently fouled to impede smooth insertion of the round. In that case, the round fired out of battery with severe damage to the rifle and potential harm to the man holding the rifle. It was not practicable, according to the ammunition manufacturers, to redesign the primers to avoid this problem. To do so would be unacceptably expensive. The solution was to lighten up the firing pin.

Next up was a controversial issue. The Army insisted on a manual bolt-closure device. The reasoning was that a positive means to ensure the seating of a round was standard in military weapons and essential if the soldier was to have confidence in his rifle. Additionally, there might be occasions when the tactical situation required silent operation, and it should be possible to ease a round into the chamber without the noise of a bolt slamming home. The point could be made that forcing a cartridge into a fouled chamber might result in a worse malfunction, failure to extract, but the Army was insistent.

Note the incident described in Chapter 2 where a 1st Cavalry Division trooper repeatedly uses the bolt-closure devices while in contact. Eugene Stoner believed it unnecessary and more likely to simply cause more trouble. In all the testing he had done with the AR15, never once had he encountered a problem that could have been resolved with such a device. It added more than $9.00 to the cost of each weapon. The Navy and Marines would accept it, the Marines qualifying their acceptance on the bolt-closure device not otherwise degrading performance. The Air Force didn't want it and did without.

All four services agreed to the one-in-twelve-inch rifling twist. At the time, there was no contention here. Three years later, the issue would come up again. There was a tradeoff with the 1:12 twist. Accuracy was improved; lethality was somewhat diminished as the bullet was less likely to tumble when it struck flesh. This remains a contentious issue and a sore point with those who continue to insist that the 5.56mm cartridge is underpowered. The bolt release was modified to function more positively and to last longer. The flash suppressor was beefed up, but still open-ended, a mud and vegetation catcher problem that would be resolved in the future. For the time being, it was useful as an expedient C-ration case opener. The material of the magazines was changed from steel to aluminum. The front takedown pin was modified so it couldn't be completely removed and become lost when cleaning the rifle.

The office of project manager for the AR15 was established on March 6, 1963, at Rock Island Arsenal, Illinois. Lt. Col. (later Col.) Harold W. Yount was appointed project manager. At about this time SecDef McNamara established a technical coordinating committee, with membership including Yount, as well as other military technical experts. The final word, however, on any changes or decisions was in the hands of McNamara's deputy secretary of defense, Roswell Gilpatric. This ensured that the project manager understood that the SecDef's office had the final word.[28] He promptly issued a directive that pushed the project along and was impatient with any delay.

Now committed to developing the M16 for military use, the service established several technical specifications. These included a muzzle velocity of 3,250 feet per second (plus or minus forty feet per second) and a firing chamber pressure not to exceed 52,000 pounds per square inch. It was determined that, despite the assurances of ArmaLite, Colt, Remington, Stoner, the Defense Department, and other proponents of the ammunition, the IMR4475 propellant used in the cartridges thus far through all the testing couldn't quite achieve the chamber pressure to bring the muzzle velocity up to now-established specifications. The muzzle velocity fell short by about one hundred feet per second (fps). To get the muzzle velocity up to 3,250 fps would increase the chamber pressure too close to the limit.[29] This generated uneconomical tolerance requirements for the ammunition manufacturers if they were to use IMR4475 propellant.

The muzzle velocity of 3,250 fps was considered necessary to achieve an effective range of 500 yards, although all the testing with the IMR-loaded ammunition met the several lethality challenges. The arbitrary increase of effective range from 300 to 500 yards was at the root of the choice of propellant problem. Rather than allow a slightly reduced muzzle velocity, the Army now insisted on compliance with its newly established muzzle-velocity requirement. Using IMR4475 propellant that would meet the specification in the now-standardized 5.56mm cartridge case would cost too much to manufacture. The standardization of the ball cartridge needed further experimentation with different propellants to enable conformance with the chamber-pressure specifications the Army insisted on. This, like the issue of the sensitivity of primers, sorely complicated negotiating ammunition contracts. The ultimate solution was to permit the use of ball propellant rather than the IMR propellant for which the AR15 and subsequently the XM16E1 had been designed. This was the principal source of major malfunction problems and came to haunt our troops in Vietnam when the new weapon was brought into play.

Frankford Arsenal had studied in 1963 the issue of compatibility of the AR15 rifle with ammunition using different propellants. On April 4, shortly after the appointment of a project manager and the establishment of the technical coordinating committee, Frankford issued its report. The data indicated that traditional compatibility trials of rifle-and-ammunition needed to be conducted, especially after one or the other was changed or modified. Both Frankford and Gene Stoner repeatedly called for such tests. OSD (Office of the Secretary of Defense) policy implemented by Gilpatric obliged the project manager to move ahead without further evaluation of rifle/ammunition compatibility tests, "in the absence of malfunction reports."[30] The rifle/ammunition mismatch was the principal source of major malfunction problems. This was no secret.

Much depended on compromise with the people in the business of making a profit. Colt needed the Army contract in a hurry to avoid shutting down its production facilities. Until contract issues were resolved, Colt would be unable to market the military version of the AR15 abroad. The acceptability standards involving all aspects of ammunition production—case hardness, chamber pressure, fouling, round-to-round consistency—had to be doable and profitable. If entire case lots failed to meet standards and had to be rejected, the cost would be too high for the Army to accept, and barely profitable for a company to produce. Driving this issue was the chamber-pressure requirement to meet a velocity specification. This could be traced back to increasing the range requirement from 300 yards to 500 yards. The ultimate compromise resulted in ammunition being loaded with the old Army standard ball propellant.

On April 11, 1963, a contract was signed with Remington Arms for 600,000 rounds of .223 ball ammunition to further support rifle evaluation. This ammunition employed the IMR propellant, with which the AR15 performed well. In September 1963, the Army type-classified the AR15 as "Rifle, 5.56mm, XM16E1" and as limited standard. At the same time, the "Cartridge, Ball, 5.56mm, M193" was standardized. On November 4, 1963, the Army signed a contract for $13.5 million as a "one-time buy" for the now-limited standard XM16E1, the U.S. military's assault weapon. On April 28, 1964, the Technical Coordinating Committee approved two propellants to replace IMR4475. They were DuPont's CR8136 and Olin Mathieson's WC846.[31]

One of the major causes of malfunctions and parts breakage was the increased cyclic rate of fire caused by high pressure at the gas port generated by WC846 ball powder. With IMR powder the cyclic rate of fire was from about 775 to 850 rounds per minute. Ball powder developed a cyclic rate of fire of up to 900 or even 1,000 rounds per minute. Using this propellant, the XM16E1s produced by Colt couldn't pass the military's quality control and acceptance tests. The pressure was on both Colt and the Army to meet the demands of M16s for American units already being deployed to Vietnam. The Technical Coordinating Committee, which represented all services using the M16 but was dominated by the Army, formally gave Colt permission in early 1964 to use any ammunition it had in stock for the acceptance tests.[32] Colt used IMR powder for the tests.

Tragically and inexcusably, the Army and Colt both knew that the malfunction problem would travel to Vietnam along with the improper ammunition.

Other cartridge propellants were also being tested in an effort to identify one that met the technical requirements regarding cyclic rate of fire and which reduced fouling. One of these was CR8136, but it was found that this propellant couldn't produce consistently acceptable chamber pressures. Remington stopped producing it in December 1964 and ". . . subsequently fulfilled its contractual commitments by loading with Olin's WC846 ball powder. This meant that all through the first 18 months of the war in Vietnam, Olin's WC846 was the only qualified propellant for the M193 round."[33] This was the propellant used in the M193 ball cartridges that went to Vietnam beginning with the first deployments of major U.S. troop commitments in March 1965.

In the next chapter we'll see where another major small arms test at Fort Benning documented the high malfunction rate of the XM16E1 but failed to emphasize the critical malfunction of "failure to extract," and didn't associate the malfunctions with the switch from IMR to ball powder.

4

THE SMALL ARMS WEAPONS
SYSTEMS TEST

One of the last major small arms tests, the Small Arms Weapons System (SAWS) test, was conducted at the U.S. Army Infantry Board (USAIB), a testing agency located at Fort Benning, Georgia, and subordinate to the U.S. Army Test and Evaluation Command (USATECOM) during the test period from July 6, 1965 to November 15, 1965, a period when major American units were already actively engaged in Vietnam.

Paul Stroessner served with Company A, 2nd Battalion (Airmobile), 7th Cavalry from July 1966 to July 1967. He describes an experience he had with his XM16E1:

> We were out on an operation when we set up for the night. We set our trip flares and claymores out and dug in for the night. I was off the M60 and point on left flank at the time. During the night while I was on guard, we heard movement and then a trip flare went off. I opened fire. One shot and it jammed. For a reason I still don't understand, I had a cleaning rod at that time. I cleared the weapon and fired, with the same results. I only remember a guy named Koonts or Koontz in the hole with me at that time. I had to turn my weapon in when we returned to LZ Betty. I was told that if the malfunction was due to a dirty rifle I'd face discipline. That was crazy because I always carried a toothbrush and oil with me to keep my weapon clean. I later found out from Swaggert [the armorer] that the problem was a bad extractor. Don't know if he was supposed to tell me that, but we trained together so he helped me out.[1]

The XM16E1 had been classified as limited standard in September 1963, so was not itself a test weapon; rather it, the M14, and the M14E2 were control rifles against which other weapons were evaluated. U.S. Army weapons tests evaluate the weapon and its ammunition as a system. Any change in one must be checked for its effect on the performance of the other. The 5.56mm cartridges employed in previous testing, however, had been loaded with IMR4475 propellant. They were now loaded principally with WC846 propellant. For the first time, testing was being conducted with cartridges using ball powder, the same ball powder in use in Vietnam. No previous testing had been conducted to evaluate the XM16E1's performance with this ammunition. Although not officially considered so by the Army, the SAWS test was, therefore, just as much an evaluation of the XM16E1 as it was of the "test weapons." In the normal order of testing, the compatibility of the weapon and ammunition should have been conducted well before the commitment of the weapon into active operations.

The Infantry Board tested and evaluated several small arms.[2] These included the following standard Army weapons: the rifle, 7.62mm, M14; the rifle, 7.62mm, M14E2; the rifle, 5.56mm, XM16E1; and the machine gun, 7.62mm, M60. Two additional configurations of the M16 were tested: the carbine/submachine gun, 5.56mm, C-SMG (Colt Patented Firearms, Colt "Shortie" Carbine/Submachine Gun) and the automatic rifle, 5.56mm, C-AR (Colt Automatic Rifle, CAR-15).The C-SMG isn't functionally identical to the XM16E1. It has a ten-inch barrel and so the gas port is closer to the chamber and the pressure at the bolt assembly is higher than in the XM16E1. Thus the cyclic rate of fire is increased. It has a lower muzzle velocity. Dimensionally, it has a shorter butt stock that telescopes to reduce its length. The C-AR is functionally identical to the XM16E1 but with a heavier barrel of the same length and a 30-round box-type magazine.[3] It accepts two types of bipods.

Additionally, three other rifles (one a Code-S rifle); one other carbine (Code-S); one other automatic rifle (Code-S); and two other machine guns (a Code-S light machine gun and a Code-S medium machine gun), were tested. The Code S weapons were designed by Eugene Stoner. These five weapons were all 5.56mm.

Only the results of the M14, the M14E2, the XM16E1, the C-SMG, and the C-AR will be included in the data presented in this chapter. All the information in this chapter is taken directly from the Small Arms Weapons Systems test report.

The test report provides the following background for the test:

The adoption of the 5.56mm M16/XM16E1 rifle for U.S. Air Force use and limited U.S. Army use has stimulated the interest of industry in developing other weapons in this caliber for military use. In 1963–64, the Advanced

Research Projects Agency (ARPA), Department of Defense, directed and coordinated with U.S. Army and Marine Corps, tests of the Code-S Weapons System. U.S. Army tests were limited to those necessary to determine the military potential of the system, while the U.S. Marine Corps conducted service and troop tests. The results of the U.S. Army tests indicated that the Code-S weapons were accurate and of good basic design, but that the machineguns appeared to be marginal in operating power and deficient in barrel life. From the final report of the U.S. Marine Corps test, it appeared that the Marine Corps favored the Code-S system as a replacement for caliber .30 and 7.62mm weapons currently in Marine Corps use.

In November 1964, the U.S. Army Materiel Command (USAMC) requested that USATECOM prepare plans for engineering and service test of the Code-S Weapons System. A USATECOM directive was issued, but planning was suspended in December of 1964 when it became apparent that the Code-S system would be tested as a part of a larger, more comprehensive program.

On 17 December 1964, the Chief of Staff of the Army directed a review and evaluation of Small Arms Weapons Systems (SAWS) either in being, or feasible for adoption within the time frame 1967–1980. This evaluation includes the current standard system of small arms (M14, M14E2, M60, and XM16E1). The objective of this program is to develop data upon which to base a program for replenishment of stocks of small arms as the inventory drops below requirements, and/or replacement of current small arms with weapons of demonstrated superiority.[4]

The Infantry Board was responsible for planning, conducting, and reporting on service and service-type tests of individual, vehicular (other than combat vehicle), and ground-mounted, crew-served weapons; and support of tests conducted by the U.S. Army Ballistics Research Laboratory (BRL) and the U.S. Army Human Engineering Laboratory (HEL) as directed by USATECOM.

The purpose of the work was to measure performance of SAWS weapons against standards provided by the U.S. Army Combat Developments Command. The testing was conducted in such a manner as to permit a comparison of effectiveness between weapons.

The results were summarized as follows:[5]

a. Findings. There are no significant differences between the SAWS weapons except for reliability. The current standard weapons are the most reliable.

b. Conclusions. The M14, M14E2, and M60 are significantly more reliable than their counterpart SAWS weapons. The use of duplex ammunition significantly increases hit capability.

c. Recommendation. USAIB recommends that no consideration be given to adoption of new weapons systems until a significant improvement over the standard 7.62mm system can be achieved.

It's interesting to note that the conclusion makes no reference to the XM16E1, although it's listed as one of the standard current system of small arms. One may wonder from this whether it's to be grouped along with the other 5.56mm weapons noted as less reliable than the 7.62mm weapons. Or was its reliability considered to be on a par with the 7.62mm weapons? Testing clearly demonstrated that the XM16E1 had a serious reliability problem.

I, Lyman Duryea, was one of the test officers for this testing and spent most of my time on the range. I helped to draft portions of the report where I had conducted the testing. I was an infantry captain at the time (infantry throughout my career). Although I can't know what, if any, guidance may have been received by USAIB regarding desired results, there was no indication that the conclusions were in any way influenced by anything other than the test.

The testing and reporting were unbiased. Note, however, the wording in the "recommendation": ". . . no consideration be given to adoption of new weapons until a *significant improvement* over the standard 7.62mm system can be achieved." This wording is curiously similar to that included in earlier decisions to stick with the .30 caliber tradition.

I had also been the primary test officer for the small starlight scope. The starlight scope or night vision weapon sight wasn't tested with any of the candidate weapons during the SAWS testing, but I stated at the time that suitable brackets could be fabricated for all the candidate automatic rifles.

Years later, when I was a student at the U.S. Army Command and General Staff College, I prepared a very detailed study of the results of the SAWS test as part of the requirement for a master's degree in Military Art and Science. The first year of this program was 1973–74, the year in which I prepared the thesis. I was principally examining the effectiveness of duplex ammunition, but my analysis included a comparison of the 5.56mm system with the 7.62mm system. A partial list of the conclusions follows:

- The weapon–duplex ammunition combinations are overall significantly more effective than the weapon–simplex ammunition combinations within the ranges of significance. Exceptions occur only during night-firing exercises and may be attributable to ballistic [mis] match of duplex and tracer ammunition, muzzle flash, and the general superiority of tracer ammunition at night. These phenomena warrant further investigation.

- The rifle 5.56mm ammunition combinations are generally more effective than the rifle 7.62mm simplex ammunition combinations.
- Other conclusions noted that the effectiveness of weapon–duplex ammunition combinations decreases with respect to that of the weapon–simplex ammunition combinations at ranges beyond those which are significant for normal tactical situations. In most situations, tracer ammunition is more effective than the corresponding ball ammunition. Exceptions appear to be the result of excessive muzzle flash. Duplex ammunition requires ballistically matched tracer ammunition to demonstrate its full potential. At night, muzzle flash not only discloses the position of the firer but seriously degrades hit capability.[6]

The focus of the thesis was the clear advantage of employing duplex ammunition. It was in analyzing all the test results that it became clear that the XM16E1 firing ball or a ball–tracer mix or tracer ammunition was measurably more effective than the M14 and M14E2 firing simplex ball or a simplex ball–tracer mix or tracer ammunition. This was an unexpected conclusion. I was aware of but did not compare malfunction issues in this study. The increased effectiveness of the XM16E1 (assuming a functional weapon) wasn't stated in the findings of the SAWS test but could be deduced by anyone taking time to analyze the results. It may be that there was an underlying prejudice for an intermediate caliber as the result of our predilection for .30 caliber weapons. The SAWS test did identify the failure-to-extract malfunction but simply noted the significantly greater reliability of the 7.62mm weapons system. The failure to extract was categorized as a "shortcoming," not a "deficiency," a serious understatement of what was really a critical deficiency. This malfunction wasn't described as linked to the unreliable, flimsy nature of the M11 cleaning rod and the absence of a chamber brush. It should have been. The brush was necessary to clean the chamber, and the cleaning rod to clear the malfunction.

The nature and seriousness of the problem, however, was clear enough to decision-makers up the chain of command. That realization didn't trickle down to commanders in Vietnam who aggressively harangued company officers and noncommissioned officers regarding lax cleaning and rifle maintenance. It took a congressional inquiry to forcibly enlighten commanders in the field and at the same time to identify the individuals responsible for failing to take immediate action. They were never held to account.

Twenty subtests were conducted by USAIB during the 1965 SAWS testing program. They were: (1) Preoperational Inspection and Physical Characteristics, (2) Training, (3) Rate of Fire, (4) Sights, (5) Magazines, (6) Ammunition and Packaging, (7) Defense, (8) Assault, (9) Mounts, (10) Record and Transition Fire, (11) Signature Characteristics, (12) Pointed Fire Accuracy, (13) Portability and Aerial Delivery, (14) Accessories and Training Aids, (15) Maintenance, (16) Durability and Reliability, (17) Versatility of Weapon Design, (18) Safety, (19) Human Factors Engineering and (20) Value Analysis. The results are presented in eight appendices: (I) References, (II) Test Data, (III) Findings, (IV) Deficiencies and Shortcomings, (V) Photographs, (VI) Maintenance Evaluation, (VII) Range Diagrams and (VIII) Distribution List.

Relevant subtests and appendices are discussed as they relate to the suitability and reliability of the XM16E1s that accompanied the first units and troops to Vietnam, before the engineering "fixes" began to address the malfunction problem. The 5.56mm ammunition employed in the SAWS test appears to have been principally ball and tracer ammunition from the same contract as that used in Vietnam, although ammunition loaded with IMR type propellant was noted as reducing muzzle flash in the C–SMG. The extent of its employment is unrecorded. Its limited use may have reduced the incidence of malfunctions. The frequent failures to extract that soldiers and Marines experienced in Vietnam were documented during the SAWS testing and were subsequently recorded in the final report. The next several paragraphs summarize the findings of the subtests:

Preoperational Inspection and Physical Characteristics: All the candidate weapons were found to be suitable. There were a few minor but not relevant comments.

Training: All the candidate weapons were found to be suitable. Initially, firers scored higher with the 5.56mm weapons, but when record firing was conducted again after firers were more accustomed to all the weapons, scores were higher with 7.62mm weapons.

Sights: The M14, M14E2, and M60 sights were superior to all the other candidate weapons except for durability.

Magazines: The XM16E1's magazines experienced a high incidence of bolt overrides and double feeds. This was listed as a deficiency.

Ammunition and Packaging: The tracer ammunition for both 5.56mm and 7.62mm weapons was satisfactory and significantly more effective as a means of target ranging and target/sector of fire designation than ball and duplex ammunition. Duplex ammunition significantly increased hit capability. There is no mention of any malfunction issues related to ammunition. At that time, we didn't associate the failure to extract with the particular propellant employed in the cartridges.

Defense, Day and Night: Duplex ammunition is the most effective. There are no comments with respect to the XM16E1.

Record and Transition Firing: The M14 produced the highest scores for the Record Marksmanship Course. There are no specific references to the XM16E1.

Signature Characteristics: There was no significant difference between the candidate rifles. Unacceptable flash was noted with the C-SMG, a short-barreled version of the M16, with standard 5.56mm cartridges loaded with ball propellant. This problem was corrected using cartridges loaded with CR propellant, a type of IMR propellant. The M14E2 produced excessive flash with M62 tracer ammunition. There are no comments with respect to the XM16E1.

Pointed Fire Accuracy: This characteristic was evaluated in both semi-automatic fire and full-automatic fire. The number of rounds fired was not limited in either the semiautomatic or automatic modes of fire. The XM16E1 is significantly less effective in the semiautomatic, pointed fire role than the other candidate rifles. Note that under circumstances that warrant pointed fire, the firer will almost surely have his selector switch on full automatic. The poorer showing in pointed fire with the assault rifle configuration will need to be addressed in training. The M14E2 is significantly less effective in the pointed fire role than other candidate automatic rifles. Note that this character-istic is one of the problems that the use of an intermediate caliber cartridge was intended to address.

Portability and Aerial Delivery: Tests included rigging with combat gear and day and night jumping with all the candidate weapons. All were suitable.

Accessories and Training Aids: The M11 type cleaning rods lack durabil-ity. Note that this was a serious deficiency when a failure to extract occurred under fire. This was noted as a shortcoming. Combined with the frequent failure to extract, it should have been a deficiency.

Maintenance: The ease of disassembly and assembly was satisfactory for all weapons. Only the 7.62mm weapons had satisfactory maintenance pack-ages. For all other weapons, including the XM16E1, the maintenance packages were incomplete and inadequate. This problem was recorded as two short-comings for the XM16E1. The first was the incomplete maintenance package and the second the missing bore brush. Because the failure to extract was such a critical malfunction, the lack of a bore brush should have been a deficiency.

Durability and Reliability: All the candidate weapons were sufficiently rugged. The 7.62mm weapons were the most rugged weapons overall. *"The*

M14 has a significantly lower, and the XM16E1 has a significantly higher, malfunction rate than the other candidate rifles and carbines" (italics added). This finding identified three deficiencies and six shortcomings for the XM16E1, overall the worst rating for any of the weapons with some of the SAWS 5.56mm candidate weapons following not too far behind.[7] It was at this point that the malfunction problem should have raised a red flag—but didn't.

Versatility of Weapon Design: Maximum commonality of parts was satisfactory for all weapons. Ammunition packaging was best provided by the standard 7.62mm family.

Safety: The XM16E1 will fire with the safety selector switch between the semiautomatic position and the fully automatic position. All the candidate weapons except the 7.62mm weapons and the XM16E1 ". . . are unacceptable for employment and use of the weapons by the infantryman."[8] Why the XM16E1 escaped the "unacceptable" category when it had the same problem as the other 5.56mm weapons isn't explained. The problem was noted as a deficiency for the other 5.56mm weapons, but only as a shortcoming for the XM16E1.

Human Factors Engineering: The only significant comment refers to the effectiveness of the safeties.

The following discussion directly addresses test results relating to reliability issues experienced with the XM16E1 during the testing. Before looking at specific malfunctions and their frequency, three comments are applicable: (1) All of the candidate test weapons were thoroughly cleaned following firing. The carbon buildup in the XM16E1 was excessive in the operating groups and the bore. The removal of this carbon was difficult and took an excessive amount of time. No chamber brush was provided in the maintenance package of the XM16E1. When questioned, the firers felt the M14 was easier to clean than the other candidate rifles. (2) The XM16E1 required more lubrication to fire sustained exercises than the M14. The XM16E1 required more frequent cleaning than the other candidate rifles to keep it operational. (3) The M11 cleaning rods furnished with the XM16E1s consisted of three separate sections that were intended to be screwed together for use. The end of a section would mushroom and flare at the female joint and frequently break. I recall one occasion in Vietnam using an already damaged cleaning rod to punch out a stuck cartridge case from my XM16E1 after a failure to extract and having to shake the individual sections out of the bore. This problem should have raised another red flag.

The maintenance issues experienced during testing should have dispelled any preconception that the XM16E1 needed less careful care and maintenance than any other firearm. That this need for special attention to individual maintenance wasn't communicated carefully to commanders, and that they, with their personal experience, didn't intuit the requirement, is incomprehensible and inexcusable.

For all the rifles, carbines, automatic rifles, and machine guns in the tests, the data bearing on durability and reliability were recorded. Special attention was given to ruggedness. Malfunctions and part breakage were recorded. Malfunctions were categorized as follows:

Category I—Malfunctions resolved by immediate action on the part of the firer. The "immediate action" taken was appropriate to the type of weapon and included such actions as manually operating the bolt or withdrawing a spent case with the fingers, but didn't include field stripping and didn't require the use of tools. Note that the malfunction of failure to extract was erroneously considered a Category I malfunction. To clear this malfunction required the use of the cleaning rod as a tool and several minutes of work. There was no time for this for a soldier in contact.

Category II—Malfunctions not correctable by Category I action but were corrected in the field by field stripping and/or cleaning, lubricating, or minor adjustment without the use of tools (other than a cartridge or other aid normally available to the firer). This category didn't include second-echelon-level work, but was intended to include actions which the soldier could take during a temporary respite in combat.

Category III—Malfunctions not remedied by Category I or Category II action, but which were correctable at second echelon, using the tools, facilities, and skills normally available at that level.

Category IV—Malfunctions not corrected by Category I, Category II, or Category III actions.

Although not documented in the report, it appears that the Category I through IV system was used during the testing to ensure that the various malfunctions were treated appropriately for each weapon, because the same malfunction on different weapons might require different levels of repair effort. For example, a damaged barrel on the XM16E1 would require the rifle to be repaired at the highest echelon of maintenance (Category IV), whereas a damaged barrel on an M60 would be changed out by the operator in the field (Category I). To understand the general severity of XM16E1 malfunctions and breakages, see the following Maintenance Allocation Chart from Technical Manual 9–1005–249–14, *Operation, Maintenance, Repair, and Replacement Parts, Rifle 5.56-MM, M16; Rifle 5.56-MM, XM16E1; and Launcher, Grenade, 40-MM, XM148*, August 1, 1966.

AR-15, CAR-15, M16

CHAPTER X
MAINTENANCE ALLOCATION CHART

10-1. PURPOSE.

To allocate specific maintenance operations to the proper level on the basis of time and skills normally available to various maintenance levels and influenced by maintenance policy and sound practices as outlined in AR 750-6 (Army).

10-2. EXPLANATION AND DEFINITIONS.

The maintenance allocation chart designates overall responsibility for the maintenance func-

tion on an end item or assembly. Repair and/or overhaul of major assemblies is designated by authority of the Army commander representative, except for the specific repair subfunctions listed in the maintenance allocation charts. Deviation from maintenance operations allocated in the maintenance allocation charts is authorized only upon approval of the Army commander representative.

SERVICE	To clean, preserve, and lubricate.
REPLACE	To substitute serviceable assemblies, subassemblies, and parts for unserviceable components.
REPAIR	To restore to a serviceable condition by replacing unserviceable parts or by any other action required utilizing tools, equipment and skills available, to include riveting, straightening, adjusting, etc.
SYMBOL "X"	The symbol "X" placed in the appropriate column indicates the level responsible for performing that particular maintenance operation, but does not necessarily indicate that repair parts will be stocked at that level. Maintenance levels higher than the level marked by "X" are authorized to perform the indicated operation.

MAINTENANCE ALLOCATION CHART

(1) Group No.	(2) Component and related operations	(3) Maintenance Levels				
		O/C	O	DS	GS	D
1	Magazine:					
	Service	X				
	Repair			X		
	Replace	X				
2	Bolt Carrier Group:					
	Service	X				
	Repair			X		
3	Upper Receiver Group:					
	Service	X				
	Repair			X		
4	Barrel and Front Sight Assembly:					
	Service	X				
	Repair				X	
	Replace				X	

10-1

AR-15, CAR-15, M16

MAINTENANCE ALLOCATION CHART - continued

(1)	(2)	(3) Maintenance Levels				
Group No.	Component and related operations	O/C	O	DS	GS	D
5	Rear Sight: Service . . . . Repair	X		. X		
6	Hand Guard Assembly: Service . . . . Replace	X		. X		
7	Lower Receiver Group: Service . . . . Repair	X		. X		
8	Stock Assembly: Service . . . . Repair . . . . Replace	X		. X . X		
9	Rifle Bipod Service . . . . Replace	X		. X		

10-3. EXPLANATION OF MAINTENANCE LEVELS.

O/C	Operator or Crew
O	Organizational
DS	Direct Support
GS	General Support
D	Depot

For all practical purposes, the chart shows that the repair of the XM16E1 was intended to be performed either at the Operator level, or at the third tier Direct Support level.

Twenty-nine different malfunctions were identified and recorded during the testing.

I have noted and commented on the normal corrective action, the first of which is applying "immediate action" (IA). This is most simply defined as instinctively doing the right thing to immediately restore a weapon to firing condition. With the M16, it includes tapping the magazine upward to make sure it is fully seated and then pulling the charging handle all the way to the rear to see if a whole cartridge or case is ejected. If so, the charging handle is released, and a new round fed into the chamber. Next, after the round has fed into the chamber, the bolt-assist is tapped to ensure that the cartridge is fully seated. If a round or expended cartridge case is not ejected, then "immediate action" has failed.[9] This is the situation with the malfunction failure-to-extract.

The malfunctions with the action to be taken are categorized as follows: (1) Failure to feed. (IA). (2) Failure to fire. (IA). (3) Failure to extract; the source of the critical problem. A time-consuming failure correctable by the firer. (4) Failure to eject. The firer could correct this malfunction by removing the expended cartridge case with his fingers or, holding the bolt carrier to the rear, by shaking out the expended cartridge case. Minimally time consuming. Where this malfunction is recorded, there is a possible misidentification of what was a failure to extract. This was the most frequent malfunction. (5) Failure of bolt to close. (IA). (6) Short recoil. (IA). (7) Inadvertent firing. Safety factor. Possible need for fix above individual level. Ignore if in contact with enemy. (8) Failure to maintain cyclic rate. Probable need for a fix above individual level. The ball propellant was the basic cause of an increase in the cyclic rate of fire that itself was a causative factor in the rate of failure to extract and necessitated the modification of the buffer. (9) Bolt underrode base of round in feeding (three occurrences with the Stoner carbine—none with the standard weapons). (IA). (10) Double feed, two rounds fed from magazine at once. Clearable by firer. Minimally time consuming. (11) Bolt hold–open catch engaged bolt carrier instead of bolt after firing the last round in the magazine. (IA). (12) Bolt failed to engage base of round in magazine. (IA). (13) Bolt lacked sufficient energy to force round from magazine. (IA). (14) Bolt over-rode base of round in feeding from magazine. (IA). (15) Failure of bolt to go forward. Probable need for fix above individual level. (16) Failure of bolt to remain at rear after last round. (IA). (17) Fired on closure of bolt. Safety factor. Possible need for fix above individual level. Ignore if in contact. (18) Failure to eject clip [sic]. (IA). (19) Failure of the magazine to lock in rifle. (IA). (20) Failure of trigger to return to forward position. May need cleaning. Possible need for fix above individual level. Bad situation if in contact. (21) Fired two rounds on one rearward movement of trigger. Might need a fix above individual level. Not much of an immediate problem. (22) Bolt catch stopped forward movement of bolt before last round of magazine was fired. IA, however, may need fix above individual level. (23) Failure to strip round. (IA). (24) Failure of bolt to sear off. (IA). (25) Failure to feed round over to stripping position. (IA). (26) Failure of bolt to sear. (IA). (27) Failure to remain in assembly. Appears to apply to machine guns. (28) Failure to load by hand charging. Repeat IA. (29) Partial strip of round from link. Applies to machine gun.

The report lists the following significant occurrences with respect to the durability of the XM16E1. These incidents don't include the durability history of the C–SMG or the C–AR: Four incidences of bolts being cracked or broken. Four incidences where the bolt carrier keys had to be retorqued. Five incidents of the buffer assembly roll pins being separated or deformed. Twenty-four incidents of the firing pin retaining pin being cracked during firing.

The C–SMG was compared with the rifles and included in the same table. The C–AR will later be compared to the M14E2. The report lists the following incident as significant with respect to the reliability of the XM16E1: one incident of the selector switch being inoperative and one incident of the front sight being frozen.

With respect to all malfunctions, the following data for the XM16E1 are derived from a total of 95,720 rounds fired. The figures are from Table 4.1. I have corrected the table which has one typo, for the most troublesome malfunction, failure-to-extract. The list of the following significant reliability problems did not, for some inexplicable reason, include failure-to-extract: 532 incidents of the bolt failing to remain to the rear after the last round of a magazine had been fired—rate: 1:180 rounds fired, or nominally one out of nine 20-round magazines or, as magazines in Vietnam were generally loaded with no more than nineteen rounds, one out of nine and a half magazines. One hundred and eighty-eight (188) incidents of the bolt overriding the base of the round in feeding from the magazine—rate: 1:509 rounds fired. Two hundred and fifty-one (251) incidents of failure to eject—rate, 1:381 rounds fired. As noted, the most serious of the malfunctions escaped inclusion in the list. The incidence of failure to extract appears in the same table, 4.1, as the foregoing data. There are eighty-six (86) incidents. The rate is 1:1,113. The frequency of this malfunction during SAWS testing was lower than experienced in Vietnam. This may be attributable to new rifles carefully maintained under ideal conditions. Also, these were XM16E1s manufactured before the pace of production was ratcheted up, and when quality control may have been more consistent. Additionally, some ammunition loaded with an IMR type of propellant was employed with the C–SMG in testing for signature characteristics and may have made its way into other tests.

It would appear that the severity of the failure-to-extract malfunction wasn't evaluated in the context of its effect in a firefight and so didn't make it into the summary of significant reliability incidents. This malfunction—failure to extract—is more than significant. It is serious, the most serious of all the common malfunctions of the XM16E1 for the soldier and Marine in contact with the enemy.

The report lists two totals: one overall total and one that excludes the failure of the bolt to remain to the rear after the last round is fired, presumably because it isn't a particularly serious malfunction. I have included both totals simply to conform to the report. The total of XM16E1 malfunctions is 710 (excluding failure of the bolt to remain to the rear after the last round) with a rate of one failure per 135 rounds fired. The total of malfunctions for the XM16E1 is 1,242 for a rate of one failure per seventy-seven (77) rounds fired, when the failure of the bolt to remain to the rear is included.

The corresponding figures for all the malfunctions of the C-SMG are again taken from Table 4.1 and are based on a total of 81,871 rounds fired.[10] I will list the same malfunctions, although no separate paragraph highlights them in the test report. There are 122 incidences of the bolt failing to remain to the rear after the last round of a magazine has been fired—rate 1:671. Eleven (11) incidents of the bolt overriding the base of the round in feeding from the magazine—rate: 1:7,443. Two (2) instances of failure to eject—rate 1:40,935. Forty-three (43) incidences of failure to extract—rate: 1:1,904. The total of malfunctions less the bolt remaining to the rear is one hundred (100) for a rate of 1:818. The total including that malfunction is two hundred and twenty-two (222) for a rate of 1:369. Note the lower malfunction rate compared to the XM16E1. This may be attributable to the use of an IMR type of powder in at least some of the testing with the C-SMG, although this is just speculation as the information is not presented in the report.

The corresponding figures for the M14, derived from a total of 518,380 rounds fired, are: A total of eighteen (18) failures to extract for a rate of 1:28,779. A total of 307 malfunctions, not including failure of the bolt to remain to the rear with a rate of 1:1,689. Including the bolt not remaining to the rear malfunction, there are a total of 313 for a rate of 1:1656. The failure of the bolt to remain to the rear malfunction rate for the M14 was 1:86,397 rounds fired.

Including the failure to extract and the total malfunctions in semiautomatic fire, the corresponding rates are:

Table 4.1

Malfunction	M14	XM16E1	C-SMG	Comparison XM16E1: M14
Failure to Eject	1:27,283	1:381	1:40,935	71.1:1
Failure to Extract	1:28,779	1:1,113	1:1,904	25.9:1
Total Less Bolt Staying to Rear	1:1,689	1:135	1:818	12.5:1
Total Malfunctions	1:1,656	1:77	1:369	21.5:1

These figures are for the XM16E1 and the C-SMG employed in the semiautomatic mode and are derived from a raw count of malfunctions, most of which can be cleared by immediate action with the M14, but with a significant number of those not clearable by immediate action with the XM16E1 or the C-SMG. The failure to extract, the most serious of the malfunctions clearable by the firer but not by immediate action, occurred, on average, once every fifty-seven magazines with the XM16E1 and once every one hundred magazines with the C-SMG, assuming each magazine was loaded with nineteen rounds. The difference appears attributable to the occasional use of an IMR type of propellant in the ammunition used with the C-SMG as well as inconsistency of results from rifle to rifle and submachine gun to submachine gun as depicted below. The recorded data from the twenty XM16E1s yields a failure to extract that varied from no such failure for four rifles; one failure for seven rifles; four failures for two rifles; five failures for one rifle; six failures for one rifle; seven failures for one rifle; eight failures for one rifle; eleven failures for two rifles; and twenty-three failures for one rifle. The number of rounds fired per rifle ranged between 3,732 and 5,868. With the C-SMG, the same malfunctions recorded for the twenty submachine guns in the test varied from no such failures for eight C-SMGs; one for four C-SMGs; two for two C-SMGs; three for two C-SMGs; four for one C-SMG; eight for two C-SMGs; and fifteen for one C-SMG. The number of rounds fired per C-SMG ranged between 1,836 and 6,224. The sample size of twenty of each type of weapon was insufficient to level out the failure-to-extract malfunction rates between the two. Nevertheless, with the XM16E1 compared to the M14, the critical failure to extract is twenty-six times greater and the total malfunction rate is twenty-two times greater. These data result from nearly ideal maintenance and cleaning situations with available cleaning rods, bore brushes, chamber brushes, and appropriate lubricants and where the temperate climate is less conducive to corrosion and pitting than a humid environment. These inconsistencies in reliability were also experienced in Vietnam as some XM16E1s often malfunctioned while others earned a reputation for good performance. As will be noted in Chapter 6, there is reason to suspect that some XM16E1s with functional problems slipped through an inadequate quality control by Colt.

The data in the report recording malfunctions by category for semiautomatic fire are in Table 4.2 and is as follows:[11]

Table 4.2

Weapon	Total Rounds Fired	Value	Category I	Category II	Category III	Category IV	Total
M14	518,380	Total	261	23	46	1	331
		Rate	1:1,986	1:22,538	1:11,269	1:518,380	1:1,566
XM16E1	95,720	Total	1,140	74	55	5	1,274
		Rate	1:84	1:1,294	1:1,740	1:19,144	1:75
C-SMG	81,871	Total	202	14	4	2	222
		Rate	1:405	1:5,488	1:20,468	1:40,936	1:369

The failure to extract—the most serious battlefield malfunction in Vietnam—is included with Category I malfunctions and it is clearly a Category II malfunction. For individual XM16E1s, the failure to extract varied from a low of 1:5,638 rounds to a high of 1:197 rounds. For individual C-SMGs, the rate varied from a low of 1:5,740 to a high of 1:208. Some of the malfunctions were relevant to safety but didn't interrupt firing when in contact with the enemy. Most could be cleared by immediate action. Some required maintenance beyond the ability of the firer and needed the attention of an armorer and in many cases, replacement of a damaged part. The failure to extract could be cleared by the firer but took several minutes at best. If the soldier or Marine wasn't directly exposed to enemy fire at the time, the malfunction was little more than an inconvenience. If, however, the infantryman was directly engaged and under fire, this particular malfunction exposed the firer to immediate peril. He became dependent upon his buddies or foxhole mate to defend him until he could clear the malfunction. If he had no M11 cleaning rod, he was dependent on someone else having one. There is at least one recorded incident where a Marine with a cleaning rod was killed while going from Marine to Marine to clear their jammed rifles.[12]

The following figures from Table 4.3 are for automatic firing and are limited to results for the M14E2, the C-AR, and the M60. The data for the latter is included as a matter of interest for comparison. The XM16E1 was not a part of these firing tests as the functionally identical C-AR was intended to provide sufficient data for comparison. These data include only total rounds fired, failure to extract, and total malfunctions.

The total number of rounds fired in automatic fire by the C-AR was 85,299, by the M60: 181,768, and by the M14E2: 107,287.

Table 4.3

Weapon	Failure to Extract	Rate	Total Malfunctions	Rate
C-AR	128	1:666	235	1:363
M60	11	1:16,524	34	1:5,346
M14E2	21	1:5,109	74	1:1,450

The rates are:

Malfunction	M14E2	C-AR	Comparison C-AR: M14E2
Failure to Extract	1:5,109	1:666	7.7:1
Total Malfunctions	1:1,450	1:363	4.0:1

These data are the result of full automatic fire. The C-AR experienced a failure to extract once every thirty-five magazines. This figure also is representative of the same failure of the XM16E1, which in close combat, generally fired in the full automatic mode. The malfunction rate of the C-AR was four times that of the M14E2. The report specifically noted that the rate of the failure-to-extract malfunction and the rate of the total malfunctions of the C-AR were significant. With respect to reliability, the report concluded that "the M14 had a significantly lower and the XM16E1 had a significantly higher malfunction rate than the other candidate rifles and carbines." What the report failed to note was the critical nature of the failure-to-extract malfunction, and it was lumped in with other Category I malfunctions mostly clearable by immediate action.

The data in the report recording malfunctions by category for automatic fire are in Table 4.4 and are as follows:[13]

Table 4.4

Weapon	Total Rounds Fired	Value	Category I	Category II	Category III	Category IV	Total
M14E2	518,380	Total	71	4	10	4	89
		Rate	1:1,511	1:26,882	1:10,729	1:26,882	1:1,205
C-AR	85,299	Total	218	0	19	62	43
		Rate	1:391	N/A	1:4,489	1:14,217	1:351
M60	81,871	Total	12	6	0	40	22
		Rate	1:8,262	1:15,147	1:30,295	N/A	1:4,544

Again, the failure to extract has been slipped into Category I and is clearly a Category II malfunction. The failure to extract rate for individual C-ARs varied from a low of 1:5,138 rounds to a high of 1:159 rounds.

The following findings are listed for "Deficiencies" under "Durability" and don't include those for the M14 or the M14E2:

- XM16E1: Excessive number of cracked bolts. Bolt carrier key became loose and required retorqueing. Cracked firing pin retaining pins.
- C-SMG: Cracked bolts.
- C-AR: Broken action spring guide assembly.

The following shortcoming was listed under Durability:

XM16E1: Separation and deformation of buffer assembly roll pins.

The following shortcomings were listed under Reliability:

XM16E1: Excessive failures of the bolt to remain to the rear after the last round of a magazine had been fired. Excessive bolt overrides. Excessive failures to eject. Inoperative selector switch. Frozen front sight post.

Note here: There were indeed excessive failures to eject. Table 4.1 cites 251 failures to eject out of 95,720 rounds fired and eighty-six failures to extract, a far more serious failure. A failure to eject is an inconvenience clearable in seconds. A failure to extract takes minutes. It is also conceivable but not ascertainable that some or many of the failures to extract were recorded as failures to eject.

C-SMG: Excessive failure of the bolt to remain to the rear.
C-AR: Excessive failures to extract.

The following were listed as deficiencies for the XM16E1: The lack of a multi-round charging device; the bolt carrier key becoming loose and requiring retorqueing; the excessive number of broken bolts and the excessive number of broken firing pin retaining pins. The deficiencies for the C-SMG listed the same lack of a multi-round charging device and cracked or broken bolts as well as excessive noise, muzzle flash, and safety issues. For the C-AR, the deficiencies included the same lack of a multi-round charging device, safety issues, and broken spring-guide assemblies.

The following were listed as shortcomings for the XM16E1: The sight doesn't have a visual scale for determining zero; the front sight requires a tool or cartridge for adjustment; the sight isn't operable with minimum motion; lack of a 50-round minimum magazine capacity; lack of adjustability of legs on bipod; incomplete maintenance package; lack of a chamber-cleaning brush; separation and deformation of buffer assembly roll pins; excessive number of failures of bolt overriding the base of round while in magazine; excessive number of failures of bolt not remaining to rear after last round of magazine was fired; excessive number of failures to eject; inoperative selector switch causes rifle to fire only semiautomatically; frozen front sight post prevents sight adjustments; weapon fires with the safety and selector switch between the safe and semiautomatic position; rapid build-up and transfer of heat in sustained fire causes difficulty in handling the weapon and poor pointing characteristics. In addition to most of the foregoing, the following additional shortcomings were listed for the C-SMG: inability of the weapon to accept a bayonet; lack of a means of carrying cleaning equipment; no carrying sling provided with weapon; and incomplete operations and maintenance instructions. For the C-AR the shortcomings were essentially a duplication of those for the XM16E1 and C-SMG.

The results of the SAWS testing conducted at Fort Benning along with a partial report of the Engineering Test conducted by the Ballistics Research Laboratory were submitted on December 29, 1965, by the Army's Test and Evaluation Command to the Commanding General, U.S. Army Weapons Command; and Commanding General, U.S. Army Combat Developments Command. By this time major Army and Marine Corps units had already been deployed to the Republic of Vietnam, equipped with the problematic XM16E1 rifle. The two test reports were forwarded with the following comments:

> *The report of the Engineering Test is partial because testing is still in progress. The final report of the engineering test will be forwarded when available. These reports are forwarded for information and to meet the deadlines established for the SAWS program. A Headquarters USATECOM position with respect to these reports and their conclusions and recommendations will be provided upon completion of detailed analysis, now in progress; pending completion of this analysis, addressees are cautioned in the use of certain of the data presented for the reasons indicated below.*

    a. Tactical Firing Exercises (USA Infantry Board Report)—The results obtained in tests of this nature are primarily dependent upon human performance; troop samples should be matched in size and quality, and test conditions should be identical for each weapon insofar as possible. However, although every effort was made, it was not possible to maintain optimum controls in SAWS testing due to circumstances that were largely beyond the control of the test agency.

(1) Weapons were not available in uniform quantity, and in some cases were delivered after testing had been initiated, because of contractor inability to meet the desired schedule. In consequence, the size of troop samples varied and in some instances the learning factor could not be kept equal for all weapons.

(2) Delays and suspensions imposed on the test agency for safety considerations and/or because of weapon malfunctioning resulted in some variance in test conditions.

    b. Reliability and Durability (Engineering and Service Test Reports)—Weapons tested varied from some which have been in production for several years to others which are in an early stage of development. Data bearing upon reliability and durability must be carefully analyzed to correlate Engineering and Service Test results and to determine, where possible, whether malperformances are considered to be correctable in future development or reflect basic design deficiencies.

Note: This caveat gave serious malfunctions too much wiggle room, given the inflexibility of the time schedule with issue of the XM16E1 and ball ammunition already in Vietnam and in the pipeline.

    c. Ammunition (Engineering and Service Test Reports)—In the SAWS test ammunition of *"average"* quality, representative of that available for issue to troops, was used. In testing it was found that occasional unacceptable wide dispersion was obtained with the 7.62mm M80 ball cartridge, and that the 5.56mm M193 ball cartridge apparently contributed to relatively low functional reliability of some weapons. The degree to which ammunition contributed to these results must be analyzed in detail.

Note: This is the heart of the matter. The cause of the failure to extract was known but the problem wasn't resolved for years, with some malfunction-prone XM16E1s still in the hands of troops as late as 1968 and even later. Many soldiers and Marines lost their lives and others were seriously wounded as a direct result of the unreliability of the XM16E1 under field conditions when employed with the ammunition that accompanied them to Vietnam.

It is clear that there was a high sense of urgency for all of the testing and evaluation; however, let's look again at the USAIB Findings, Conclusions, and Recommendations.

a. Findings. There are no significant differences between the SAWS weapons except for reliability. The current standard weapons are the most reliable.

b. Conclusions. The M14, M14E2, and M60 are significantly more reliable than their counterpart SAWS weapons. The use of duplex ammunition significantly increases hit capability.

c. Recommendation. USAIB recommends that no consideration be given to adoption of new weapons systems until a significant improvement over the standard 7.62mm system can be achieved.

There is no mention of the XM16E1, yet this was the individual weapon already in the hands of thousands of American soldiers and Marines in Vietnam. The USAIB "Recommendation" seems to have been shortsighted. There was clearly no perception of the fact that modern war had entered the era of the assault rifle. Infantrymen would need an individual weapon that could produce the greatest amount of immediately available firepower. This was a certain clue that the infantry firearm must be a weapon capable of fully automatic fire, irrespective of its caliber or configuration.

The dramatic increases in the rate of malfunctions of the XM16E1 should have been a red light. Even though the recommendation was that the XM16E1 not be adopted as a new weapons system, it was already in the hands of soldiers and Marines in combat. There should have been a clear statement to the effect that immediate action was needed to correct the malfunction problems that the USAIB confirmed. The failure to extract was more than a "shortcoming."

The contract that resulted in the use of ball powder reflected not a lack of communication between responsible military developers and decision-makers with Stoner and Colt, but rather an unwillingness to take stock of their cautionary guidance. There was an ongoing contract for ammunition. One may speculate as to whether some abrupt change could have been made here that would have met the existing and anticipated requirements for 5.56mm ball ammunition. No action was taken with respect to the ammunition, and the fix had to be made to the XM16E1 itself to accommodate the propellant. One by one the "upgrades" were accomplished, although the most basic—chroming the bore of the rifle—was something that should have been noted and corrected before even initial testing was conducted. The increased rate of fire resulting in the change from IMR propellant, with which the M16 had been developed, to ball propellant was identified early on, but the modification of the buffer to accommodate this increased rate of fire lagged behind the known fix. The sense of urgency was insufficient. Soldiers and Marine infantrymen paid the price in blood.

In the next chapter we will look at the problems with the XM16E1 experienced by the soldiers and Marines in Vietnam. Many in the chain of command, including senior officers, did not listen to the troops, blamed them for poor maintenance, and failed to address the problem. The XM16E1 "limited standard" rifle was not ready for combat.

5

CYA—THE NAME OF THE GAME

The XM16E1 rifle that accompanied U.S. soldiers to Vietnam in 1965 (or was issued to them in-country) and was distributed to American Marines in the same time frame wasn't altered in any significant way from the AR15 that had done well in most of the testing with ammunition using IMR propellant.

It had, however, been shown to have significant reliability issues when employing the ammunition loaded with the Army's standard ball propellant, the ammunition that was issued in Vietnam. With the ammunition it was engineered to employ, it would have been an effective weapon until pitting and corrosion set in. Corrosion and pitting were a sure thing in the hot and humid Vietnamese climate. With ball ammunition, a bore that wasn't chromed, and absent proper cleaning material and maintenance guidance, poor performance was assured.

Mike Handley was a combat medic attached to the 3rd Platoon, Company A, 5th Battalion, 7th Cavalry, 1st Cavalry Division (Airmobile) in 1966. He outlines his experience with the XM16E1:

I carried an M16, ammunition, and grenades as well as the medic stuff. I was allowed by my Platoon Sgt. to have free reign until someone was wounded. The 5th Battalion trained as a unit in Fort Carson, Colorado and the entire Battalion shipped to Vietnam on the USNS Gaffney from Oakland, California in August 1966. Except for a few, most of us had no experience in Vietnam. The 5th of the 7th rounded out the 3rd Brigade of the 1st Cav. Once arriving we were exposed to low key missions and Air Assaults to gain experience operating in the Central Highlands, generally around An Khe. The first significant engagement for A Company was on Oct. 4, 1966 in Binh Dinh Province where we did a sweep through a broad valley. This lasted all day and involved sloshing most of the way through rice paddies for 10–15 clicks. Toward the end of day 2 helicopter pilots were shot down near us in an area called the Salt Dikes and Mangrove Swamp near the ocean or South China Sea. A Company went in to rescue the pilots.

When the action started, several, not all, of us in 3rd platoon experienced jams after the first shot was fired from our M16s. The shell would not extract and stayed lodged in the chamber. Fortunately, our platoon Sgt. took out his cleaning rods and was able to push the spent round out of the chamber. This worked to the best of my recollection for all who experienced jams. After that the weapon worked for the rest of that engagement. Leading up to that day, many of us had not fired or cleaned our weapons for several days. My theory is that dirt and corrosion on the cartridges that were chambered several days caused the shell to hang up from expansion from firing and dirt on the cartridge. The ejector [sic] pulled notches on the end of the shell rather than eject it. I specifically remember seeing this on the spent cartridge pushed out of my M16.

After that we didn't have to be reminded to pull a little PM [preventive maintenance] on our M16s. This for me was simple, periodically cleaning the chamber with a cotton swab with a little oil on it, wiping off the cartridge and reloading. To the best of my recollection no one experienced any more problems.

I give the M16 an A– based upon that experience and which could have been prevented. I would and did stake my life on the M16.[1]

Many units didn't have an opportunity to train with the rifle. It was issued to troops with no or inadequate cleaning equipment. There were neither bore nor chamber brushes available. Some units weren't issued enough cleaning rods to provide one for every soldier or Marine. The three-piece cleaning rods were fabricated of aluminum and were flimsy. They were easily damaged after very little use. The rifle came with no instructions. These rifles were employed under adverse conditions, not simply to be used for a week or two of hunting, then cleaned under ideal conditions, and perhaps fired a few times at a range or out in the country. They were employed as weapons and were used roughly.

The men who depended on them were dirty, hot, tired, and hungry—just as men fighting on the ground have always been. Dirt, mud, and rain in intensive combinations was a nearly constant environment. Of course, with the ammunition that accompanied the XM16E1, malfunctions were assured irrespective of the training, cleaning equipment, instructions, lubrication, and supervision available. Sooner or later, and all-too-often sooner, the rifle would simply fail to extract a fired cartridge. As soon as this problem occurred, it was likely to repeat itself. Good officers and noncommissioned officers make the best of any difficult and challenging situation: bring order out of chaos, and lead with good humor. That's what they are trained and paid to do.

Sooner or later, even with proper ammunition, the humid and wet Vietnamese climate would have taken its toll. The bores and chambers would have corroded. The rifles would have needed more maintenance than the individual rifleman could provide. The military plans for maintenance challenges and provides spare parts and maintenance specialists who are trained to make repairs. What happened in Vietnam, however, was quite different.

The XM16E1, with known design deficiencies and incompatible ammunition, as issued to Vietnam-bound troops and to units in-country, was programmed to fail. The rate of malfunctions, under the adverse conditions of employment in combat, was much higher than anticipated. Senior leaders, initially even at battalion level, and generally further up the chain of command, including general officers with long experience, exhibited an indifference to reports from men doing the fighting, an example of incompetence and lack of responsibility that is painful to contemplate. Back in the States, military and civilian decision-makers had sent a defective rifle/ammunition system to the front. They denied the existence of a problem. Here is a comment by Vern Humphrey, an infantry advisor in Vietnam and an infantry company commander at Fort Polk, Louisiana, and the exchange that followed:

> *In 1967 after my first tour* [in Vietnam], *I was an* AIT [Advanced Individual Training] *company commander at Fort Polk. Before going to the range, we would thoroughly clean and lube all the rifles, then take them to the range in a truck, covered with ponchos. They still kept the NCOs busy running from one trainee to another clearing stoppages. One trainee wrote to President Johnson, complaining about the M16. The President's inquiry was sent to me. I wrote a draft response, but the post headquarters didn't send it. Instead they used it to send their own response. In my draft response, I stated frankly that we had many stoppages, but inadvertently said I couldn't tell him if that particular trainee had a stoppage, because the NCOs were so busy they couldn't remember any particular soldier who needed help. That was rewritten at Post level to say the NCOs couldn't remember any particular soldier having a stoppage.*[2]

I (Duryea) responded that his comments tied right in with the general cover-up that was a major contributing factor to our problems with fixing the XM16E1 and to problems in Vietnam in general—sometimes poor and unethical leadership. In our continuing dialog, he comments *"I call that era, 'The Age of Midgets.' We needed leaders who were giants and look what we got."*

He (Vern Humphrey) continues:

> *I always think of Bruce Palmer. His book,* The 25 Year War, *is an indictment of Lyndon Johnson. But in the book, he says he only met the President twice. The first*

time was for a photo, and the other time Johnson asked everyone what they thought of his strategy. He went around the room asking each person there individually. Palmer's comment, "It was obvious no one was going to tell him they disagreed." "What the Hell, General!?! The President asked for your professional opinion and you didn't have the cojones to give it to him? What were you afraid of, that they'd send you to Viet Nam?"

This hesitancy and failure to speak out frankly and honestly reflects a greater concern with self-interest than with more important general welfare concerns. It started at battalion level with politically sensitive issues and infected the chain of command all the way up. It's probably one of the major reasons we lost the struggle to preserve an independent South Vietnam.

The XM16E1 with the issued ball ammunition was a problem for men in combat. No one took responsibility. No one was held accountable. In Vietnam, leaders who should have had more faith in their men, the ones who depended upon them, didn't pay attention to their problems with the XM16E1, even when it was brought clearly to their attention. They curried favor with their own senior leaders, looking up the chain of command when they should have been looking down. They had a duty to pay attention to what was happening with their men in the fight.

It's consistently more informative when looking for answers to just about any military situation, condition, or problem to consult experienced noncommissioned officers on the ground, an officer here and there, as well as some troopers, than it is to look for unbiased judgment somewhere up the line. It's a mistake to believe that the men on the ground can't figure out what is going on and who is or is not acting in their—the troops'—welfare, or the country's best interests. Senior officers who don't talk individually with their men on a regular and candid basis are missing an important and unbiased source of information. This is too often reflected in the erroneous reports they send up the chain of command until just about everyone who isn't on the ground has been misled. This happened with the XM16E1 in the first few years in Vietnam.

Misleading reports took on a more serious aspect as the war dragged on. Senior leaders promoted the expectation that success was right around the corner. They misled the military decision makers, who in turn misled the senior political leadership. By failing to accurately analyze and report events, the military raised unrealistic expectations and misled the press. As a result, the press, tired of deception, didn't recognize or report good news, and unhappy with being deceived, told their own story, frequently wrong. Popular support for the war, very strong for a couple of years, collapsed.

When I completed a tour as a district senior advisor in the Mekong Delta in the summer of 1969, we were on a path to success. To my surprise, Phong Dinh Province, in the center of the Mekong Delta, under severe Viet Cong (VC) threat in 1968, was nearly secure by the summer of 1969. There was sporadic contact with the VC. Mortar attacks, which had occurred regularly in the summer of 1968, had ended. The local economy was rapidly improving. Fish ponds, flocks of ducks, market construction, all represented progress. Unfortunately, by that time, in contrast with calling "wolf" too often, we had boasted too often. The good news was no longer believable.

There is an active tendency in the military to distrust the press and blame them for what happened. In fact, the loss of support for the war in Vietnam was, if not self-inflicted, nevertheless partly the result of intentionally misleading the press. Journalists simply discovered that they weren't getting the truth at briefings. The ones in the field with the troops, and there were many, couldn't offset the stories coming out of Saigon from the REMF[3] types. It was all over. One can't manage the press. The only successful course of action is to conduct all aspects of a war in an honorable manner and to be scrupulously honest in reporting what is going on. Informational deception must be reserved as an instrument to deceive the enemy.

Information now moves on an almost instantaneous basis. It moves rapidly up the chain of command and even faster via the news media. The same tendency to boast of success in a career-enhancing display of optimism is alive and well. That's what senior officers too often do as they massage information on the way up the chain of command. Pubic information officers respond to the guidance they receive. All information should be prepared with the interests of the country in mind, not the careers of those who prepare it. This is such a simple principle that it shouldn't even need to be mentioned.

This same aversion to directly addressing problems created somewhere up the chain of command played its part in Vietnam. Leaders who had a duty to know better aggressively maintained their own ignorance and blamed the troops for XM16E1 malfunction problems. In combat men do their best to keep their weapons clean. They know that their lives depend on a working rifle. The "brass" knew this, or should have.

In 1965 and 1966 in the 1st Cavalry Division, during brief periods in base camp between operations, the XM16E1s received particularly thorough cleanings and inspections. But malfunctions continued, just as they had during extensive testing by the Infantry Board in 1965 following very professionally supervised cleaning after every firing.

There was clear evidence of fouling, and that acted to deflect attention from other problems: the too-high cyclic rate of fire and the incompatible ammunition. These issues were unanticipated. Engineering and design details and ammunition compatibility should have been resolved before weapons were issued to troops. To the chain of command in the field, the causes of the failure to extract looked like poor maintenance.

The first military reaction to poorly functioning weapons is to blame it on inadequate maintenance by the troops. A little bit of professional communication would have revealed that the problem wasn't with the men. Many commanders looked no further. They tried to shift the blame for malfunctions on to the soldiers and Marine infantrymen. The Marines in the Hill Fights in the I Corps area of operations, including the fierce Khe Sanh fighting in 1966 and 1967, endured brutal casualties unimaginable to anyone who hasn't served in combat. A very significant number of the Marines killed and wounded may be attributed to the failure of the XM16E1 to fire more than a few rounds, sometimes only one. Marines would search for a working rifle from among the dead and wounded, just as we did in the 7th Cavalry. Senior Marine commanders were particularly vocal in their criticism of what they alleged were poor maintenance practices. This is a perfect example of senior officers out of touch with the men doing the fighting. The greater the distance from the action, the greater the tendency to discount reports from the field. This is a problem that extends into all manner of important decisions. The decisions respond to political interests and reflect a concern with appearance and approval, neither of which contribute to success in the field or the welfare of the troops.

In many units, Marines and soldiers were ordered not to talk about the problem with the XM16E1 with journalists who frequented some of the bloody battlefields, generally but not always after the shooting had stopped. What sort of self-serving order was this, and where did it originate? A few very courageous troopers dared to defy this "guidance." They were poorly treated by the chain of command; some careers were shortened. Senior commanders attempted to keep outspoken soldiers and Marines away from journalists, technical inspectors, and congressional investigators.

The malfunction problem was the result of decisions made by people far from the shooting. Adding to the basic problems of design deficiencies and unsuitable ammunition was a basic lack of planning for the deployment of a new weapon. There was no instructional package or guidance and no weapon-specific cleaning kits or lubricants. There were no bore brushes for the .22 caliber bore, and no chamber brushes. There was a shortage of cleaning rods.

Sometimes even magazines were in short supply. These planning issues may be attributable to the way the XM16E1 came into service through a "back door," as an interim weapon filling the gap between the M14/M14E2 (re-designated M14A1 in 1966) and the anticipated SPIW.

The combat conditions that men fight and live with make everything more difficult. Beyond the risk of not coming home whole or coming home at all, the combat environment is always mean, dirty, and difficult. The maintenance requirements for military weapons should be anticipated to accommodate these conditions. The AK47 falls far short of the M16 family of weapons in many respects, but in the early years in Vietnam it was far more reliable than the XM16E1. It functioned reliably under adverse conditions. It was a weapon of choice for American infantrymen and Marines whose XM16E1s proved unreliable. In 1965 and early 1966, as numerous AK47s were captured, it wasn't unusual to find several men in a rifle company armed with them.

The XM16E1 with the ammunition that accompanied it to Vietnam wasn't yet fit for service. As commanders followed the tradition of faulting troops for poor maintenance, that attitude provided cover for military and contractor investigators when they arrived in Vietnam to confront the problem in October 1966. They noted maintenance issues which were largely legitimate. After all, the "maintenance packages" were incomplete and the conditions appalling. The inspectors were defending their product as well as earlier poor decisions regarding quality control and ammunition compatibility. They were critical of what they described as poor maintenance. They attempted to avoid acknowledging the basic cause of the malfunction. The maintenance shortcomings made it easier for military inspectors to absolve the military and enabled the contractor's inspectors to divert responsibility from themselves.

Some officers and other inspectors contended that poorly motivated draftees were indifferent about caring for their rifles. This is the epitome of arrogance and ignorance coming from people mostly isolated from serious danger. Frontline draftees fought with all the courage and tenacity of any and all earlier warriors. There were no distinctions between draftees and volunteers with respect to audacity and courage. They all did the best they could to maintain their rifles. After all, their own lives were at stake.

In February 1967 the XM16E1 was officially type-classified as Standard "A" by the Department of the Army. The normal practice is not to classify a weapons system until it has been thoroughly tested and evaluated (not in combat), modifications incorporated, and bugs worked out. The standardization of the M16A1 didn't conform to established practices. There were still problem areas. There was an ongoing effort to identify a propellant that met the velocity and chamber-pressure specifications while not contributing to malfunctions. The cyclic rate of automatic fire exceeded design limitations. There was the basic problem of chamber corrosion. Chroming the chamber wasn't even approved until late May 1967. There was still some contention regarding the optimal rifling twist. Ball powder caused excessive fouling. The design specifications for tracer ammunition were pending. There were other product improvements still to be worked out.[4]

The Special Subcommittee on the M16 Rifle Program Richard H. Ichord Committee Investigation got under way in May 1967. In addition to sending members of their own committee and staff to Vietnam, they also called on the services of a retired officer, Col. E. B. Crossman. He would go to Vietnam and, working independently, interview Marines and soldiers in the field. As an independent observer, he would be free of any political pressure, financial, or other interests. As a senior and experienced officer, he would know what to look for. To compile statistically significant data, Crossman would talk with 250 soldiers and Marines in different parts of the country. Other committee investigators arrived in Vietnam in June 1967. They finally zeroed in on the malfunction problem and its causes, after initial deceptive attempts by in-country military leaders to convince them that poor maintenance was the issue became all too obvious.

This reaction of the military to resist political scrutiny is an example of the tendency to distrust politicians. All too often an attempt to protect what are perceived to be military interests by intentionally deceiving or withholding information from political representatives or their inspectors turns out ultimately to damage the military. The congressional inspectors had every reason to be objective and none to be professionally or personally wary of the results of their investigations. Perhaps they missed some of the finer points; after all, they weren't small-arms experts, but they aggressively waded through resistance and obfuscation to get to the heart of the matter. They were very critical, some would say too critical, but the buck must stop somewhere.

Colonel Crossman prepared a "Report of Investigation of M16 Rifle in Combat" dated June 16, 1967, and presented it to the committee. His conclusions confirmed what the committee had pretty much determined for itself. About half the men with whom he spoke had had serious malfunctions with their XM16E1s. About 90 percent of these malfunctions were failures to extract. About half the men he interviewed said they would rather be armed with an M14 rifle. He found that there was generally a supply of one or another kind of cleaning material and lubricants, but many men didn't have a cleaning rod, the essential tool to clear a stuck cartridge case. He noted very few rusty chambers. He couldn't correlate ammunition type with malfunctions.[5] This latter was possibly because at that time the ammunition of Army and Marine units was almost universally ball powder, apart from a type of IMR powder used in tracer ammunition. He thus had insufficient evidence to compare the relative performance of rifles employing both types of cartridges. He went on to recommend that soldiers be given the choice of being armed with the M14 rather than the XM16E1. His personal opinion regarding an appropriate caliber of cartridge for a military rifle was unspecified.

With regular and careful cleaning under ideal conditions, before they had been in several engagements, new XM16E1s might have been expected to incur malfunction rates on an order of about thirteen times the rate of M14 malfunctions, not counting instances of the bolt not remaining to the rear after the last round in a magazine had been fired. Somewhat less than one in ten of those malfunctions would be a failure to extract—and could kill you. After being exposed to conditions in Vietnam, and after a few firefights and "mad minutes," the XM16E1s and early follow-on M16A1s were much less reliable. Passed from one generation of infantryman to the next, sometimes a very short "generation," they were well worn. With the failure to extract, you had a weapon that wouldn't fire. Retired Marine Corps Major Dick Culver describes it as a "magazine fed, air cooled, single shot, muzzle ejecting shoulder weapon."[6]

By June 1967 the M14s in Vietnam had been replaced. U.S. troop units were armed with the XM16E1, now designated the M16A1, some of which had received some upgrading. Chromed chambers had been approved in May 1967 but not until late 1968 were all chambers being chromed, and so this remained an issue in Vietnam. By August 1967 over a third of M16A1s still had unmodified buffers. It may have been called the M16A1, but upgrades were in progress and the rifles in the hands of the troops represented various degrees of evolution and upgrades.

The same malfunctions continued to plague the troops. Until all the weapons conformed to the now-recognized needed modifications, the only way to reduce the problem was to concentrate on maintenance. In 1967, cleaning rods, including a new four-piece cleaning rod, were still in short supply. In March, chamber brushes entered the supply chain, but there weren't enough to go around.

In August 1967, the Army produced an M16 rifle maintenance card, which superseded an earlier version dated April that same year. It was the size of a playing card and provided basic instructions for maintaining the XM16E1/M16A1. It was a necessary thing to do, and one wonders why it hadn't been done, say, in 1965. I would comment here that in 1968–1969 on a second tour in Vietnam, as an advisor and not in a U.S. unit, I never saw such a card, nor any instructions, nor any sort of special cleaning material for the M16A1s. As an advisor, however, we could pick and choose whatever individual weapon we preferred.

Generally, cleaning and maintenance is taught in basic training or Marine boot camp. The fundamentals pretty much apply to all individual and crew-served weapons firing a cartridge that launches a bullet through a bore. Rifles, submachine guns, machine guns, handguns, and any variation fall into this category. Perhaps for this reason no special effort was made to provide training guidance and instructional material for the XM16E1, a weapon that, after all, was an interim development presumably awaiting the arrival of a much better individual weapon.

Whatever instructions the troops had received regarding rifle maintenance for the M14 should have been adequate for just about any other rifle, including the XM16E1. This reasoning was, if uncharacteristic of military practice, nevertheless optimistically sound. Add to this the wishful thinking that the "black rifle" needed less, much less, cleaning and we have the basis of institutional complacency. The problem was that the XM16E1, unlike other rifles in the hands of Marines and soldiers, was still in an incomplete stage of development, one that demanded special attention to maintenance. Add to this the tough Vietnamese environment. Add to this the intense confrontations that worked this new rifle hard and the scope of the problem becomes magnified.

The maintenance card provided necessary guidance, although it was no substitute for cleaning rods, bore and chamber brushes, patches, or proper lubricants. The card covers all the basics. Clean your rifle every day, more frequently if necessary. It describes cleaning all metal surfaces with bore cleaner. It addresses cleaning and maintenance of the chamber using a chamber brush and substituting one intended for a different caliber if the "regular brush" is not available. It addresses cleaning the bolt carrier group, the magazine, the barrel bore, and the receiver. It goes on to discuss lubrication in some detail and specifies a particular lubricant: lubricating oil, semifluid, Mil-L-46000A (LSA), designed for use in a warm, humid environment. It discusses cleaning and examination of ammunition. It warns about the tendency of the barrel to retain water if immersed and advises to check for damaged magazines. The last bit of advice appropriately refers to the failure-to-extract malfunction and advises the individual to turn his weapon in to field maintenance at the first opportunity. Not particularly helpful in a firefight. The presumption here is that there is a better, modified XM16E1 or M16A1 waiting to be issued, standing by as a replacement.

In July 1969, the Department of the Army published one of its ever-popular maintenance pamphlets using a comic-book design, always a tried and effective device to get a young soldier's attention. DA Pamphlet 750–30, *The M16A1 Rifle: Operation and Preventive Maintenance*, superseded an earlier DA pamphlet 750–30 published in June of the previous year. The 1969 version of the pamphlet is probably the surest sign that the Army had finally accepted the small-caliber high-velocity concept in an assault rifle configuration.

This publication, designed to make easy reading for the young soldier and Marine, featured as narrator and weapons maintenance advisor an attractive young woman and employed a mildly seductive dialog. This young lady and her advice was featured in other maintenance publications. In the new instructional pamphlet for the M16A1, the instructions just inside the cover start off: "Gettin' to know all about you," a take-off on a popular song, and continue: "How to Strip your Baby." There follow detailed illustrated instructions on field stripping and reassembling the rifle. These instructions continue onto page four. The next page describes immediate action. The last comment on immediate action deals with a failure to extract: "However, if you do find a cartridge or case in the chamber [following immediate action], be sure you remove it before you try to reload and recycle your weapon." At least this is an acknowledgement that a cartridge might lodge in the chamber, although not very helpful otherwise.

The pamphlet goes on to itemize the items essential for maintenance. It describes ammunition and magazine inspection and maintenance, bore and chamber cleaning, and details proper lubrication. It suggests the proper way to carefully employ the still flimsy new M11E3, five-piece cleaning rod. "Do it the right way and you won't hurt the rod." It cautions the soldier to make sure the threads of the bore and chamber brushes match the threads of the particular cleaning rod you have. If you don't have patches of the size designed for the .223 caliber bore, cut standard patches into four pieces, presumably using your razor-sharp bayonet or a suitably sharp pocket knife.

The pamphlet is well written, provides excellent advice on cleaning and maintenance, and positively and optimistically promotes the M16A1. Firearms buffs will see a few subtle caveats in the descriptions of maintenance material. A version of this pamphlet should have been ready with the first issue of the XM16E1. Many lives would have been saved.

In the next chapter we'll describe the rapid deployment of major combat units to Vietnam, some with the XM16E1, others to be issued the rifle in-country, and with inadequate training on its maintenance. We'll take a close look at the technical problems of the XM16E1 being employed with ammunition for which it hadn't been designed and engineered.

6

THE TROOPS DEPLOY—AN
AUTOPSY OF THE PROBLEM

S tarting in 1965, American units began to move to the conflict in Vietnam,
responding to increased pressure from North Vietnamese forces and supplies moving south along the Ho Chi Minh Trail. The Army of the Republic
of Vietnam (ARVN), assisted by American advisors and by a significant presence of Special Forces, needed help. Some units arrived equipped with the
M14 and the M14E2. They were issued the XM16E1 in Vietnam with little
or no prior experience with the weapon. Airborne units and the 1st Air Cavalry Division arrived with the XM16E1, and most of them had done at least
some training with this new rifle.

Dan Brodt, long range reconnaissance patrol team, 1st Battalion (Airmobile), 7th Cavalry, relates his experience with the XM16E1 during Operation
Pegasus in April 1968, long after the defective early XM16E1s should have
been replaced or upgraded:

> My very 1st experience (Marine Operation Scotland-1st Cav Op-Pegasus) with this
> piece of crap was when my one-one's (team leader) M16 jammed after about 5–6 rounds.
> He was KIA. We were not even off the helo yet. Mine jammed repeatedly after hours/
> days on operations in the humidity and heat. Most of us would pick up AKs from dead
> NVA and use them until we finally got a new version M16. My understanding was that
> ArmaLite/Colt screwed up the barrel alloy [failure to chrome bore] and that the
> intense heat and humidity contributed to the casing jamming upon extraction [corrosion
> and/or pitting]. Anyway, many, MANY incidents were M16s jammed in my unit
> and line units. Khe Sanh was primo here—Tet also. No problems after late Feb-Mar

1968, but I always carried a .45 and if I could muster an AK we would [use it]. *Always had a M14 on hand also.*[1]

The XM16E1 came with the previously described military modifications of the AR15, as more or less agreed upon by the Army and Marine Corps. What was distinctly different, however, was the ammunition, now loaded with ball powder, the source of most malfunctions, including the most serious, failure to extract. This same ammunition had been used during the SAWS test, with the malfunctions noted and recorded. The Army, at least, was aware of the problems to come, but seemed unconcerned. Most commanders had no idea of the malfunction issues with the XM16E1, which were downplayed by those associated with the acceptance of the weapon, who knew of its problem. It was close hold in the office of the project manager, and the problem, by directive, was kept out of in-house documents. The chain of command plodded along with this example of subterfuge and forbade the men in the field from talking about the problem with journalists. This restriction on discussing the XM16E1's malfunction problems extended to military training back in the United States in 1966.

Mike Mantegna, a 2nd Battalion, 7th Cavalry veteran, relates his experience with the continuing deception effort upon his return to the States.

When I returned to Fort Benning, I volunteered as Senior Tactical Officer for 72nd Company in the expanded OCS. While at the M16 firing range, I noticed that the instructor did not mention the potential jamming and other mechanical problems which the troops in RVN had been experiencing. When I questioned him about it, he said that he had been told by his department head at Building 4 [Infantry School headquarters] that all such info was classified. Immediately thereafter, I visited every company in my battalion, and met privately with all the officer candidates, and shared with them everything that I had learned about the Black Rifle.[2]

On March 8, 1965, elements of the 3rd Marine Division's Battalion Landing Team 3/9 came ashore toting their M14 rifles at Da Nang. By the end of March, the 9th Marine Expeditionary Brigade (MEB) was ashore with a strength of nearly 5,000, including two infantry battalions, two helicopter squadrons, and supporting units. The stated mission of the Marines was to secure the American air base at Da Nang. It soon became apparent that this was completely unrealistic, and they initiated aggressive offensive operations that involved some of the bloodiest fighting of the war.

One of the early major engagements was Operation Starlight, known to Marines as the Battle of Chu Lai, in August 1965. The Marines exchanged their M14s for XM16E1s after they arrived in Vietnam and were not at all pleased. They experienced a high rate of malfunctions, mostly failure to extract. Edward F. Murphy in his book *The Hill Fights* describes the problem with the XM16E1:

> *Almost immediately the rifle displayed its tendency to jam. Often, after just a few rounds, a spent cartridge stuck in the breech. To remove it, a cleaning rod had to be shoved down the weapon's barrel, but only one cleaning rod was issued for every four men. So a Marine with a jammed rifle could either borrow the pieces of a cleaning rod or try to pry the jammed cartridge loose with the tip of a knife or bayonet. That took time and rarely worked.*[3]

Not only had the Marines received no extensive training with the rifle, they had received no familiarization at all with it. It came without cleaning equipment. There were no bore or chamber brushes. Cleaning rods that were required to pound out stuck cartridges that hadn't ejected after being fired were in short supply and proved to be flimsy. Marines cleaned and maintained their XM16E1s as best they could with available cleaning materials. They ordered lubricants and other cleaning paraphernalia from family and friends back home. There were no maintenance instructions. In fact, some Marines had been advised that the rifle needed very little maintenance.

When malfunctions became a serious problem, the senior Marine command ignored constant reports from the field that something was wrong with the rifle. It aggressively blamed the problems on lax maintenance. In fact, no amount of maintenance or cleaning could have solved the failure-to-extract problem. It was possible, with very careful frequent cleaning and correct lubrication, to reduce the frequency of this malfunction, but it would continue to recur even under the most diligent care. It took moral courage for enlisted Marines and junior officers to confront senior leaders and insist on being heard. Some of them stepped forward and wrote letters to family, friends, and members of Congress. This had a negative effect on their careers. Some in the Marine chain of command considered them disloyal.

The Marines paid a high price in blood and earned the right to be heard. They should have been heard. How their chain of command could have ignored the information coming from the men doing the fighting is hard to understand and reflects unfavorably on senior leadership.

Arriving at about the same time as the 3rd Marine Division, the 7th Marine Regiment of the 1st Marine Division also saw action in Operation Starlight. It then conducted a follow-up operation to Operation Starlight,

Operation Piranha. In March 1966 the division established its headquarters at Chu Lai. By June, the entire division was in Vietnam and operated in the southern two provinces of I Corps. During the next two years, the 1st Marine Division conducted forty-four named operations and saw fierce fighting in Huê during the 1968 Tet Offensive. Other operations and battles included Napoleon-Saline II; Oklahoma Hills; Pipestone Canyon; Imperial Lake; Da Nang; Dong Ha; Qui Nhon; Phu Bai; Quang Tri; and Operation New Arrivals. In 1971 the division returned home to Camp Pendleton, California. The two Marine divisions suffered the highest casualties of any U.S. divisions in the war, followed closely by the 1st Air Cavalry Division.

Next on the scene were the first Army units to arrive, the 1st and 2nd Battalions of the 503rd Airborne Infantry Regiment of the 173rd Airborne Brigade. They began arriving on May 7, 1965. These units arrived with supporting U.S. elements and additionally had attached a battalion of the Royal Australian Regiment as well as a New Zealand artillery battery. In November of 1965 they fought a major engagement in Operation Hump, just north of Biên Hòa, close to Saigon, where in severe fighting they endured heavy casualties. They also engaged the enemy in the Iron Triangle, an enemy stronghold north of Saigon. In January 1966, they launched the first U.S. military operation in the Plain of Reeds, Operation Marauder. In the same year they participated in Operation Crimp. Later, in August 1966, they were joined by the 4th Battalion, 503rd Infantry. In February 1967, the 173rd conducted Operation Junction City, the only combat parachute assault of the Vietnam War. In June 1967, elements of the brigade conducted Operation Francis Marion and engaged NVA units in the Dak To area. Soon thereafter, in September of that year, the 3rd Battalion of the 503rd Infantry joined them. The brigade returned stateside in 1971.

The 1st Brigade of the 101st Airborne Division, the "Screaming Eagles," deployed to Vietnam in July 1965 with the remainder of the division arriving in Vietnam in November 1967. In July 1968, the division renamed itself the 101st Air Cavalry Division. In August 1969, it changed its name again to the 101st Airborne Division (Airmobile), making it the Army's second airmobile division. Helicopters were the most practical means of combat assault and insertion. From 1965 to 1967, the 1st Brigade of the 101st operated throughout South Vietnam, moving where needed and employed as a fire brigade.

With the whole division in-country, the 101st deployed to the north, to the I Corps region and operated against North Vietnamese forces coming down the Ho Chi Minh Trail through Laos and into the A Shau Valley. One of the major battles was the vicious fight for Hamburger Hill in 1969. The division was involved in other major fighting at Firebase Ripcord in 1970, fighting off North Vietnamese regulars outnumbering them almost ten to one in a twenty-three-day siege until the division was withdrawn. The 101st fought in Vietnam for nearly seven years, participating in fifteen campaigns. One of its final operations was in support of the ARVN Operation Lam Son 719 in 1971. The division returned to Fort Campbell, Kentucky, in late 1971 and early 1972.

The long range reconnaissance patrols of the 101st participated in constant and high-risk missions. The problems they experienced with their XM16E1s were particularly problematic as they operated in small groups of six men. When in contact, the loss of fire from a single rifleman put the whole patrol at increased risk. Reynel Martinez, in *Six Silent Men*, describes one experience in early 1968 when his long range patrol team was in heavy contact.

I got my second magazine in, rolled to the left, and opened up again. All of a sudden, I was empty again. Man, that was fast! I inserted my third magazine and hit the release on the bolt receiver when I realized I had a ruptured brass stuck in the chamber. Oh shit! The horror of horror—a jammed rifle in a firefight.[4]

Next in-country was the 2nd Brigade of the 1st Infantry Division, the "Big Red One," arriving in July 1965. The rest of the division soon followed and participated in three major operations in 1965: Operations Hump, Bushmaster I, and Bushmaster II. In 1966 it fought in Operations Marauder Crimp II, Rolling Stone, and Attleboro as well as several battles: Ap Tau O, Srok Dong, and Minh Tanh Road. It fought in five more operations in 1967, among them Cedar Falls, Junction City, Manhattan, Billings which included the battle of Xom Bo II, and Shenandoah II. In October it fought the battle of Ong Thanh. In 1968, during the Tet Offensive, the division secured the U.S. air base at Tan Son Nhut. In April 1968 it participated in Operation Toan Thang. In 1969 it conducted several operations including Atlas Wedge and participated in Operation Dong Tien. The division fought additional battles along National Highway 13 as a part of Operation Thunder Road in 1969 before returning to Fort Riley, Kansas, in January 1970.

When members of the Special Subcommittee of the House of Representatives (the Ichord Committee) visited Vietnam in 1967 to investigate the reported problems with the XM16E1, "75 members of the 1st Infantry Division units in Task Force Oregon, almost 40 percent stated a preference for the M-14 rifle over the M-16. Malfunctions were: selector switch sticking, stoppage due to dirty ammunition, failures to extract, and failures to extract rounds left in chamber overnight. There was evidence of some shortages of cleaning materials. Some men were having to share cleaning rods."[5]

Next up was the 1st Air Cavalry Division. The 11th Air Assault Division (Test) was reflagged as the 1st Cavalry Division (Airmobile) in 1965 at Fort Benning, Georgia. The advance party arrived in Vietnam on August 16, 1965, and began to prepare the ground for the arrival of the rest of the division. The division arrived by sea on three naval transports, the USNS Buckner, the USNS Geiger, and the USNS Rose. By September 20 the division was on the ground and establishing itself in its new location and base camp at An Khê, named Camp Radcliff after the Cav's first casualty. The men of the 1st Cav had been issued their XM16E1s at Fort Benning a few weeks prior to deployment and had undergone familiarization training with the new rifle.

As reported by Mike Mantegna,

When the M16 was distributed to us just a few weeks prior to deployment, I was the only officer in the 2nd of the 7th who had any prior experience with the new rifle. Hence, I was familiar with its tendency to jam; but I had no idea just how serious or widespread the problem was. I volunteered to supervise the battalion's POR [Preparation of Replacements for Oversea Movement] qualification with the test firing of all its personnel and weapons. When I reported to the battalion commander about the number and kinds of mechanical issues, he ordered his S-4 [supply officer] to obtain enough cleaning rods to be passed out with every rifle. We also recommended that everyone carry a shaving brush and a can of Dry Slide, [a multi-purpose lubricant, a synthetic polymer] *and clean his weapon religiously.*[6]

During the four-week trip by sea the men had a further opportunity to become more familiar with their new rifle.

We constructed a wooden target and towed it behind the ship. Adjusting the length of the rope, we used it for target practice off the fantail. This marksmanship training exercise confirmed the need for cleaning rods and better lubricant. During our initial firefights with the VC, rifles jammed and otherwise malfunctioned regularly, but nobody died as a result.[7]

In fact, as time went on during the first years of deployment, the failure to extract caused many casualties, including men killed in action.

The 1st Cavalry Division (Airmobile) established itself and began operations to help relieve the siege of Plei Me near Pleiku. This led to the first major and one of the bloodiest battles of the war, the Battle of Ia Drang and the fighting at LZ X-Ray and LZ Albany, in November 1965, described in the book *We Were Soldiers Once . . . And Young* (Harold G. Moore and Joseph L. Galloway, 1992). The vicious fighting was just beginning. In 1966 there followed many more battles and operations: Operation Masher, Operation Crazy Horse, and Operation Thayer. In 1967, the division conducted a major operation, Operation Pershing, to destroy communist base areas in the II Corps area of operations. The 3rd Brigade also participated in Operation Wheeler/Wallowa in the Que Son Valley in October 1967.

During the Tet Offensive in February 1968 the 3rd (Garry Owen) Brigade moved to intercept NVA forces pouring into Huê. In March 1968 the division conducted Operation Pegasus to break the siege of the Marine combat base at Khe Sanh. In April the 2nd Battalion of the 7th Cav linked-up with Marines at Khe Sanh, ending the seventy-seven-day siege. More heavy fighting followed, including Operation Delaware in the A Shau Valley. In May 1970 the division participated in the incursion into Cambodia. The bulk of the 1st Cav returned to Fort Hood, Texas, in April 1971. The final Cav unit to depart Vietnam was the 1st Battalion, 7th Cavalry in August 1972, the last U.S. Army combat unit to depart from Vietnam.

By mid–August 1965, 2,200 men of the 25th Infantry, "Tropic Lightning" Division, were employed in Vietnam in construction programs at Cam Ranh Bay. In December 1965, the division began deploying its 3rd Brigade, reinforced to task force strength, from Hawaii to Pleiku in the Central Highlands area of Vietnam. Deployment was complete by mid–January 1966, and the division fought in several major engagements, including the Tet Offensive and the incursion into Cambodia (Operation Junction City). The division began its return to Schofield Barracks in Hawaii in December 1970. The last element to leave the country was the 2nd Brigade in May 1971, returning to Fort Lewis, Washington.

The 196th Infantry Brigade, "The Chargers," was reactivated at Fort Devens, Massachusetts, in September 1965 and arrived in Vietnam in August 1966, settling in at the Tây Ninh combat base. It participated in Operations Cedar Falls, Gadsden, Lancaster, Junction City, Benton, and Attleboro. In April 1967, the brigade became part of a division-sized task force, Task Force Oregon. It was joined by the 1st Brigade of the 101st Airborne Division and the 3rd Brigade of the 25th Infantry Division to form the 23rd Infantry Division, the "Americal Division," in October 1967. The brigade departed Vietnam in June 1972.

The 4th Infantry Division deployed from Fort Lewis, Washington, to Vietnam in September 1966. The 3rd Brigade was deployed northwest of Saigon and participated in Operation Attleboro in September and November

1966 and subsequently in Operation Junction City in 1967. This unit returned stateside in April 1970 and was deactivated. The 1st and 2nd Brigades conducted operations in the Central Highlands, from the South China Sea to Cambodia, and engaged in fierce fighting with NVA units in the mountains surrounding Kontum in 1967. Subsequently, they participated in the Cambodian incursion. They returned to Fort Carson, Colorado, in December 1970. The division was subsequently rejoined by its 3rd Brigade, which had been made a part of the 25th Infantry Division in exchange for elements of that division.

Notice here how the Army tends to re-flag units in a manner convenient to the needs of a particular time and place. This has a destructive effect on the very significant regimental traditions that leaders strive so valiantly to impress upon the troops and which—as they bond during combat—have a great significance for them. It is no laughing matter to be stripped suddenly of the regimental history and traditions of an organization with which one identifies. This is another one of those types of decisions that contradicts basic leadership principles.

The 11th Armored Cavalry Regiment, the "Black Horse" Regiment, arrived in Vietnam in September 1966 and was actively engaged the following month. They employed various configurations of armored personnel carriers, principally a modified M113 employed as an Armored Cavalry Assault Vehicle or "ACAV." The regiment also employed Sheridan tanks, or M551s, as well as other armored vehicles. The regiment participated in Operations Hickory, Cedar Falls, Junction City, Manhattan, Kittyhawk, Quicksilver, Fargo, the Tet Offensive, Adairsville, and Alcorn Cove. Although an armored unit, many men were armed with the XM16E1. The unit was inactivated in Vietnam in early 1972.

The 9th Infantry Division, the "Old Reliables," was reactivated on February 1, 1966, at Fort Riley, Kansas, and arrived in Vietnam in mid-December of that year. It operated in the Mekong Delta area and worked frequently with the U.S. Navy, patrolling the extensive rivers and canals in the Delta. The division's 2nd Brigade was the Army contingent of the Mobile Riverine Force, and conducted operations in coordination with Navy SEAL teams, South Vietnamese Marines, and the 7th ARVN Division. The division was active in the Delta during the Tet Offensive and took part in twenty-two major combat engagements. It returned to the United States in August 1969.

The 23rd Infantry Division, the "Americal Division," was reactivated in Vietnam in 1967 from units already in-country: the 3rd Brigade of the 25th Infantry Division; the 1st Brigade of the 101st Airborne Division; and the

196th Infantry Brigade and newly arrived units. The organization from which the 23rd was constituted was Task Force Oregon. As new units arrived in-country, the 25th and 101st Divisions got their brigades back. The division now consisted of the 196th, 11th, and 198th Infantry Brigades. The division participated in several major battles, among them: the Battles of Kham Duc, LoGiang, and Nui Hoac Ridge. The 11th and 198th returned to the United States in November 1971 and the division was inactivated. The 196th remained in-country until June 1972 with one battalion, the last maneuver battalion, the 3rd Battalion of the 21st Infantry, remaining until August.

The 82nd Airborne, the "All American" Division, was America's strategic reserve force, and remained stateside until the Tet Offensive, when it was hurriedly deployed to Vietnam. The 3rd Brigade was en route to Chu Lai within twenty-four hours. The 82nd remained in Vietnam for twenty-two months, participating in the fighting during Tet at Huê and Phu Bai and subsequently in the Mekong Delta, the Iron Triangle, and then along the Cambodian border. It returned to Fort Bragg in December 1969 to resume its strategic reserve role.

All these units were deployed and served for extended periods of time while the XM16E1 rifle was consistently malfunctioning, which, in many close and violent engagements, was the direct cause of American casualties. The positive features of the XM16E1 don't excuse the many failures of leadership and management that allowed an incompletely developed weapon system to be deployed with soldiers and Marines engaged in war.

There were standards for military firearms, including chromed bores and chambers, but these weren't included in the rifle's development by ArmaLite. The civilian engineers who developed the XM16E1 prototypes didn't have military specifications—the result of long experience in military arms development—in mind. Weapons and ammunition development must necessarily proceed in tandem. In all phases of testing, with the exception of the SAWS tests, the AR15 employed a type of powder propellant, Improved Military Rifle (IMR4475), which it had been designed to use. Although the name Improved Military Rifle would seem to imply a new and improved type of propellant, it was an older type of propellant than the ball powder propellant that subsequently caused so many problems.

The performance of the AR15 was engineered to accommodate IMR4475 propellant. This linkage of rifle and cartridge was shattered when the Army's contract for ammunition permitted the employment of a different propellant. Ultimately, a ball propellant, WC846, was used in the manufacture of most of the cartridges that accompanied the major troop deployments to

Vietnam. Both Stoner and Colt attempted to bring the services on board with the critical need for ammunition compatibility with the AR15 design, but the military didn't buy into it, thereby paving the way for devastating problems.

IMR 4475 is a double-based propellant that follows a specific formula employing tubular nitrocellulose propellants developed during the two world wars and modified for civilian use by DuPont for target shooting and hunting. M193 cartridges loaded with this propellant functioned without problems in the AR15. They caused no problems with those AR15s that initially went to Vietnam for evaluation. This powder burns faster but produces less fouling than types of ball powder such as WC846. It generates a higher peak pressure in the chamber but a lower pressure at the gas port than ball powder. The XM16E1 was specifically designed to use this type of powder.

Ball propellant in fact takes the form of small balls. Because the granules of powder are spherical, their surface area with respect to their volume is the geometric minimum. This means that the propellant burns more slowly than the tubular propellants of IMR powders where the ratio of surface area to mass is greater. The result is a lower peak pressure but an extended pressure curve that delivers a higher pressure at the gas port. Ball propellant can be manufactured more rapidly and with greater safety and lesser expense than extruded propellants. It can be stored longer and requires less specialized equipment for manufacture. It is the standard propellant used in military firearms. The WC846 ball propellant has a more consistent high pressure than IMR propellant types. It was easier to manufacture it to conform with the pressure muzzle-velocity requirement, while not exceeding the maximum chamber pressure. Its higher pressure than IMR powder at the gas port increases the cyclic rate of fire. It also burns dirtier. These characteristics—increased cyclic rate and fouling—both contributed to malfunctions in Vietnam.

The only military requirement of note was that the round be capable of penetrating a steel helmet at 500 yards, an increase from the original design objective of 300 yards. (Ironically, Viet Cong combatants seldom wore headgear, while North Vietnamese Army troops generally wore soft pith helmets, so the steel-helmet requirement was irrelevant in Vietnam.) This was to accommodate an anticipated requirement from the Army staff in the Pentagon. Colt had claimed that the muzzle velocity was 3,250 feet per second, but the measured velocity fell about one hundred fps short. The Army insisted on the claimed muzzle velocity, and with a chamber pressure not to exceed the design parameter of 52,000 pounds per square inch. With an effective range of 300 yards, there was some flexibility in the manufacture of the propellant. When it was belatedly determined that cartridges loaded with this propellant sometimes produced a less-than-acceptable muzzle velocity, ammunition manufacturers began looking for alternatives that would comply with the muzzle-velocity requirement of 3,250 fps, plus or minus forty fps. It seemed not to matter that the performance during evaluation trials and the lethality tests had been satisfactory with a slightly lower muzzle velocity. The "specification" was now cast in stone.

The Ichord Report notes that when the range was increased to 500 yards, the chamber-pressure requirement, while unchanged, meant that the propellant specifications to conform to velocity and pressure requirements became more sensitive. A very conservative margin would need to be maintained between the typical chamber pressure of production lots and the maximum level permitted. To meet this requirement, IMR propellant would have to be loaded in each cartridge with more precise tolerances. Quality control would have to be tightened to a point where it would be difficult and costly. There would still be a risk that whole lots of ammunition would not meet the muzzle-velocity requirement or would exceed the chamber pressure limit and would be rejected.

The Army's Frankford Arsenal in Philadelphia noted that cartridges loaded with IMR4475 couldn't reliably achieve the now-specified 3,250 fps muzzle velocity without exceeding the allowable chamber pressure. The evident choices were either to lower the velocity, increase the acceptable pressure, or change the propellant. Frankford Arsenal recommended another possibility. Employ a different bullet with an improved aerodynamic design that required a lower chamber pressure. Such a cartridge would at the same time improve impact energies at all ranges beyond one hundred yards. But the recommendation wasn't approved.

To quote Major Dick Culver, a Marine veteran of Vietnam and small arms specialist who encapsulates the technical details and the result:

Had we but known, the problem was not simply dirty powder or a lack of regular and conscientious cleaning by the operator but was due to the burning rate(s) and burning temperature of the powder coupled with varying gas-port pressures depending on the powder. It seems that the AR-15/M16 was developed and tested with extruded IMR powder. This powder is relatively clean burning but has a relatively high peak pressure during its initial ignition. Remington had been using some stuff called IMR4475 that worked extremely well but wasn't terribly consistent from lot to lot. Remington had solved the problem by using selected lots of the powder to obtain the desired burning rates and functioning in the M16. In fact the entire testing had been accomplished by using such ammunition [not in the SAWS test]. The double based [extruded] powder (so called because it used both nitroglycerine and nitrocellulose in its manufacture) [IMR4475] *burned hotter than ball powder due to the nitroglycerine content, and the chamber pressure tended to be a bit higher than with say, ball powder. Because of the quality control problems with the double-based extruded IMR powder that had been used by Remington, all manufacturers of the 5.56mm cartridge preferred to use a less finicky ball powder. The argument was essentially that ball powder burned cooler, thus giving less barrel/throat erosion, and had a lower peak pressure, and would stay well within the pressure limits prescribed for the cartridge. . . . While it was true that the ball powders did have a lower "peak" pressure, **they also had a higher port pressure.** (last seven words in italics in the original)*[8]

According to the Ichord Report:

On May 23, 1962, the Air Force awarded a contract to Colt Patent Firearms Manufacturing Co. (Colt's Inc.) for 85,000 rifles, spare parts, and 8,500,000 rounds of ammunition. Colt subcontracted manufacture of the ammunition to Remington Arms Co., Inc., with inspection and acceptance of ammunition to be based on independent laboratory certification that ammunition conforms to established commercial standards. The Remington specification was the same as that tested three months earlier by the Air Force at Hill Air Force Base, Utah.[9]

This ammunition employed the IMR 4475 propellant. The Army, in March 1963, had been designated the procurement agency for all users of the AR 15 and ammunition and established an AR 15 project office; however, the Air Force had already been actively arranging ammunition contracts for 5.56mm ammunition. Continuing from the Ichord Report:

The Air Force change of ammunition from the single-base [actually double-base] *extruded to the double-base ball propellant* [WC486] *occurred in the subsequent procurement of ammunition in October 1963.*[10] This latter contract was coordinated with the Army, which in March 1963 had been designated the procurement agency for all users of the AR 15 and ammunition and which established an AR 15 project office. The Army elected for the time being to stay with IMR 4475.

Note that IMR propellant is sometimes described as single-base, as in the Ichord Report. In fact, IMR 4475 is a double-base propellant. The ball propellant WC486 has several components. The "C" in WC486 stands for "cooler."

A contract with Remington Arms for 19 million rounds called for the use of IMR 4198 propellant. This propellant was considered the equal of IMR 4475, the propellant that had functioned satisfactorily in earlier testing. According to the Air Force, the contract further allowed that any propellant meeting the pressure, velocity and environmental requirements of the specification would be acceptable. Remington chose to load the ammunition using the propellant WC486, the ball powder, even though this was a propellant produced by Olin Mathieson and not by Remington. This was a response to the requirement to produce large lots of ammunition within tight specifications, something apparently more difficult and more expensive to achieve with IMR propellants. WC486 propellant met the specifications.

The Army's 1964 5.56mm ammunition requirement was now 150 million rounds. In January 1964, a meeting was held at Frankford Arsenal to resolve various issues with ammunition manufacturers. Representatives of Remington; Olin; Federal Cartridge; DuPont; the Air Force; and the Army were at the meeting. The response from commercial ammunition producers was that the requirements would have to be relaxed before they would be able to produce ammunition in the quantities needed by the military. The Army agreed to allow a maximum chamber pressure increase to 53,000 psi. Remington and Olin agreed to produce 500,000 cartridges each under this waiver, enabling the production of a final one million rounds loaded with IMR4475. The issue now was how to get contracts for the remaining ammunition. Remington indicated that if ballistic requirements were to be met in the future, some change in the design of the commercial .223 cartridge might be required to meet large-scale production.

In February 1964, three propellant manufacturers were invited to submit proposals for propellants that would meet the military requirements as well as being not significantly inferior to IMR4475 with respect to smoke, flash, fouling, and other characteristics, when produced in large quantities. Unfortunately, the initial ammunition specification of the Air Force contract didn't include a reduced fouling requirement. Both a DuPont product, CR8136 (a type of IMR propellant), and the Olin Mathieson product, WC846, were recommended as permissible alternatives to the IMR4475 propellant and were supposed to be an improvement regarding consistency of velocity and chamber pressure. In 1964, Olin opted to load with WC846. Remington started out using IMR8136 but switched to WC846 in December 1964 after about 50 million rounds had been produced with the IMR powder.

The XM16E1 and the 5.56mm ball cartridge M193 were both officially adopted in 1964, but the M14 was still the Army's standard rifle. The XM16E1 was an experimental weapon now needed for the special conflict that Vietnam—at that point in time—was perceived to be. There was still the expectation that something better was on the way, the Special Purpose Individual Weapon, or SPIW. This apparently dulled any sense of urgency on the part of the Army to expedite a correction of problems with the sometime-in-the-near-future-to-become-history XM16E1 rifle.

From July to mid-November 1965, during testing conducted at Fort Benning by the Infantry Board,[11] using carefully cleaned and maintained rifles, the failure-to-extract malfunction occurred frequently. While the normal malfunctions with the M14 and the M14E2 were clearable with immediate action, the failure to extract with the XM16E1 was not. Using data from that test, for semiautomatic fire, and including all malfunctions, the XM16E1 has a malfunction rate of about twenty-two times that of the M14. Also, for semiautomatic fire and not counting the malfunction of the bolt not staying to the rear after the last round has been fired, the XM16E1 has a malfunction rate of about twelve times that of the M14. The comparative failure to eject and failure to extract rates are, respectively, seventy-one to one and twenty-six to one favoring the M14.

When XM16E1 malfunction reports began to trickle in from Vietnam in 1965, increasing in 1966, they confirmed what the Army already knew was a problem. There were two ways to fix it: Go back to IMR propellant or modify the rifle. Going back to IMR propellant would have necessitated acceptance of a slightly reduced muzzle velocity, something the Army was apparently not prepared to do. More significantly, the Army, with a large ammunition contract on its hands and XM16E1 rifles in the hands of thousands of troops in Vietnam, and with more of both on the way, was reluctant to acknowledge any fault if it could be placed elsewhere. The Army chose to modify the XM16E1 rifle, as described in subsequent paragraphs.

The WC846 ball propellant was the basic cause of the failure to extract problem. The Air Force and Army had both bought off on the contract that permitted this change of propellant. Eugene Stoner at the time of this decision was working at Cadillac Gage. After the contract allowing the use of ball powder was already in effect, Stoner in 1964 was asked his opinion by Frank Vee of the Office of the Secretary of Defense's Comptroller's office. Stoner responded; "I would advise against it, because . . . All of our experience was with the other cartridge, with the other propellant, and I [don't] quite see changing . . . without an awful lot of testing before. . . ." Stoner was then asked what was going to happen and was told that the decision had been made. Stoner then asked, "Why are you asking me now?" and was told by Vee that he, Vee, would have felt a lot better if Stoner would approve the technical package that authorized the change of cartridge. Stoner responded, "Well, now we both don't feel so good." Colt had not approved the change of propellant to ball either.[12]

The rifle was designed to use cartridges loaded with IMR4475 propellant. The ammunition that went with the rifle to Vietnam used the less-expensive, easier-to-manufacture and readily available propellant, WC846. Firing cartridges loaded with this propellant was the principal cause of expended cartridge cases lodging in the rifle's chamber after firing, sometimes when firing in the single-shot mode, quite frequently when firing in the full automatic mode.

Soldiers and Marines are trained on a procedure known as "immediate action" to clear any type of individual weapon of a malfunction. This worked sometimes when the cartridge case failed to extract, but only if it wasn't firmly lodged in the chamber, as was the usual case with rifles that weren't new and that didn't have chromed chambers and when those chambers had some corrosion. There was no such thing as effective immediate action when the cartridge case was seriously stuck in the chamber and the soft metal of the case expanded into the corroded pits of the rifle's chamber. The original cartridge cases met commercial standards but were insufficiently hardened to work consistently well in a weapon firing in the full automatic mode. Their relative softness made them more liable to bind in a corroded chamber. Years later in 1970, Dr. Carten, the principal foe of any rifle that threatened his M14, still chief of the Technical Evaluation Branch of Army Materiel Command's RRD&E Directorate, prepared a report, *The M16 Rifle—A Case History*. It stated in part: "It was not until October 1964 that Frankford Arsenal identified case hardness as a significant factor in AR-15 weapon malfunctioning."[13] Colt was under pressure to produce enough rifles to meet the requirements, and McNamara's Defense Department was applying the pressure. Until complaints came in and began to build, the emphasis was on finding more obvious solutions to the problem even though insufficient case hardness had been earlier suggested as a possible contributing factor. Finally, in 1966 Frankford began to study the role of case hardness, and in August 1967 ammunition manufacturers were given six months to adjust their production to resolve the issue.[14]

The following, from the *10th Revised Edition of Small Arms of the World*, describes the operational sequence of the AR15 and thus the XM16E1:

> *With the weapon loaded and the selective fire-lever on "Semi," pulling the trigger causes the hammer to strike the firing pin, which detonates the primer.*
>
> *When the bullet passes beyond the gas port, gas passes through the gas tube and into a chamber formed by the bolt carrier and bolt. At this time, the bolt is in the locked position, acting as a stationary piston. The entering gas pressure causes the bolt carrier to move to the rear. In moving rearward, the bolt carrier rotates the bolt, unlocking it and carrying it rearward. As the bolt assembly travels to the rear, the gas is exhausted through a port in the side of the bolt carrier. The cartridge case is then extracted and ejected in the usual manner.*

When the selective-fire lever is on "Auto," the automatic sear holds the hammer in cocked position. Upon locking of the bolt, with the trigger held to the rear, the bolt carrier trips the automatic sear, firing the weapon.

When the selective-fire lever is on "Semi," the sear holds the hammer in cocked position. The hammer is released by pulling the trigger.

The firing pin can strike the primer only when the bolt is completely locked.[15]

The basic cause of the failure-to-extract problem was the higher pressure at the gas port caused by the ball powder. The higher pressure at the gas port was transmitted through the gas tube to the bolt. This caused a very slight speedup of the unlocking of the bolt carrier and its rearward movement along with the extractor. This slightly early unlocking of the bolt carrier and its movement involved a very small fraction of time, but it was time subtracted from that during which the residual pressure in the cartridge case might drop and facilitate extraction, before the pressure in the expended case had dropped enough to allow it to loosen its firm grip within the chamber. "There was still high residual pressure in the chamber and the cartridge cases did not have time to contract to be easily removed from the chamber."[16] Where the extractor engaged the rim of the cartridge case it sometimes stripped off a piece of the rim, leaving the expended cartridge case stuck in the chamber. With an uncorroded chamber, the incidence of failure to extract was reduced but not eliminated. If a cartridge case failed to extract, and if the chamber wasn't corroded and the extractor had just slipped off the rim as it moved to the rear, or hadn't completely sheared the rim, the malfunction could sometimes be cleared by immediate action; the rifleman recycling the bolt by hand. This was not a sure thing. More often the case was lodged in the chamber. When the chamber was corroded, the case would be even more firmly lodged in the chamber and couldn't be extracted, whether or not rim-shear was an issue. This was more likely if the chamber was pitted and exacerbated by cartridge cases that were not hardened to military specifications.

With the expended cartridge case stuck in the chamber, the rifleman had an inoperable weapon. To clear this malfunction, the man had to screw together three pieces of a cleaning rod, if he had one, and punch the expended case from the chamber. There was a shortage of cleaning rods. The M11 cleaning rods were flimsy, and after some use the female end of the sections flared and the pieces could no longer be screwed together. After inserting the often loosely-fitted-together pieces of the cleaning rod into the muzzle of the rifle, the rifleman had to punch out the case and then remove or shake the pieces of the cleaning rod out of the barrel or otherwise pry the case out of the chamber with some other makeshift tool, such as a pocket knife.

The higher pressure at the gas port also caused an increase in the cyclic rate of fire. The rate of fire in the full automatic mode increased from the allowable maximum of 850 rounds per minute up to 1,000 rounds per minute. This increased the rate of malfunctions. Colt somehow convinced the Army to increase the allowable rate of fire to 900 rounds per minute.[17] The increased rate of fire caused parts failures: cracked or broken bolts, broken firing pins, and broken spring guide assemblies. It was directly related to high residual pressure in a fired cartridge case and the failure to extract.

This rifle/ammunition combination was issued to troops on the way to and in Vietnam, with full knowledge of the malfunction problem. The solution involved several modifications to allow the rifle to function with the ball powder. Be that as it may, the early successful test results employing M193 cartridges charged with the IMR type propellant failed to alert anyone to the looming disaster that ball powder would immediately produce in new XM16E1s, long before problems of cleaning, maintenance, or corrosion would complicate matters. The soldiers and Marines in Vietnam lived with this problem, groused about it, but soldiered on.

Some XM16E1s, for one reason or another, functioned more reliably than others, probably as a result of inconsistent quality control of the rifles sent to Vietnam. The Aberdeen Research and Development Center in its *Technical Report No. 1* dated July 1968 investigated issues related to problems with the XM16E1. The report specifically stated that it was seeking information and its purpose was not to place blame. A visit to Colt to evaluate quality control was a part of this report, and a small portion follows. "*The system of applying individual sampling plans* to each individual component and subassembly (say 1% for each characteristic major defect) is basically unsound and could permit a high percentage of defective materiel, say 20% to remain in the process without being detected. . . . *The in-process roving inspections* were conducted in a manner which could permit appreciable defective materiel to be produced with a very low probability of being detected on the basis of the weak sampling plans which were being used during the visit" (italics reflect underlining in original).[18] This inadequate quality control probably accounts for at least some of the spread in frequency of malfunctions between different XM16E1s. When there were casualties, men would trade their poorly functioning rifle for one that had a better "reputation," and return theirs to the rear with the wounded soldier or fatalities.

The ball propellant worked just fine in the M14 and earlier military small arms. It didn't work well at all in the XM16E1. The problematic ammunition was already in the pipeline and was sent to Vietnam for use in XM16E1 rifles.

Although there were other problems with both the rifle itself (the chamber in particular) and with the ammunition (the degree of hardness of the shell cases), the propellant was the main culprit. Coupled with the lack of chroming of the chamber, the quality of the shell casings, and the need for some mechanical modifications, principally to the buffer to bring the cyclic rate of fire to within design specifications, the ball propellant was inevitably going to cause problems. But by then production of M193 ammunition was in full swing. Cartridges employing the WC846 propellant—the main source of the malfunction—were in and on their way to Vietnam.

By August 1966, Col. Harold W. Yount, the Army's AR15/M16 project manager, was briefing Army Materiel Command on the results of SAWS testing. Included in these discussions was the collapse of the SPIW Program. The Army would instead be relying on the XM16E1.[19] The SPIW was not to be, something that should have become evident much sooner. This eliminated the expectation that some weapon of "demonstrated superiority" was on the horizon and the 5.56mm fixation would become history.

In December 1966 a new buffer was designed for the XM16E1 that reduced the excessively high rate of fire when ball powder was used.[20] In February 1967 the XM16E1 was standardized as the M16A1. It was not until May 1967 that the chrome plating of chambers was approved.[21] In December 1967 the Army ordered that all M196 tracer cartridges bound for Southeast Asia be loaded with an IMR propellant, not with WC846.[22]

It was not until late 1968 that all M16A1s produced by Colt had chrome-plated chambers.[23] This didn't ensure, however, that all soldiers and Marines would be armed with upgraded XM16E1s or with the now-standard M16A1. Some unmodified and partially modified XM16E1s still lingered in service. Those that performed with few problems or in the hands of soldiers and Marines infrequently exposed to combat tended to escape upgrade or replacement. Malfunction problems were only finally resolved when new M16A1s or upgrades to the in-service XM16E1s replaced the problem rifles on hand in Vietnam.

Every adjustment affects other aspects of performance. For example, chrome-plated chambers somewhat increased the cyclic rate of fire, one of the basic causes of malfunction problems with the XM16E1. Since chroming of the chamber preceded the buffer fix, the effect on rate of fire was presumably considered when the buffer was modified. The critical changes included the chrome-plated chamber, and bore, and the redesigned buffer to reduce the cyclic rate of fire.

In 1969 the M16A1 officially replaced the M14 and became the standard service rifle. During the 1969 to 1970 timeframe, malfunction problems with the rifle were addressed at the production level. In January 1970, Olin Mathieson, following two years of testing by Frankford Arsenal, accepted the unfortunate reality that lots of WC846 propellant that performed acceptably in 7.62mm NATO ammunition were at an end of the tolerance range regarding fouling, and could cause gas tube clogging in XM16E1 and M16A1 rifles. They reduced the acceptable amount of calcium carbonate in the propellant intended for the 5.56mm ball ammunition from 1.0 to 0.25 and re-designated it WC844.[24]

The M16 rifle program came into being through a back door, avoiding long military experience in the production of serviceable combat weapons. The problem worsened as poor decision-making delayed both identifying and addressing critical design deficiencies.

In the following chapter we'll contrast the incidents experienced by soldiers and Marines with the information, filtered through the chain of command, that made its way into official reports from the field.

7

WEIGHED IN THE BALANCE—A JAMMED M16 CAUSED MY FIRST KIA

by Lyman Duryea

On May 6, 1966, the 1st Cavalry Division (Airmobile) kicked off Operation Davy Crockett. It was another 3rd ("Garry Owen") Brigade operation beginning with an air assault. It was in the same general area of Bong Son as Masher/Whitewing and was known to the men of Garry Owen as Bong Son 2.

Compared to LZ Albany and Bong Son 1, this operation, at least for Charlie Company, 2nd Battalion, 7th Cavalry, began with little action. Other units weren't as fortunate and endured significant casualties. Charlie Company got through the first day with only one casualty, a man wounded by friendly artillery fire. We brought the artillery in very close. It wasn't a particular risk here, but it wasn't uncommon to be so close to an enemy when in contact that supporting fire, artillery, and aerial rocket artillery risked inflicting friendly casualties, and sometimes did.

In this operation the company cleared a good-sized village, Thanh Son 2, that had been occupied by elements of the 9th Battalion of the North Vietnamese Army's Qyet Tam Regiment. This unit had been established a sufficiently long time in the village to not only completely entrench it and build coconut-log and hard-packed mud bunkers (hard as concrete), at intervals of the trench line, but also to live there.

They had started raising families there, and this was deep into South Vietnam. During the day, following a heavy strike by air and artillery, we moved slowly through the village, clearing trenches and bunkers as we progressed.

117

Charlie Company cleared the bunkers with CS tear gas grenades, or smoke grenades when the men had expended the available incapacitating agent. This spared both NVA and civilian lives. It also provided a supply of prisoners. Whether or not the information they ultimately provided to interrogators proved useful wasn't evident to men at company level. They may have provided useful order-of-battle information. For search and destroy operations, the intelligence provided by interrogation is often fed back to the troops too late to be useful. Insurgents generally anticipate compromise and move well ahead of the intelligence curve. When the North Vietnamese established themselves in places where they apparently considered themselves secure and thought they would never have to leave, good intelligence would lead us to them.

The company moved completely through the village and believed it was cleared. As they were to discover, the sweep missed several concealed NVA soldiers. Most had made good their escape before the 3rd Brigade had surrounded the village. Those enemy personnel still in the village began their exfiltration that night. The infantrymen, conveniently positioned in the NVA trenches they had "cleared," were oriented facing back toward the village. To their rear, beyond the village, was a large paddy field where the supporting Huey lift company had laagered their helicopters for the night. Other elements of the brigade to the flanks and rear secured the rest of the field.

At some point in the early hours of the morning, firing broke out, apparently coming from the village or somewhere near its perimeter. Several helicopters were hit by automatic weapons fire, and some helicopter crew members became casualties.

One young Charlie Company trooper, Private First Class Joseph Reid, coming up on his fourth month in-country—alert in a portion of the trench line—heard noises to his front at about this same time. With the selector switch of his XM16E1 on full automatic, he raised his rifle as three North Vietnamese soldiers materialized in the darkness. He fired one round but suddenly his weapon jammed, and he was killed by return fire.

The enemy vanished into the night, making good their escape. This soldier was the first man I lost as a company commander. This frequent XM16E1 malfunction had claimed another casualty.

Depending on who was speaking or writing, the M16 rifle in the Vietnam War was either a superior revolutionary firearm handicapped perhaps by poor cleaning and maintenance discipline among frontline infantrymen, or a flawed, unreliable weapon rushed into production without adequate field testing by a civilian-military bureaucracy that failed shamelessly in its responsibility to provide its soldiers and Marines with an automatic weapon that could stand its own against the enemy's AK47.

What follows is a sampling of commentary—pro and con—about the M16 rifle's performance in Vietnam:

> In my time in Vietnam, I was issued numerous M16s, and none of them functioned properly. Every fourth Marine in our company carried an M14 as we could not depend on the M16.
>> Lt. Col. Duane "Dutch" Van Fleet, USMC (Ret.)

> The over-all performance of the M16 rifle in Vietnam has had the revolutionary impact of dramatic improvement of the combat capability of U.S. ground maneuver units in all types of operations. This is in spite of reliability problems caused by its accelerated issue and employment on a large scale, and the less than adequate preparation, training and discipline of U.S. forces for its support and maintenance.
>> U.S. Army Report of the M16 Rifle Review Panel, June 1, 1968 (originally graded confidential, regraded unclassified Febuary 1, 1994).

> One Army report, classified at the time, but available in archives now, showed that 80 percent of 1,585 troops queried in 1967 had experienced a stoppage while firing. The Army meanwhile, publicly insisted that the weapon was the best rifle available for fighting in Vietnam.
>> C. J. Chivers, *New York Times*, "How Reliable Is the M-16 Rifle?" November 2, 2009.

> Our M-16s aren't worth much. If there's dust in them, they will jam. Half of us don't have cleaning rods to unjam them. Out of 40 rounds I've fired, my rifle jammed about 10 times. I pack as many grenades as I can plus bayonet and K-bar (jungle knife) so I'll have something to fight with. If you can, please send me a bore rod and a 1 1/4 or so paint brush. I need it for my rifles are getting a lot of guys killed because they jam so easily.
>> U.S. Marine in letter to parents in Idaho, quoted by James Fallows in "M-16: A Bureaucratic Horror Story," *The Atlantic* magazine, June 1981.

> There are no major problems being experienced in the field with the M16 rifle at this time that have not been identified and for which corrective action had not been instituted. There are minor problems remaining which are within the purview of the product improvement program for the weapon.
>> Report of the Army's M16 Rifle Review Panel, June 1, 1968.

Seeking an independent, unbiased report of the true field performance situation, the Ichord Congressional Subcommittee selected a retired officer, Colonel (Edward B.) Crossman, as their representative and sent him to Vietnam. In the course of his investigation, he interviewed 250 soldiers and Marines throughout South Vietnam, fully 50 percent of whom reported malfunctions with their M16/M16A1 rifles.

Of these malfunctions, 90 percent were failures to extract. Colonel Crossman found 22-caliber cleaning kits in short supply and concluded many of the problems were due to lack of maintenance and cleaning. He also felt there was room for improvement in the rifle. He concluded, "It was not possible to correlate ammunition make or type with malfunctions." His final report, dated June 16, 1967, included the statement that the rifle needed a complete overhaul in design and manufacture.

Christopher R. Bartocci, *Gun Digest*, July 16, 2012.

The weapon has failed us at crucial moments when we needed fire power most. In each case, it left Marines naked against their enemy. Often . . . we take count after each fight, as many as 50% of the rifles fail to work. I know of at least two Marines who died within 10 feet of the enemy with jammed rifles.

Letter from Marine officer to Sen. Gaylord Nelson of Wisconsin, quoted by James Fallows in *The Atlantic* magazine, June 1981.

The great preponderance of riflemen, their commanders and support personnel accept the M16 as the proper infantry rifle for use throughout Vietnam and like it as an individual weapon. Only thirty-eight out of more than 2,100 surveyed stated they would exchange their M16 rifle for another weapon. Of this group, thirty-five wanted the shorter, lighter version of the M16—the CAR-15.

Report of the Army's M16 Rifle Review Panel, June 1, 1968.

I was walking point a few weeks back and that piece of you know what jammed 3 times in a row on me. I'm lucky I wasn't doing anything but reconning by fire or I wouldn't be writing this letter now. When I brought the matter up to the Captain, he let me test fire the weapon—well, in 50 rounds it double fed and jammed 14 times. I guess I'll just have to wait till someone gets shot and take his rifle because the Captain couldn't get me a new one.

Letter received by Rep. Charles W. Whalen Jr. of Ohio, quoted by James Fallows in *The Atlantic* magazine, June 1981.

The general performance of the M16 rifle has been satisfactory in Vietnam. Since June 1967, it has improved steadily as a result of increased training and discipline of the rifleman in the care, cleaning and maintenance of the weapon.

Report of the Army's M16 Rifle Review Panel, June 1, 1968.

Beginning intensely in 1966, soldiers and Marines complained of the weapon's terrifying tendency to jam mid-fight. What's more, the jamming was often one of the worst sorts: a phenomenon known as "failure to extract," which meant that a spent cartridge remained lodged in the chamber after a bullet flew out the muzzle.

　　C. J. Chivers, *New York Times*, November 2, 2009.

In general, men armed with the M16 in Vietnam rated this rifle's performance high. Most frequently lauded were its light weight and its firepower. However, many men entertained some misgivings about the M16's reliability (33 percent made adverse comments on either the rifle's sensitivity or its reliability).

　　Report of the Army's M16 Rifle Review Panel, June 1, 1968.

One of the most dramatic moments in the (Ichord Subcommittee) hearings came when a letter from a soldier was entered into the record. This poignant letter read in part, "Before we left Okinawa, we were all issued this new rifle, the M-16. Practically, every one of our dead was found with his rifle torn down next to him where he had been trying to fix it."

　　From weaponsandwarfare.com, March 21, 2017, "M-16 Fiasco in Vietnam or Not?!"

When asked what weapon they would prefer to carry in combat, 85 percent of the men wanted either the M16 or its submachine gun version, the XM177.

　　Report of the Army's M16 Rifle Review Panel, June 1, 1968.

Interviews were conducted with units from all Marine regiments presently in Vietnam. Of the Marines interviewed, approximately 50 percent had experienced some type of malfunction. Of these malfunctions, the most prevalent and most serious is the failure to extract, which comprised about 80 percent of the total malfunctions. Most, if not all, of the others can be corrected with the individual's bare hands or by using a knife or bayonet. In the case of a failure to extract, it usually requires a forceful push of the cleaning rod from the muzzle of the rifle barrel. Since the cleaning rods are to be carried disassembled in the carrying case, it takes time to locate and assemble the rod before one can remove the stuck cartridge. If a soldier fails to carry a cleaning rod, this necessitates borrowing a rod from another soldier, hopefully nearby.

　　Report of the Ichord Subcommittee, October 19, 1967.

Dear Sir:

　　On the morning of December 22nd, our company . . . ran into a reinforced platoon of hard core Viet Cong. They were well dug in, and boy! was it hell getting them out. During this fight and previous ones, I lost some of my best buddies. I personally checked their weapons. Close to 70 per cent had a round stuck in the chamber, and take my word it was not their fault. "Sir, if you will send three hundred and sixty cans along with the bill, I'll 'gladly' pay it out of my own pocket. This will be enough for every man in our company to have a can."

Spec. Fourth Class. Letter to commercial manufacturer of a rifle lubricant called Dri-Slide, quoted by Fallows, *The Atlantic* magazine, June 1981.

Adequate quantities of repair parts and cleaning materials and equipment were found to be generally available in Vietnam. However, unbalanced distribution among depots resulted in temporary shortages which did affect using units.

Cleaning materials such as the cleaning rod, lubricant, brushes, and patches, were generally available to the rifleman and he usually carried most items with him in the field. Pipe cleaners and bore cleaners, however, were often not available.

Report of the Army's M16 Rifle Review Panel, June 1, 1968.

Shortages of cleaning equipment and lack of proper training and instructions contributed to the excessive malfunction rate of the M-16.

Report of the Ichord Subcommittee, October 19, 1967.

The reported death of one (Marine) corporal, killed while running up and down the line of his squad pushing out cartridges which failed to extract with the only cleaning rod in the squad, was confirmed by our investigation.

Report of the Ichord Subcommittee, October 19, 1967.

As far as the adequacy of support in terms of parts, cleaning equipment, and so forth, we had no indication that there was any lack of actual quantities in the-ater. There may have been a distribution problem when the actual unit got its rifles. There was a team sent when we got these reports, as we did in the fall of last year (1966) when the units were first issued the rifle, to cover the matter of proper training and maintenance and operation of the rifle in the field. That appeared to solve the issue, because since then we have had no such reports through Army channels, at any rate, of any problems with jamming or malfunc-tioning of the rifle. This was a problem that occurred just when the exchange (of M14 rifles for M16s) was taking place in-country.

Testimony of Dr. Robert A. Brooks, assistant secretary of the Army for installations and logistics, before the Ichord Subcommittee, May 15, 1967.

Out of millions of rounds of 5.56mm ammunition expended, very few ammu-nition malfunctions were reported. Where rifles were given proper care, indi-vidual riflemen were unable to discern any difference in performance or carbon build-up between ammunition loaded with either ball or IMR propellant from different manufacturers.

Report of the Army's M16 Rifle Review Panel, June 1, 1968.

The culprit, it turns out, wasn't the gun but the ammunition, and it was the result of a bad decision by Ordnance. The report (of the Ichord Subcommittee) concluded that the M-16s jammed because the Ordnance Department insisted on changing the cartridge propellant from extruded or stick-type powder to ball-type powder, which tended to leave a residue in the rifle after repeated firing . . . Stoner insisted that stick powder be used in his weapon, and it is not fully understood why Ordnance insisted on changing his recommendation. The subcommittee noted that the army had a cozy relationship with Olin Mathieson, the ball-powder manufacturer, which may have influenced the decision to change powder.

From weaponsandwarfare.com, March 21, 2017, "M-16 Fiasco in Vietnam or Not?!"

The major contributor to malfunctions experienced in Vietnam was ammunition loaded with ball propellant. The change from IMR extruded powder to ball propellant in 1964 for 5.56-mm ammunition was not justified or supported by test data.

The Army's decision-making on ball propellants from sole-source provider Olin Mathieson Chemical Corporation may have been influenced by the company's "close relationship" with three Army commands involved with ammunition procurement.

Report of the Ichord Subcommittee, October 19, 1967.

And so those conflicting points of view about the M16 rifle echoed the broader, more all-encompassing quandary about what America was doing in South Vietnam, how we were going about it, and what ultimate conclusion to the war was being sought from our murky strategy.

In some respects, the controversies over the AR15/XM16E1 rifle and its readiness for combat can be viewed as microcosms for the amorphous decision-making that characterized LBJ's White House, McNamara's Pentagon, and Westmoreland's MACV headquarters at Tan Son Nhut Air Base near Saigon. The factors that weighed heavily in the balance and were found wanting with respect to the rifle program also characterized the flawed TFX/F-111 fighter-bomber program (Chapter 10). Some of the same elements, in fact, would still be around in the 1990s to plague the development of the Lockheed Martin F-35 Lightning, described as the most expensive military weapons system in history.

In the context of America's overall mission in South Vietnam and the strategies developed and resources committed, the misfires involving the M16 rifle can be perhaps viewed in the following perspectives.

A war was being waged half a world away. The slain young president had promised to "pay any price, bear any burden, meet any hardship, support any friend, oppose any foe to assure the survival and the success of liberty."

His successor was torn between the conflicting priorities confronting him. With all his heart he yearned to forge what he termed a "Great Society," in which poverty and racial injustice would be defeated by new spending programs and intense federal emphasis on schooling, medical care, reduction of urban blight, and the tragedy of American citizens being relegated to poverty because our nation had failed them.

And yet there was the burgeoning conflict in Southeast Asia that he believed mistakenly and disastrously, that he had no option but to pursue. Along with a number of social-improvement initiatives he had inherited from John Kennedy—known as the "New Frontier"—Lyndon Johnson had also been bequeathed a legacy of 16,000 American military advisors operating in South Vietnam and neighboring Laos, among them many holders of the prized green beret of which Kennedy was so enamored.

Then there was the financial burden LBJ had inherited from Kennedy, amounting to half a billion dollars in aid to South Vietnam in 1963 alone, an onus that sorely threatened to disrupt Johnson's focus on his Great Society goals.

His solution? Guns and butter. A nation as prosperous as ours, he and his advisors reasoned, could prosecute its national-security obligations in Southeast Asia while at the same time maintaining focus on the domestic agenda Johnson desperately sought. America could wage a war that was consistent with its post-World War II policy to contain the spread of communism (guns), while at the same time its citizenry would be able to enjoy the fruits of a thriving national economy (butter).

It didn't work. "That bitch of a war," Johnson complained during the latter years of his all-too-short life, "killed the lady I really loved—the Great Society." He was only sixty-four years old when he died in January 1973 of a massive heart attack at his ranch in Stonewall, Texas. Two days before his death, Richard M. Nixon, who had been elected president in 1968 only because a heartbroken LBJ in effect decided to abdicate the White House that year, was sworn in to his second term as president, a post from which he would resign in disgrace in August 1974.

To a large degree, Johnson's ambivalence about the war he really didn't want in Vietnam—but had no recourse except to pursue—caused the American public to similarly wonder why we were there and what our end-game strategy was for winning it. In the conflict's early stages with American combat units engaged—1965–1966—much of the public was patriotically supportive of the Vietnam War. Sgt. Barry Sadler wrote a No. 1 hit record about the Green Berets in 1966, and even as late as 1968 John Wayne's movie entitled *The Green Berets*—filmed mainly in the summer of 1967—was a box-office success even as it was roundly and deservedly panned by movie critics.

With the enemy's unexpected Tet Offensive in late January and February 1968, however, all bets were off in the public's perceptions about the war. General Westmoreland's optimistic progress reports, the "Five O'clock Follies" daily press briefings in Saigon, Secretary McNamara's relentless quantifications of enemy bodies being tallied and hamlets and villages being pacified turned out to be illusory, Potemkin village-like fabrications—much like the fake portable villages built in Russia in 1787 to impress Empress Catherine II, but which turned out to be only false fronts.

In the midst of everything, the American soldiers fighting in Vietnam—75 percent of them enlistees into the armed forces, 25 percent draftees—stood face to face with a determined enemy who seemed to have an endless supply of soldiers coming south down the Ho Chi Minh Trail to do battle in South Vietnam, encouraged by leaders in Hanoi who had no qualms about sizeable battlefield losses as long as American public opinion and America's will to continue the fight were being systematically eroded.

The Chinese military strategist and general Sun Tzu (544–496 BC) served as an important influence on the thinking of North Vietnamese general Vo Nguyen Giap and other leaders of his nation. So when they read in Sun Tzu's writing, "One need not destroy one's enemy. One need only destroy his will to engage," it resonated with them, and they proceeded to follow it to the letter. Ultimately, of course, America's resolve to continue the war in Vietnam simply disappeared and Sun Tzu was proven correct.

When Walter Cronkite made his post-Tet visit to Vietnam in February 1968 and subsequently aired his CBS News Special the evening of February 27, declaring that the war was unwinnable and it was time to begin a withdrawal of our forces, LBJ realized that the "bitch of a war," as he described it, had cost him much of his Great Society ambitions, had aged him well beyond his fifty-nine years, and had cost him much of his credibility with the American people.

Five weeks later he chose to speak to the nation on March 31 in a televised prime-time address to announce that he would not seek, nor would he accept, the nomination by his Democratic Party for another term as president. The failure of his Vietnam War policies had humbled this once proud man.

That war, of course, also killed 58,300 of America's finest young men out of an estimated 2.7 million who served there. As described in other chapters of this book, unsound decision making at the highest levels of our nation's civilian and military leadership produced what ultimately came to be called the "quagmire" of Vietnam, so that it's now *de rigueur* among many contemporary historians and op-ed columnists to preface each mention of the Vietnam War with adjectives such as "disastrous," "ill-fated," "catastrophic," and "cataclysmic."

And yet the tragedy of Vietnam—much like the tragedy of the flawed introduction of the M16 rifle into combat there—is that it was all avoidable, all preventable. As Robert McNamara finally admitted in his memoir twenty years after the Vietnam War had ended, "We were wrong, terribly wrong. We owe it to future generations to explain why."

It was McNamara, Westmoreland, and others who, in the words of the Old Testament's Book of Daniel, were weighed in the balance and found wanting. Johnny Cash's 1957 recording of the song "Belshazzar," about the arrogant, imperious Babylonian king of that name who failed to see the handwriting on the wall and was therefore weighed in the balance for his sins, has a refrain which goes in part:

> *He was weighed in the balance and found wanting*
> *His houses were built upon the sand.*

In the final analysis, the decision makers in Washington and Saigon who mismanaged the war in Vietnam to its lamentable conclusion were building unstable, unsupportable castles in the sand. Committing thousands of America's young men into combat with an unproven, insufficiently tested weapon such as the XM16E1 was just one tragic instance of the many misguided decisions that characterized the Vietnam War.

For PFC Joseph Reid—Capt. Lyman Duryea's first combat loss, slain when his XM16E1 rifle jammed as three NVA soldiers were advancing on him—John Kennedy's promise that our nation will "pay any price, bear any burden, meet any hardship" offers small consolation. He and 58,300 others whose names are etched in black granite at the Vietnam Veterans Memorial in Washington, DC, deserved much, much more.

8

SOMEONE HAD BLUNDERED

Forward, the Light Brigade!
Was there a man dismay'd?
Not tho' the soldier knew
Someone had blunder'd.
Theirs not to make reply,
Theirs but to do and die.
Into the valley of Death
Rode the six hundred.

—Alfred, Lord Tennyson, "Charge of the Light Brigade"
1854, memorializing events in the Battle of Balaclava,
October 24, 1854, during the Crimean War

B y the beginning of 1967, complaints originating from troops in Vietnam about their new XM16E1 rifles had risen to near-epic proportions as soldiers and Marines in pre-internet days snail-mailed back home to loved ones their tales of ongoing frustrations with the "black rifles" that kept jamming and all-too-often failed to function satisfactorily in the close quarters of combat. As wives and parents besieged their congressmen and congresswomen for explanations and assistance in keeping their loved ones alive in the face of a formidable enemy, and as the news media pondered what was going on, it became incumbent upon Congress to respond.

It was clear that the U.S. military's new XM16E1 rifle—a weapon which Secretary of Defense Robert McNamara had endorsed and had ordered standardized in September 1963—wasn't doing the job in Vietnam that had been promised and promoted. In the process, the "black rifle" was jeopardizing

American lives and compromising the American mission in Vietnam, which Presidents Kennedy and Johnson had sworn to fulfill.

The 89th U.S. Congress, which had met from January 1965 until January 1967—peak years of the U.S. buildup in Vietnam—was called by *The Washington Post* "arguably the most productive in American history," having enacted watershed legislation such as creation of Medicare and Medicaid; Voting Rights Act; Higher Education Act; Freedom of Information Act; National Foundation on the Arts and the Humanities Act; Highway Safety Act; National Historic Preservation Act; Comprehensive Health, Planning, and Service Act; etc.

Led by Democratic Party supermajorities (i.e., controlling two-thirds of the votes) in both houses of Congress, largely as a result of Lyndon Johnson's sweeping victory (61 percent of the popular vote, plurality of 486 to fifty-two in the Electoral College) over Republican candidate Barry Goldwater in the 1964 presidential election, Congress—with Johnson in the White House as an overwhelmingly popular president—had been fully empowered to pass important legislation.

Many of those legislative accomplishments helped fulfill LBJ's vision of a "Great Society," as he tried to balance "guns and butter" (i.e., military versus civilian priorities). As quoted in *The Nation* magazine in 2001, Johnson lamented about Vietnam toward the end of his life, "That bitch of a war killed the lady I really loved—the Great Society."

But the 89th Congress (1965–1967) had in fact accomplished many of Johnson's New Deal/Great Society goals. Yet, even as progress was being made on his legislative agenda, on the other side of the world half-a-million young Americans were embroiled in a worsening war, confident that they had the support of the American people and were being furnished the finest arms and equipment that modern technology could provide. Unfortunately, both of these assumptions would prove to be erroneous.

Perhaps it's worth noting at this point that the American public in too many instances perceived the typical American soldier in Vietnam as a combat infantryman, opposing a Viet Cong or North Vietnamese enemy with his rifle, machine gun, grenade launcher, or, as a last resort, his pistol or bayonet.

But such was not the case. In the peak war year of 1969, for example, with 540,000 U.S. troops on the ground in Vietnam, it's been estimated that only 30 percent of them—maybe fewer—ever saw combat of any kind during their twelve- or thirteen-month tour of duty in Vietnam.

In other words, out of 540,000 American military personnel in-country in 1969, estimates are that only 60,000 of them (about 11 percent) were actually rifle-toting front-line infantrymen, of whom—on any given day—maybe

40,000 were actually engaged in seeking and establishing contact with the enemy. Meanwhile, however, other Americans were firing artillery pieces; conducting riverine patrols along the Mekong River; piloting attack, medevac, and resupply helicopters; manning tanks as crewmen; flying F4 Phantoms; operating Navy Swift boats; or firing at targets in Vietnam from naval vessels in the South China Sea.

But in terms of infantry combatants, only a relatively small number of U.S. military personnel in Vietnam fought eye to eye with the Viet Cong or North Vietnamese. These were the unfortunate few—theirs not to reason why—who paid the price for the troubled rifle issued them by Pentagon planners and logisticians.

When the new 90th Congress convened on January 3, 1967 (the same day that Jack Ruby, convicted assassin of Kennedy assassin Lee Harvey Oswald, died of a pulmonary embolism at Dallas's Parkland Hospital, where JFK had also died), Democrats still maintained a two-to-one 64–33 advantage in the Senate (one seat vacant) and a substantial 247–187 plurality in the House. John W. McCormack of Massachusetts served as Speaker of the House, with Carl Albert of Oklahoma as its majority leader and Gerald R. Ford of Grand Rapids, Michigan, as minority leader of the lower chamber.

Ford, an All-Star center and long snapper on the University of Michigan's national championship football teams in 1932 and 1933, once caused Lyndon Johnson to comment to reporters that Ford—LBJ's Republican adversary in the House—had sustained so many hits on the head at the center position wearing his old-style leather helmet that he "can't fart and chew gum at the same time."(Reporters tactfully changed the off-color verb to "walk" in their news coverage.) But in 1973 and 1974 Ford became the only person in American history to serve as both vice president and president without having been elected to either office under terms of the 25th Amendment to the Constitution, adopted in February 1967 as one of the aftereffects of the 1963 Kennedy assassination. Coincidentally, Ford had been a member of the Warren Commission which investigated the Kennedy shooting and at one point was contemplating writing a biography about assassin Lee Harvey Oswald and Oswald's motivation.

It was Ford as president who would officially pronounce an end to America's involvement in the Vietnam War during a speech at Tulane University in New Orleans on April 23, 1975. "Today," Ford said, "America can regain the sense of pride that existed before Vietnam. But it cannot be achieved by refighting a war that is finished as far as America is concerned."

Even as Ford was speaking, the North Vietnamese Army was finalizing preparations for its all-out assault on the South Vietnamese capital of Saigon. News of America's decision to abandon the South proved devastating to many South Vietnamese, who pleaded for last-ditch U.S. support. But in the face of overwhelming public opposition to the war, Ford and Congress had no alternative other than to put an end to the U.S. misadventure in Vietnam.

On April 30, 1975, NVA tanks smashed through the gates of the Presidential Palace in Saigon, South Vietnam surrendered, and the Vietnam War had ended: Saigon was renamed Ho Chi Minh City by its conquerors. The last American combat troops had been withdrawn two years earlier, on March 29, 1973.

At home, the American public watched on their TV sets as UH-1H "Huey" helicopters—workhorses of the combat in Vietnam—were jettisoned over the sides of aircraft carriers to make room for other aircraft evacuating American and Vietnamese civilians from the beleaguered city of Saigon. The American public just scratched its collective heads and wondered: What in the hell is happening? Why were we there in the first place? Who's responsible for this disaster?

Why did so many thousands of young Americans have to die if this is the god-awful result?

Responding to the growing national uproar in early 1967 about the M16 rifle's shortcomings in Vietnam (Chapters 5, 6, and 7), the House of Representatives delegated its Armed Services Committee (HASC) to conduct all necessary investigations. Accordingly, a three-person bilateral subcommittee was established May 3, 1967, and was "directed to make inquiry into the development, history, distribution, sale, and adequacy of the present M-16 rifle." The subcommittee was also tasked to "determine the advisability of relying on a sole source for production of the rifle and any military proposals for a follow-on weapon."

The HASC subcommittee was chaired by Congressman Richard H. (Dick) Ichord, Democrat of Missouri. Ichord (pronounced EYE-cord) had served in the Navy's air arm as an enlisted man in the final two years of World War II and had a reputation as a staunch foe of communism. Between 1969 and 1975, as the Vietnam War was peaking and then winding down, Ichord served as the last chairman of the House Un-American Activities Committee (renamed the Committee on Internal Security), a controversial panel that investigated suspected communist activity in the United States. One of the committee's early members was California congressman Richard M. Nixon, whose political career was substantially advanced in the 1940s by the committee's spy hearings.

Joining Ichord on the subcommittee investigating the XM16E1's problems were Representative Speedy O. Long, Democrat of Louisiana, and William G. Bray, Republican of Indiana. Bray had served in World War II as an Army captain with a tank company in the Pacific Theater, earning a Silver Star for gallantry in action, and left active duty in 1946 as a colonel.

The Ichord Committee undertook its assignment in a determined, no-stone-unturned manner, holding extensive hearings of witnesses between May 15 and August 22, 1967, and also conducting field investigations at Fort Benning, Georgia; Camp Pendleton, California; and Hamilton Air Force Base, California. The group visited several military hospitals to interview wounded soldiers and Marines and traveled to South Vietnam for fact finding. The committee also toured the Colt M16 production plant in Hartford, Connecticut, and visited facilities of two former M14 rifle producers, Olin Mathieson of Stamford, Connecticut, and Harrington & Richardson, largest single manufacturer of the M14 rifle and later a major producer of the M16A1.

Shortly after the subcommittee returned from its trip to Vietnam, it submitted an interim report on June 30, 1967, to HASC chairman L. Mendel Rivers, Democrat of South Carolina, a staunch supporter of the Vietnam War, for whom the U.S. Navy in 1971 would name a nuclear-powered attack submarine. Rivers was sometimes dubbed the "servicemen's best friend" because of his strong support of military projects—accompanied by the commitment of appropriations—including a road in Vietnam near Cam Ranh Bay dubbed the Mendel Rivers Parkway.

The final report of the committee—*Report of the Special Subcommittee on the M-16 Rifle Program*, dated October 19, 1967, was a damning indictment of the M16 rifle's development and implementation processes. Here's one instance, quoted verbatim from the committee's report:

> *At the present time the two major publications providing training and maintenance instructions on the M-16 rifle are the Army Field Manual FM 23–9, and a technical manual TM-9-1005-249-14. An examination of the manuals indicates unnecessary duplication on one hand, while providing a lack of information and instructions on the other. For instance, the field manual fails to contain adequate instruction on stoppages and actions for correction. Also, certain training publications appear to provide misleading instructions in that the language tends to oversell the overall reliability of the rifle.*
>
> *Examples of this language are as follows:*
>
> *"This weapon requires the least maintenance of any type weapon within the Army arsenal today."*

"This rifle will fire longer without cleaning or oiling than any other known rifle."
"An occasional cleaning will keep the weapon functioning indefinitely."
"Working parts can be cleaned by wiping with a clean cloth."
    The recent experience in Vietnam tends to refute the above statements. In fact, military personnel are now instructed to provide what some consider to be an excessive amount of care and cleaning to the weapon.

So what was essentially promotional material from a Colt Firearms sales brochure touting the many advantages of its product began finding its misleading way into official Army publications. Army Field Manual FM 23–9, "Rifle, 5.56-MM, XM16E1," had been published July 16, 1966, and was subsequently updated on February 2, 1968, just as the Tet Offensive was commencing. The Army's doctrinal updates stressed the need to field strip the weapon for proper cleaning and maintenance, a far cry from the original "no maintenance" claims provided by Colt. With publication of illustrated DA Pamphlet 750–30 on June 28, 1968—further refined on July 1, 1969—the Army had belatedly taken steps to train and educate its soldiers on care and cleaning of the "black rifle." Not that any of these publications were of much use to soldiers and Marines already in combat with their M16s. The pamphlets and manuals were rarely distributed to front-line combatants but were perhaps helpful back in the training base in the Continental United States (CONUS).

These actions by the Army—together with other serious missteps by the Defense and State Departments—caused an untold number of American battle casualties when XM16E1 rifles in combat failed to fire when needed.

A largely unnoticed—even to this date—finding of the Ichord Committee, even as U.S. and ARVN soldiers were still using older weapons, was the sale of AR15s/M16s to foreign markets just as the Vietnam War was escalating. The committee took note of the fact that Colt sold 5,000 AR15s to England in 1963, with a sale of 20,500 to Singapore during 1967 and 1968, when U.S. infantry divisions were arriving in Vietnam with the older M14 and M14E2. The committee's final report said:

> The one sale to Singapore causing the subcommittee to be greatly concerned was that of 20,500 rifles to Singapore. The concern was not one of fear that the weapon would fall into unfriendly hands or that the security forces of Singapore should not be equipped with a modern and effective weapon, but whether or not the U.S. inventory of this weapon was sufficient to provide the quantities needed for our fighting forces in South Vietnam, including the United States and allies. In addition, there existed at the time of the approval of the Singapore sale an unfulfilled requirement for M-16 rifles for training of

U.S. military personnel prior to their deployment to Southeast Asia and for equipping support units in Southeast Asia.

State Department witnesses admitted in testimony that someone "goofed" in failing to obtain proper approval from the Department of Defense prior to issuing the export license. Subsequent to that instance the coordinating instructions have been reemphasized and now require approval of the military department involved prior to the issuance of export license [sic] *for weapons.*

Placing this "goof," as the committee termed it—or blunder—in perspective, the 20,500 M16s sold by Colt to Singapore could perhaps have been better used for issue to U.S. infantry divisions and/or brigades while they were still in CONUS or Hawaii, allowing time for more thorough training and maintenance guidance, along with marksmanship practice with the new rifles prior to actual deployment to Vietnam. Twenty-thousand five-hundred M16s, for example, could have just about fully equipped the 1st Infantry Division at Fort Riley, Kansas, as well as the 25th Infantry Division at Schofield Barracks, Hawaii, *before* their arrivals in Vietnam and commitment into combat. Would additional operations and maintenance training at their home bases perhaps have averted the difficulties arising from in-country weapons switchovers? It's worth considering.

Thus, the failure of one department of the federal government—State—to coordinate with another one—Defense—while a major war was taking place involving hundreds of thousands of American soldiers is yet another example of the mismanagement of the war in Vietnam at all-too-many levels of government, industry, and the military establishment.

Shortly after beginning its inquiry, the Ichord Committee reported that it "witnessed two malfunctions during rifle demonstrations on the range at Fort Benning, Ga., and Camp Pendleton, Calif. Many reports of similar or worse malfunctions being experienced in Vietnam continued to come to our attention. In view of these reports and the malfunctions personally witnessed by members of the subcommittee, the chairman of the House Armed Services Committee, the Honorable L. Mendel Rivers, directed the subcommittee to visit Vietnam and attempt to determine the extent of the problem and the possibility of immediate corrective action, if such were necessary."

Accordingly, the three subcommittee members, accompanied by aides to record events and findings, departed for Vietnam on June 1, 1967, returning home June 11. While there, they visited "units representing all infantry divisions of the Army and Marine Corps in Vietnam," along with meetings with "logistics support and maintenance personnel at various levels."

The committee's report stated,

Interviews were conducted with units from all Marine regiments presently in Vietnam. Of the Marines interviewed approximately 50 percent had experienced some type of malfunction such as: failure to fire, failure of the bolt to close, failure to feed, failure to eject, failure of the selector lever, and failure to extract. As noted earlier of these malfunctions, the most prevalent and most serious is the failure to extract, which comprised about 80 percent of the total malfunctions. Most of the malfunctions, with the exception of failure to extract, can be corrected with the individual's bare hands or by using a knife or bayonet. In the case of a failure to extract, it usually requires a forceful push of the cleaning rod from the muzzle of the rifle barrel. Since the cleaning rods are to be carried disassembled in the carrying case, it takes time to locate and assemble the rod before one can remove the stuck cartridge. If a soldier fails to carry a cleaning rod, this necessitates a rod from another soldier, hopefully one nearby.

Some soldiers bungeed an assembled cleaning rod to the side of their rifle for immediate access.

The reported death of one corporal, killed while running up and down the line of his squad pushing out cartridges which failed to extract with the only cleaning rod in the squad, was confirmed by our investigation.

The committee determined that because

of the malfunctions personally experienced or reported by others, many of the Marines lacked confidence in the M-16 rifle. In addition to the malfunctions experienced, much of the dissatisfaction with the M-16 might be attributed to a lack of proper training and familiarity with the rifle. None of the enlisted Marines had possession of preventive maintenance pamphlets, manuals, or other written instructions. Many had received very little oral instruction in the care and cleaning of the weapon. While it was reported that sufficient cleaning materials were on hand at the battalion levels, numerous shortages were noted at the company and squad units.

Some Army brigades and divisions reported better experiences with the M16, such as members of the 173rd Airborne Brigade, who

stated that they had no problems with the M-16 rifle as long as it was properly assembled and adequately cleaned. They stated that under extreme conditions, the unit commander issued orders during halts and rest periods for half of the men to disassemble and clean their weapons while the other half remained alert for action. This practice was repeated whenever possible. The men stated a preference for the M-16 but indicated that it required more detailed and frequent cleaning than the M-14.

A unit of the 4th Infantry Division which "had just completed a severe firefight" reported "very few malfunctions during the fight," the committee found in interviews. Despite the 20-round capacity of the M-16 magazine,

> the members of the fire teams loaded only 17 to 18 rounds to insure that the weapon would fire the first time. The platoon leaders supervised the daily cleaning of the rifles and the loading of the magazines. This unit believed that the magazine and ammunition played a great role in the malfunctions experienced.

Other Army divisions reported similar satisfaction with their M-16s—assuming thorough cleaning and maintenance—

> with the exception of the 1st Cavalry Division and the units participating in Task Force Oregon. Of approximately 75 members of the 1st Infantry Division units in Task Force Oregon, almost 40 percent stated a preference for the M-14 rifle over the M-16. Malfunctions experienced were: selector switch sticking, stoppages due to dirty ammunition, failures to extract, and failures to extract rounds left in chamber overnight. There was evidence of some shortages of cleaning materials. Some men were having to share cleaning rods.
>
> Of the 30 members of the 1st Cavalry Division interviewed, 24 had experienced failures to extract at one time or another. Some of these men lubricated the ammunition in the magazine, which is not in accordance with instructions. At least four of the men interviewed did not have cleaning rods and a similar number were without brushes.

The committee found it "most disturbing" that their on-the-ground findings with the 1st Cavalry Division were in stark contrast with a December 1966 report of the Army Weapons Command which reported that this "Division stated that they were not having any troubles with the rifle." It's worth noting that back in early May 1966, then-Captain Chan Duryea, commanding an airmobile rifle company of the 1st Cavalry Division, reported that the first man he lost in combat was as a result of a jammed M16.

The fifty-one-page report of the Ichord Committee concluded with a total of thirty-one "Findings and Recommendations." Foremost among them were:

- Both Army and Marine Corps personnel experienced "serious and excessive malfunctions with the M-16 rifle, the most serious being failure to extract the spent cartridge."

- Proper care and cleaning are of "utmost importance to the effective operation of the rifle."
- "Shortages of cleaning equipment and lack of proper training and instructions contributed to the excessive malfunction rate of the M-16."
- Various levels of command in the Army and Marines Corps "have been negligent in failing to provide proper supervision in the care and cleaning of the rifle, as well as failing to distribute cleaning material and written instructions."
- The Army was remiss in not alerting Marine units to the M-16's problems "when the weapon was issued to them in Vietnam."
- The "major contributor to malfunctions experienced in Vietnam was ammunition loaded with ball propellant." The "change from IMR extruded powder to ball propellant in 1964 for 5.56-mm ammunition was not justified or supported by test data."
- The Army's decision-making on ball propellants from sole-source provider Olin Mathieson Chemical Corporation may have been influenced by the company's "close relationship" with three Army commands involved with ammunition procurement.
- "Some of the modifications to the M-16 became necessary only after ball propellant was adopted for 5.56-mm ammunition."
- The AR-15/M-16 rifle "as initially developed was an excellent and reliable weapon." Some modifications made by the Army "were unnecessary and were not supported by test data. Two such modifications "increased the unit cost of the rifle substantially and another decreased its performance characteristics. These modifications were the bolt closure device, chrome plating of the barrel chamber, and the change in barrel twist." (Note that the Army insisted on the bolt closure device. See the experience of Robert Towles as expressed in Chapter 2. The chromed chamber was an essential modification to reduce the failure to extract malfunction. The lethality of the 5.56mm round was reduced by increasing the rifling twist from one in fourteen inches to one in twelve inches, since the bullet was less likely to tumble when it struck flesh. However, accuracy was significantly increased, a reduction of maximum spread at one hundred meters from 7.2 inches to 3.6 inches.)
- Corrective action on reported M-16 deficiencies and product improvement "have been unnecessarily delayed."
- "A sole source of production of both the ball propellant and the M-16 rifle have contributed to the delay in product improvement and the corrective action required."

- Army officials "were aware of the adverse effects of ball propellant on the cyclic rate of fire as early as March 1964 . . . yet continued to accept delivery of thousands of rifles that were not subject to acceptance or endurance tests using the ammunition of greatest density in the field and in the supply system (ball-propellant-loaded ammunition). Up to September 1966, about 99 million rounds of 5.56-mm. ammunition were consumed in Vietnam, of which 89 million rounds were loaded with ball propellant."

- Army officials "and others as high in authority as the Assistant Secretary of Defense for Installations and Logistics knowingly accepted M–16 rifles that would not pass the approved acceptance test. Colt's officials advised the Army that more than half of the rifles would not pass the acceptance test on cyclic if they were made to use both ball propellant and IMR extruded propellant in their testing procedure. Colt's was allowed to test using only IMR propellant at a time when the vast majority of ammunition in the field, including Vietnam, was loaded with ball propellant."

- The "failure on the part of officials with authority in the Army to cause action to be taken to correct the deficiencies of the 5.56-mm. ammunition borders on criminal negligence."

- The "fouling characteristics of ball propellant will require continued emphasis on proper care and cleaning of the M–16 rifle."

- There was a "shortage of M–16 rifles for training purposes both in the United States and Vietnam at the time of the approval of the sale of 20,500 rifles to Singapore," resulting from "a lack of proper coordination between the State and Defense Departments."

- The "bias and prejudice of individuals associated with Army commands or agencies responsible for development and testing of new weapons made it extremely difficult for higher authority to obtain objective information upon which decisions should have been made." Additionally, "the Army system of development, production, and introduction of a new weapon into the inventory should be thoroughly reviewed to determine if the rifle program is typical of the manner in which the Army operates. The manner in which the Army rifle program has been managed is unbelievable."

- It was "at least unethical" for the commanding general of the Army Weapons Command—Maj. Gen. Nelson M. Lynde Jr.—to accept employment with Colt, producer of the M–16 rifle, upon his retirement from the Army. General Lynde had overseen the "negotiations for the first Army procurement of the M–16 rifle and in fact approved the terms of the contract negotiated by his subordinates." In August 1964, Lynde was hired as an executive consultant by Fairchild Whitney, which became Colt Industries. The committee noted, without "passing judgment on the legality of General Lynde's activities since becoming associated with the company that produced a rifle contracted for by his immediate command while he was on active duty, that the subcommittee does seriously question the wisdom of such action in view of the suspicion aroused by this type of association."

• The Army and Defense Department expended "minimum effort" in "attempting to acquire the production rights and technical data package for the purpose of establishing additional sources for production of the M–16 rifle."

• Based on "information and records available to the contractor and the Army, it appears that Colt's has enjoyed an excessive profit on M–16 production contracts to date." The report then detailed the excessive profits enjoyed by Colt's and recommended that the General Accounting Office "conduct a complete audit of Colt's military contracts to determine actual profit rates experienced."

• Summing up, the Ichord Committee "recommended that proper action be taken by the Secretary of Defense and the Secretary of the Army to insure that the design, contracting, procurement, manufacture, development, supply, and testing of future weapon systems not suffer the same fate." Further, the committee recommended that "the Secretary of the Army make adequate studies to determine if the abolishment by the Secretary of Defense of the Office of the Chief of Ordnance (which was accomplished along with abolishment of the position of other chiefs of various Army services in 1962) could have been partly responsible for the failure of proper control and supervision in the matter of the M–16."

HASC chairman L. Mendel Rivers signed off on the Ichord Committee's report, writing, "I have read the foregoing report and find myself in full accord with the views and recommendations of the subcommittee."

Language used in the Ichord Committee's report (goofed; remiss; bias and prejudice; unethical; unbelievable; borders on criminal negligence; etc.) constitutes a damning indictment of the chain of command's role in committing young American men into combat with a far-less-than-perfect weapon

Capt. Lyman Duryea (left), commanding officer of Company C, 2nd Battalion (Airmobile), 7th Cavalry, with his executive officer in Vietnam in 1966.

Capt. Lyman Duryea, commanding Company C, 2nd Battalion (Airmobile), 7th Cavalry, 1st Cavalry Division (Airmobile), 1966.

Specialist 4 Vernon Miller, a rifleman in Capt. Lyman Duryea's airmobile infantry company in Vietnam, was a former ROTC cadet of Capt. Bob Orkand's in Rockford, Illinois. Miller, shown here in July 1966 with his M16 rifle in the Company C, 2nd Battalion, 7th Cavalry tent area, was the common denominator that brought Duryea and Orkand together as co-authors of this book.

Army chief of staff Gen. Creighton W. Abrams visited the 197th Infantry Brigade—the prototype unit for the Modern Volunteer Army concept— in February 1973 at Fort Benning, Georgia. Here Abrams questions Lt. Col. Bob Orkand (right), commander of the brigade's mechanized infantry battalion, about the M114 command and reconnaissance vehicle. Orkand told him the vehicle was underpowered, tended to overheat, and spent too much of its time in maintenance bays. Photo by Columbus, Georgia, Ledger-Enquirer *newspaper.*

Lt. Col. Bob Orkand was invited to speak to a civic club in Union, South Carolina, in 1973 about the Volunteer Army and was presented with a plaque.

Col. Lyman Duryea, with a doctorate in military history and a master of arts degree in modern languages, served as defense military attaché in El Salvador from 1983 to 1985. Here he is shown conversing with an El Salvadorian Army officer.

Chaired by Congressman Richard H. Ichord Jr. (Democrat of Missouri), the three-man special subcommittee appointed to address M16 rifle problems in Vietnam found numerous faulty decisions in the weapon's development and pointed specifically to the usage of ball powder in the ammunition.

REPORT

OF THE

SPECIAL SUBCOMMITTEE
ON THE
M–16 RIFLE PROGRAM

OF THE

COMMITTEE ON ARMED SERVICES
HOUSE OF REPRESENTATIVES

NINETIETH CONGRESS

FIRST SESSION

OCTOBER 19, 1967

[Pages of all documents printed in behalf of the activities of the House
Committee on Armed Services are numbered cumulatively to
permit a comprehensive index at the end of the Congress. Page numbers lower than those in
this document refer to other subjects.]

U.S. GOVERNMENT PRINTING OFFICE
WASHINGTON : 1967

85-06g

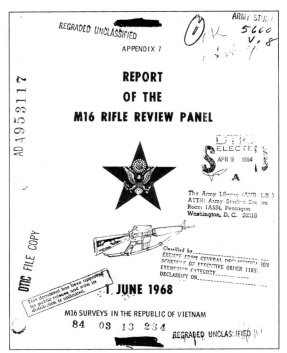

Originally classified confidential, this 1 June 1968 study by the Office of the Director of Weapons System Analysis in the Office of the Chief of Staff of the Army was downgraded to unclassified on 1 February 1994. Despite evidence to the contrary, the report—issued four months after the Tet Offensive—concluded that the M16 rifle was performing well in Vietnam.

DA Pamphlet 750-30 on M16A1 operation. It took the Army until 1 July 1969 to come up with a definitive training manual on care and cleaning of the M16A1 rifle, which combat units had begun using beginning four years earlier in 1965. By then, numerous soldiers and Marines had experienced jamming problems with their rifles, usually attributed by developers and proponents of the "black rifle" to poor care and cleaning practices among improperly supervised riflemen. Problems with the M16A1, it turned out, went much deeper and included a lack of cleaning equipment in too many instances.

and ammunition. The report seems to carefully avoid making specific allegations of malfeasance, but the implications are clear that blunders, lack of coordination and communication among governmental departments, coziness in business relationships, and incompetence at too many levels of administration and command jeopardized American lives on the battlefield and resulted in numerous casualties.

Not everyone agreed with the Ichord committee's conclusion that "the major contributor to malfunctions experienced in Vietnam" was improper substitution of the M16's prescribed IMR 5.56mm ammunition. Writing in *Small Arms Review* in February 2006, Christopher Bartocci concluded, "The principal and most serious cause of the malfunctions of the AR-15/M16 rifle in Vietnam was the failure to chrome plate the chamber."

C. J. Chivers, in his *The Gun*, pretty much agreed with Bartocci, saying, "Ichord's subcommittee did not get everything right. Its emphasis on the IMR-ball powder controversy implicitly missed other causes of jamming, including problems relating to corrosion. It attached little importance to chroming the bore and chamber."

Gordon L. Rottman, who served with the 5th Special Forces Group in Vietnam in 1969–1970 and who retired from the Army after twenty-six years of active duty, has authored excellent, comprehensive books on the M16 and AK47. In analyzing the factors leading to the M16's failures in Vietnam in his 2011 book, *The M16*, Rottman wrote:

> *Several problems contributed to these issues. The first was the failure to chrome-plate the chamber. Under the high heat conditions, extensive rapid fire and high cyclic rates, the chamber quickly became pitted or eroded. The use of improper oil and lubricants gummed it even more and, coupled with poor or no cleaning, quickly led to, [sic] frequent stoppages. . . .*
>
> *The real problem was the propellant ordered by the Chief of Ordnance. The Army successfully used ball powder in all its ammunition. This was more prone to fouling, but had little effect on weapons like the M14 rifle and M60 machine guns. The M16, though, had a sensitive gas system which directed the gas down the very narrow tube over the barrel directly to the bolt carrier—direct impingement. There was no conventional operating rod or gas piston to "block" propellant residue from fouling the entire tube and system. This meant that propellant residue was vented into the receiver and built up rapidly on the bolts and carrier, as well as fouling the gas tube. This system reduced the number of parts and weight, but with the wrong kind of propellant it was a recipe for disaster.*

In a highly influential but often inaccurate article ("M-16: A Bureaucratic Horror Story") in *The Atlantic* magazine's June 1981 issue, James Fallows—a national correspondent for *The Atlantic* who had once served as chief speech-writer for President Jimmy Carter and reportedly had also written policy papers for President Bill Clinton, but who had no military training or experience—penned a damning indictment of the Army's incompetence in developing and procuring the M16. The mismanagement of the AR15/M16 program by the Army brass and also by their superiors at the Defense Department had been well documented by the Ichord Committee, which faulted both the Army and DoD, along with the State Department, for creating many of the M16's misfires.

Much of what Fallows reported in his lengthy article was correct, but misstatements such as "As the fighting in Vietnam grew more intense, in late 1963, procurement of the rifle began," undermine Fallows's arguments, since the first U.S. troop units—beginning with the 9th Marine Expeditionary Brigade—didn't arrive in South Vietnam until March 1965. He also speaks of the "Army's airborne units in Vietnam" being issued the AR15 in 1963, when the first airborne unit, the 173rd Airborne Brigade, didn't arrive in-country until May 1965. (Fallows was apparently referring to Special Forces advisors and their ARVN counterparts.)

Fallows also erred in saying that the "regular Army and Marine units carried the old M-14" in 1965 when they "began full-fledged ground combat in Vietnam." As pointed out in Chapter 1 and elsewhere, the entire 1st Cavalry Division (Airmobile), the 173rd Airborne Brigade, and the 1st Brigade of the 101st Airborne Division arrived in 1965 bearing the new XM16E1. Follow-on Army units, however, brought their M14 rifles with them when arriving in the war zone and transitioned to XM16E1s as they became available. (Not all soldiers and Marines were comfortable about turning in their M14s, however, as the Ichord Committee discovered.)

Be that as it may, Fallows focused on two modifications imposed on the AR15 by what he repeatedly refers to as the "Army ordnance corps," which had been disestablished in 1962 and became the Ordnance Branch, a component of the Army's deputy chief of staff for logistics. In explaining how the Army "militarized" the AR15 "into the M-16," Fallows cited the addition of a "manual bolt closure, a handle that would permit the soldier to ram a cartridge in manually after it had refused to seat properly by itself." The modification, Fallows noted, was opposed by both the Air Force and Marine Corps, both of which "objected vehemently to this change." The Marines went along with the device as long as it didn't affect normal functioning. The Air Force, however, refused to accept the modification.

The second modification that Fallows took issue with was "to increase the 'twist' of the rifle's barrel (the spiral grooving inside the barrel that gives the bullet its spin. The rate of twist was changed," Fallows continued, "from one-in-14-inches to one-in-12. More twist made the bullet spin faster as it flew, and therefore made it hold a more stable path; but it likewise made the bullet more stable as it entered flesh, and thereby reduced, by as much as 40 percent, the 'shocking' lethality that had so distinguished the AR-15."

Fallows called this modification—barrel twist—the most important, saying that "it was apparently motivated by two other forces: the desire of some Army bureaucrats to discredit the AR-15, and the widespread tendency to overlook the difference between meeting technical specifications and producing a weapon that would perform reliably in the real circumstances of combat."

In addition to these problems, Gordon L. Rottman noted that most Marine units receiving the XM16E1 in 1967 "received little if any cleaning gear beyond some cleaning rods and bore brushes. Some units," he wrote, "had never heard of chamber brushes. Colt had hyped the weapon as futuristic, requiring little maintenance owing to new materials. This was interpreted to mean the black rifle was 'self-cleaning.'"

Writing in the Marine Corps's *Leatherneck* magazine in March 2016, retired Lt. Col. Duane "Dutch" Van Fleet recounted how, as a private first class/corporal from March 1967 to March 1968, he served with Company D, 1st Battalion, Seventh Marine Regiment, surviving Tet '68 and twice being wounded in action. Responding to a letter to the editor published in the magazine's January 2016 issue, Van Fleet reiterated some of the M16's problems: "failure to extract spent brass, weak extractor, weak buffer, someone official said the flash suppressor had something to do with all of the above."

Van Fleet concluded that "the weapon was poorly engineered and not adequately tested in Vietnam battlefield-type environments," adding, "There was trouble with the ammo as well. The ammo came from two different depots, one in California and the other in Utah, if I remember correctly."

"In my time in Vietnam," Van Fleet concluded his letter, "I was issued numerous M16s, and none of them functioned properly. Every fourth Marine in our company carried an M14 as we could not depend on the M16."

Retired Marine Major Dick Culver published a lengthy essay entitled "The Saga of the M16 in Vietnam," in which he states that his "experiences with the 'Matty Mattel Mouse Guns' in Vietnam were not pleasant ones." His unit, the 2nd Battalion, Third Marine Regiment, was given a "quick trip out of Vietnam" back to its home base on Okinawa in 1967 for a "refurbishment of web gear, worn out equipment, and the fleshing out of a casualty riddled Battalion with fresh replacements."

"Shortly after 2/3's arrival on Okinawa," Culver continued, "the Battalion learned that it was scheduled to draw a new 'experimental' rifle . . . the XM16E1. 2/3 dutifully turned in their M14s to draw a curious little plastic thing that drew in lots of snickers and comments from the old timers (we still had a few WWII vets in those days). The Battalion was given an orientation lecture in the Camp Schwab Base Theater by some ordnance folks, sent to the range for some sighting in rounds, and pronounced properly prepared for combat . . . little did they know!"

After describing what he termed "several flies in the ointment (only one cleaning rod per rifle with no replacements available, there were only enough magazines to issue three per rifle, a full fifty percent of the rifles wouldn't shoot semi-automatically)," Culver went on, "The first clue (for 2/3) that something was wrong came during the battle of Hill 881 North . . . but *all* the Hill Fights at Khe Sanh in April '67 came up the same—dead Marines with cleaning rods stuck down the barrel of their M16s to punch out cartridge cases that refused to extract."

Culver noted that "ordnance had only enough magazines to issue three (3) per rifle, and they were '*twenty rounders.*'" The thirty-rounders in those days were only being used by the Special Forces.

Fingering SecDef McNamara, Culver said that "he had decreed that the 20 round magazines were more cost effective than the 30 round magazines (this from the guy who was responsible for marketing the Edsel!)!"

Culver added, "Our confidence level would probably have been considerably higher if we had been issued more than three 20 round Magazines [*sic*] per gun. We were promised more of course, and as it turned out, it became true, but only because we were able to pick up those left behind by the casualties. The long and the short of this lesson, however, was that they were trying to get the M16 into action well before adequate supplies were available to support the weapon, even if it had been functioning properly."

The failure to extract problem, pervasive among many Army and Marine units in Vietnam, derived directly from the ammunition snafu identified in the Ichord Committee's report and in the above comments by Gordon Rottman and Lt. Col. Van Fleet, among many others who have written on this debacle.

For example, C. J. Chivers, in a pair of articles published in *The New York Times* in November 2009, wrote:

> Beginning intensely in 1966, soldiers and Marines complained of the weapon's (M16's) terrifying tendency to jam mid-fight. What's more, the jamming was

often one of the worst sorts: a phenomenon known as 'failure to extract,' which meant that a spent cartridge case remained lodged in the chamber after a bullet flew out the muzzle.

The only sure way to dislodge the case was to push a metal rod down the muzzle and pop it out. The modern American rifle, in other words, often resembled a single-shot musket. One Army record, classified at the time but available in archives now, showed that 80 percent of 1,585 troops queried in 1967 had experienced a stoppage while firing. The Army, meanwhile, publicly insisted that the weapon was the best rifle available for fighting in Vietnam.

"The principal and most serious cause of the malfunctions of the AR-15/M16 rifle in Vietnam," wrote Christopher R. Bartocci in *Small Arms Review* in February 2006, "was the failure to chrome plate the chamber. From experience in the Pacific Theater during World War II, it was found that chrome plating a chamber of a firearm would prevent many serious failures to extract."

Bartocci then asks, "If we learned this lesson in World War II and made it a military specification on all U.S. small arms, why did the AR-15/M16 rifle not have it? The blame here goes not to the Ordnance Corps but to the 'Wiz Kids' [*sic*] on Secretary of Defense McNamara's staff who made all the decisions. This micromanagement of money in resources and decisions was made by people who had not the slightest clue about small arms."

The chrome plating problems arose from several issues. Bartocci's reference to the Pacific campaigns of 1941–1945 evokes images of heat, humidity, sand, and salt air, all of which can conspire to foul the workings of a precisely machined weapon of war, such as the XM16E1 rifle was designed to be, and to be employed in Vietnam's semitropical climate, which was much like the Pacific Theater's.

Given conditions of warm temperatures, full-automatic firing in close combat, along with higher cyclic rates produced by use of the wrong ammunition, it was perhaps inevitable that the chambers of many M16s would become pitted or eroded before long. In units where improper oiling and lubricating occurred, the problem became even more pronounced.

Asked by Chairman Ichord of the House subcommittee about why the chamber of the AR15/M16 hadn't been chrome-plated, Army Col. Harold W. Yount, M16 project manager from March 1963 to June 1967 at Rock Island Arsenal, Illinois, offered a less-than-candid answer:

The M-14 rifle does have a chrome plated chamber, as well as a bore, and in this particular rifle (M-16) it has a chrome-molyvanadium barrel, the best machinegun barrel steel there is. It does not have a plated chamber or bore. Initially in the program we did not feel that chrome plating was necessary because of the good steel that was in this particular barrel. It was considered as gold plating, actually, at the time.

However, since that time we feel that the corrosion resistance of chromium plating within the chamber is a thing that is necessary to help us lick this extraction problem, inasmuch as a chrome plated chamber will not corrode, such as a plain chrome-molyvanadium would do.

The contract modification has been made with the Colt Co. and the initial production of barrels with chrome plated chambers is scheduled for the month of August (1967). However, the strike may have an effect on this.

Yount's reference to "the strike" was a five-week walkout by Colt employees, represented by the United Auto Workers, which took place in July 1967 after Colt had licensed production of the M16 family of weapons to the federal government. At the time, Colt Industries and its Firearms Division, headquartered in Hartford, Connecticut, was the sole manufacturer of the M16 rifle. By 1966, Colt had 1,800 employees, nearly half engaged in manufacturing M16 rifles. In 1969, Colt delivered its one-millionth M16, an M16A1.

Because of the work stoppage at Colt in 1967, the availability of new and/or replacement M16s, designated the M16A1 in February of that year, was being short-circuited even as the troop buildup was escalating. A shorter two-week company-wide walkout at Colt in 1969 resulted from a DoD requirement to increase M16 delivery rates. It's unclear why McNamara's Pentagon—which was building up to a troop strength in Vietnam of more than half-a-million men—continued to rely upon a sole-source manufacturer of the M16A1—Colt—that had a long history of labor unrest.

So even though Colonel Yount unwisely felt that chrome-plating the M16 constituted "gold plating," battlefield findings and reports were belying the decisions he and his associates had made. As Bartocci reported in his *Small Arms Review* article, the chrome-plating problem was easily and "simply corrected."

First to appear were barrels manufactured only with chromeplated chambers. The barrels were marked "CMPC" (Colt magnetic particle inspected and proof tested). Barrels were also sent to Rock Island to have the chambers modified and chrome plated. This prevented the serious failures to extract and made the chamber easier to clean. Later in the war, the barrels were chrome plated in both the bore and chamber. These barrels were marked "CMPB" or "CMP Chrome Bore."

With this modification the failures to extract became a thing of the past in the rifle, but it was late 1968 before Colt managed "to chrome-plate the chambers of all M16A1s leaving Hartford," according to Chivers.

The Ichord Committee noted in its report that chrome-plating of the chamber "was expected to begin in August (1967) on new production barrels. This was delayed by more than a month by the July strike at Colt's plant. It is said that by chrome plating the chamber, the possibilities of carbon buildup and scoring of the chamber walls are reduced, and cleaning of the weapon is facilitated."

On February 28, 1967, the XM16E1—as the rifle had officially been known—was standardized by the Army as the M16A1 rifle, even as complaints from troops in the field were mounting, as families back home were receiving letter after letter detailing problems with the rifle, and as confidence in the weapon was steadily eroding. Two months later, the Ichord Committee would begin its hearings to determine what had gone off-target with the M16 rifle, an inquiry into what really became a microcosm of all that had gone wrong with our nation's goal of containing the spread of communism in Southeast Asia.

Eugene M. Stoner, chief engineer with the Costa Mesa, California-based ArmaLite Corporation, a division of Fairchild Aircraft and Engineering Company, was instrumental in the development of the AR15 and filed patent applications in 1956 for design elements that would become components of the weapon. In May 1957, he was invited to the Army's Infantry School at Fort Benning to demonstrate his AR15 which took place, coincidentally, just a few days after the Army had officially installed the in-house-developed, traditional M14 rifle as its primary small-arms weapon.

From the outset, Stoner had told the Army that—to function effectively—the AR15 required a commercially produced propellant called Improved Military Rifle powder, which was slightly more expensive to manufacture than the Army's traditional ball powder, of which the Army had large stockpiles.

IMR propellants, developed by the DuPont Chemical Company early in the 20th century as a miniaturized modification of propellants used in Army artillery pieces, consist of nitrocellulose, a compound formed by nitrating cellulose through exposure to nitric acid. Highly flammable, it has sometimes been referred to as guncotton.

With the U.S. military's adoption of the .223-caliber rifle cartridge in September 1963 (much to the everlasting dismay of the U.S. Army, with its longstanding penchant for .30 caliber and 7.62mm rounds), DuPont's IMR

4475 gunpowder—first introduced in 1936—was the only propellant sanctioned by the military establishment for use in the M193 cartridge.

One problem with the IMR powder was that it was slightly more expensive than the alternative: ball (or spherical) powder. To Secretary McNamara's bean counters in DoD, that raised concerns when many millions of rounds were going to be expended. But perhaps more importantly, large quantities of ball powder had been stockpiled over the years at Army depots. Could it conceivably be used in M16s, thereby saving millions of dollars?

As the Ichord Committee reported, "The M-16 (AR-15) rifle was initially developed, tested, and evaluated using commercial ammunition loaded with IMR 4475 propellant." Despite this, and despite Eugene Stoner's concerns about using a different gunpowder for the M16, ball powder was shipped to Vietnam for use in M16s."

The Ichord Committee reported this about the ammunition problem:

> *According to Dr. Wilbur B. Payne, Chief, Office of Operations Research, Army, for 26 years the military has been locked into a sole-source procurement of a propellant for which the design objective was to permit reuse of scrap and surplus cannon powder.*
>
> *Dr. Payne stated in a memorandum of February 10, 1967, to the Under Secretary of the Army that ball propellant was adopted with a total absence of comparative tests from the time of its adoption to the M-16 rifle experience.*
>
> *In April 1954, the Chief of Ordnance directed that all military small arms ammunition should eventually be loaded with ball type propellant powder which was (and is) produced only by Olin Mathieson. This is a double-base (nitrocellulose-nitroglycerine) propellant commonly called ball powder and is a spherical grain coated with dibutylphthalate.*

Rottman explained the decision to ship the Olin Mathieson WC 846 ball powder to Vietnam as follows:

> *The ammunition used by the Army to test the AR-15 came from the 8.5 million rounds procured by the Air Force, and was loaded with IMR powder. This gave good results, but it was found that IMR powder caused erratic chamber pressures and muzzle velocities. After a great deal of hot debate the Army decided on ball powder, a disaster in the making. After making the decision the Army approached Stoner, asking if this was a good decision. They had hoped for his reassurance; instead, Stoner stated that any change in the ammunition affected a weapon's performance, and refused to endorse the change.*

As a result of the decision to use ball powder, not only did weapons foul up, but the M16's cyclic rate of fire increased to 1,000 rpm, caused by higher gas port pressure. "High port pressure, high chamber pressure and carbon corrosion were ultimately to blame," wrote Martin K. A. Morgan in *American Rifleman*'s September 20, 2017, issue, "for the outbreak of XM16E1 extraction failures in Vietnam."

The Ichord Committee's final report recommended discontinuing the use of Olin Mathieson's ball powder in the M16 rifle and that chrome-plated chambers be immediately included on all M16s being produced.

As summarized by Morgan in *American Rifleman*:

> *Thus, at about the same time as the Tet Offensive in early 1968, the often tragic malfunctions experienced with the XM16E1 began to fade away . . . From the violent battles in the A Shau Valley in 1969 to the incursion into Cambodia during the summer of 1970, the rifle proved itself a highly effective infantry weapon.*

But as a result of the Tet Offensive in January–February 1968 and the American public's subsequent dismay at this shocking, unforeseen turn of events, the inevitable outcome of the war in Vietnam had been pretty much decreed. By the time the M16 rifle proved itself to be battle-worthy, the hearts and minds of the American people had been irretrievably lost.

The *Report of the Special Subcommittee on the M-16 Rifle Program*, prepared by Congressman Richard H. Ichord and his two colleagues and dated October 19, 1967, remains the most authoritative and complete documentation extant about the fatally flawed AR15/M16 rifle program.

Even as disagreement persists about whether the primary cause of M16 malfunctions in Vietnam was failure to chrome-plate, ill-advised ammunition substitutions, buffer-design problems, faulty magazines, inadequate training, lack of cleaning/maintenance emphasis, or inadequate cleaning materials—and very likely all of the above collectively—there remains one inescapable conclusion:

The AR15/M16 rifle was rushed into combat in Vietnam without adequate testing, troop training, or provision for an adequate supply train for the rifle's ammunition and care and cleaning equipment.

Who blundered? Who was at fault? (Perhaps the question might more accurately be posed, "Who *wasn't* at fault?" in terms of decision-making from the top down.)

In Chapter 9, we'll try to come to grips with the many wrong-headed decisions concerning Vietnam and the M16 rifle and how they might have been averted.

9

IN COUNCIL ROOMS APART

All wars are planned by older men
In council rooms apart,
Who call for greater armament
And map the battle chart.

But out along the shattered field
Where golden dreams turn gray,
How very young the faces were
Where all the dead men lay.

Portly and solemn in their pride,
The elders cast their vote
For this or that or something else,
That sounds the martial note.

But when their sightless eyes stare out
Beyond life's vanished toys,
I've noticed nearly all the dead
Were hardly more than boys.

—Grantland Rice (1880–1954), foremost American sportswriter
of the first half of the 20th century and occasional poet

NO, THE NEWS MEDIA DIDN'T LOSE
VIETNAM FOR US, BUT . . .

By Bob Orkand

Co Rentmeester walked into my tiny office at Headquarters Area Command in Saigon and plunked down in a chair. The tall Dutchman, a finalist in

148

sculling (two-oared rowing) for the Netherlands at the 1960 Summer Olympics in Rome, was in Vietnam as a staff photographer for *Life* magazine. In fact, he'd win the World Press Photo of the Year competition that very year (1967) for his photo of a U.S. tank gunner peering through his gunsight—which became the first color photograph ever to win the coveted award.

But Rentmeester's visit came earlier in 1967, maybe March, as I recall, and I was on my first assignment in Vietnam, as spokesman for the Saigon area command. In addition to logistical responsibilities, the command's structure included the 716th Military Police Battalion, which bore responsibility for deterring any and all acts of terrorism in and around the South Vietnamese capital. The 716th, which had participated fifteen years earlier in helping enroll James Meredith at the University of Mississippi in Oxford, would distinguish itself during the forthcoming Tet Offensive by engaging "in ten separate major confrontations with the enemy in an area that roughly formed a semicircle around the city" of Saigon, according to its citation. Additionally, the battalion's MPs took part in numerous small firefights and killed nineteen Viet Cong attackers at the American Embassy, capturing another. Not one of the 130 facilities for which the 716th had responsibility was seized by the enemy during the Tet Offensive.

But Tet was almost a year down the road. Rentmeester, very much aware of his international reputation and his affiliation with *Life* magazine—a highly influential American periodical of that day and age—let me know in no uncertain terms what he had in mind. He wanted to photograph, for a forthcoming *Life* cover, an MP jeep on patrol in Saigon, with one MP behind the wheel and a second MP standing in a ready position at the jeep's pedestal-mounted M60 machine gun. All this would be set against a background of the sun rising over the Saigon River at dawn.

From 4 to 6 a.m. Rentmeester posed that jeep and its occupants—two MPs from the 716th MP Battalion—in every conceivable position, with the river as backdrop. As the sun rose incrementally, he fiddled with different cameras, different exposures, etc., before finally expressing grudging satisfaction with the early morning's endeavors.

When the finished product appeared in *Life* a few weeks later, it was a truly dramatic photo: night patrol; war zone; vigilance against an unseen enemy; daylight breaking; all framed against the Saigon River. The problem was: How real was it? After all, it wasn't a live-action photo. It was a posed set piece, photographed over a period of several hours until the artist (Rentmeester) was satisfied that his "brush" had painted on "canvas" what he was depicting as reality. But the reality was that the event never really occurred as it was portrayed in *Life* magazine. Oh yes, it happened after a fashion, but it was stage-managed to create a certain effect, which happened all too frequently in the media's faulty coverage of the Vietnam War.

It's been estimated that in 1968 the number of accredited journalists from around the world in South Vietnam had swelled to 600, up from fewer than two dozen in 1964. The reporters from America worked for the wire services (AP and UPI), radio and TV networks, major newspapers, large newspaper corporations, and magazines such as *Life* and *Time*. More than sixty journalists, including a number of South Vietnamese photographers and TV cameramen working for U.S. media, were killed during the war.

No, Walter Cronkite didn't lose the war for America; that dubious distinction belongs to Lyndon Johnson, Robert McNamara, his whiz kids; and William Westmoreland. But a February 2018 letter to *The Wall Street Journal* by a former West German reporter, Uwe Siemon-Netto, helps set the record straight.

Siemon-Netto, born in Leipzig, who later became North American correspondent for *Stern*, a weekly news magazine published in Hamburg, covered the Tet Offensive for West German newspapers.

His letter to *The Journal* read in part:

> There were three different sets of reporters accredited to Saigon at that time (i.e., Tet, 1968). The first category accounted for some 70% who hardly ever left the Saigon region. Category II consisted of fewer than 30% who did spend a lot of time in the field. I knew many of those well, including Peter Braestrup. We were far too busy reporting what we had seen to squander our time producing fake news. These combat reporters knew and wrote that the North Vietnamese and Viet Cong had lost the Tet Offensive militarily. But they were overshadowed by category III. These were the media stars flown in from New York or Washington for brief stints who often made ideologically motivated pronouncements on camera that were really a form of malpractice.
>
> I remember how furious Peter Braestrup, I, and others were when Walter Cronkite stated in front of millions of U.S. viewers that the war couldn't be won, when in fact we had just witnessed American and South Vietnamese soldiers shed their blood vanquishing the communists and destroying their infrastructure. I stood next to Braestrup at a mass grave filled with the bodies of old men, women, and children (i.e., South Vietnamese civilians slaughtered by conquering communist forces during Tet). A U.S. television team walked idly about this site. Braestrup asked them: "Why don't you film this scene?" "We are not here to spread anticommunist propaganda," one answered.

The references to Peter Braestrup are to *The Washington Post*'s Saigon Bureau chief during the Tet Offensive. Braestrup was a former Marine lieutenant wounded during the Korean War. His book *Big Story: How the American*

Press and Television Reported and Interpreted the Crisis of Tet 1968 in Washington and Vietnam, was called by distinguished military historian Col. Harry G. Summers Jr. "the essential reference work for serious research on the Tet Offensive."

The first category of reporters, who Siemon-Netto says "hardly ever left the Saigon region," was for the most part billeted in Saigon's modern, downtown, ten-story Caravelle Hotel, built in 1959. The Caravelle also housed a number of news bureaus, such as ABC and CBS, along with the embassies of Australia and New Zealand.

From the Caravelle, reporters could stroll each afternoon at five over to the Rex Hotel for the daily press briefing at JUSPAO (Joint U.S. Public Affairs Office), which they facetiously (and perhaps with some accuracy) dubbed the "Five O'clock Follies" (see Chapter 1). At night, Siemon-Nieto wrote, "Category 1 news types could lounge in the Caravelle's rooftop Saigon Bar and gaze out across the Cuu Long Delta to observe mortars being fired and tracer rounds from rifles and machine guns lighting up the night sky, just in time to pen the following day's 'dispatches from the front.'"

An uncredited website about the Caravelle and its media occupants reports the following:

> For the most part, the ambience at the Caravelle was one of relaxed conviviality. The rooftop bar was the centre of operations—both professional and social—for the international media. From their tenth-floor perch, cold beers in hand, journalists could, by the war's closing days, see the front line from their bar stools. If things got lively enough, they would ride the elevator down to the lobby, take one of the hotel's swanky American limousines out into the field and be back in time for cocktails and note comparing. By the end of the war journalists claimed that they could cover the action without even leaving their bar stools.

It wasn't the press that "lost the war" in Vietnam for the United States. The war's outcome, to the contrary, was a self-inflicted wound resulting from decisions made by our nation's totally befuddled military and civilian leadership. But the American news media did indeed play a major role in debunking the optimistic forecasts emanating from General Westmoreland and his spokesmen. Unlike Simeon-Netto, Braestrup, Nelson Benton of CBS, and several dozen other "scribes" (our code name for reporters who accompanied troops into battle) who legitimately covered the war, too few in the media ventured afield to see for themselves what was taking place in the boondocks.

One conspicuous exception in courageous reporting was Charlie Black of the *Columbus Ledger-Enquirer* newspapers in Georgia, with whom comparisons to World War II's Ernie Pyle are accurate. A 2001 website by Michael P. Enders memorializing Black (charlieblack.net) says, "His unique approach to covering the war was to put on a uniform, lace up his combat boots, hump his own gear (manual typewriter and weapon included) and slog through the mud, heat, and bugs alongside the soldiers he wrote about. Most of the other reporters relied on headquarters briefings and rear-echelon interviews for their information."

Because Black was sending his typewritten dispatches only to the newspapers in Columbus, Georgia (adjacent to Fort Benning, home of the infantry), his reporting never received the national attention it warranted. But twenty-three-year-old Joseph ("Joe") L. Galloway of UPI was embedded with the 1st Battalion (Airmobile), 7th Cavalry at the historic Battle of the Ia Drang Valley in November 1965 and reported heroically from Landing Zone X-Ray and its surroundings. Galloway was later awarded a Bronze Star Medal for coming to the aid of wounded soldiers during the battle, and in 1992, he co-authored with battalion commander Lt. Col. Harold ("Hal") G. Moore (later a lieutenant general) an important book about the early stages of the Vietnam War, *We Were Soldiers Once . . . and Young.*

While the follow-on paperback version of the book depicted Mel Gibson on its cover, with Gibson portraying Moore in the successful 2002 movie *We Were Soldiers*, the original hardback printing showed on its cover an unnamed, haggard grunt with no insignia, bearing his M16 rifle with fixed bayonet, in a photo taken by the Associated Press's Pulitzer Prize-winning reporter Peter Arnett, a New Zealander. It was later learned that the unidentified soldier was twenty-six-year-old Lt. Cyril ("Rick") Rescorla, born in Cornwall, England, whom Moore called "the best platoon leader I ever saw."

On September 11, 2001, Rick Rescorla, director of security at Morgan Stanley (the international financial services company) in the South Tower of the World Trade Center, is credited with saving the lives of an estimated 2,700 of the building's occupants by calmly escorting them down the stairs to safety—while singing Cornish songs learned during his youth in Cornwall—moments after United Airlines Flight 175 was crashed into the building by terrorists. Rescorla gave his life going back into the building and was last seen climbing up a flight of stairs at the tenth floor in search of anyone still in the building. His body was never recovered.

In another instance of fourth-estate bravery, in November 1967 a rifle company of the 1st Battalion (Airmobile), 7th Cavalry found itself pinned down by elements of the 2nd NVA Division along a stream near the seaside fishing village of Hoi An in the northern provinces. Radio calls went out for immediate tactical air support. But the two F-4 Phantom pilots—arriving on scene—found themselves unable to distinguish between friend and foe beneath the dense tree canopy overhanging the stream. "Pop a smoke!" the Marine Corps pilot ordered so he could identify where the friendlies were, but they were all immobilized by enemy AK47 fire. One unidentified Associated Press scribe—who had combat-assaulted that morning with the cavalrymen—began a slow crawl under fire toward a wooden case of variously colored smoke grenades. He removed one from its cardboard container and pulled the pin to release the harmless smoke. "I identify lavender!" the leatherneck pilot called out as the purple smoke drifted over the firefight, indicating where the friendly front lines were. With that information originating from a brave scribe, the jets were able to decimate the enemy as the cavalrymen regained the initiative.

During World War II, reporting from the battlefields in the European and Pacific theaters of operation was subject to rigorous censorship so that U.S. military movements and operations wouldn't be compromised. But no such censorship existed in Vietnam and, for the first time in the history of warfare, television cameras were frequently on hand to record combat actions. Film was airlifted to Tokyo for processing and was then flown to the States for final editing before being aired.

In the process, television viewers learned from Vietnam combat footage that warfare is a particularly nasty endeavor conducted by human beings. In the history of human experience, no more cataclysmic events than war—other than natural disasters—ever take place. Scenes of a naked little Vietnamese girl fleeing napalm attacks or of a captured Viet Cong officer being executed in 1968 by a bullet to the head by the South Vietnamese police chief justifiably horrified the American public. The public was thankfully spared scenes of the March 1968 My Lai massacre because no scribes were present and the Army managed to cover it up until freelance investigative journalist Seymour Hersh broke the story in November 1969, a full year and a half after the event.

But the public's parents and grandparents never had the opportunity in the 1940s to watch on not-yet-widely-available RCA, DuMont, Farnsworth, and Belmont television sets the February 1945 firebombing of the German city of Dresden. On that occasion, a combined force of U.S. and British heavy bombers incinerated and killed an estimated 25,000 old men, women, and children who lived in the historic German state capital on the Elbe River. Four waves of more than 1,300 allied heavy bombers dropped almost 4,000 tons of high explosive and incendiary bombs on Dresden, a city with no strategic importance whatsoever; its principal attribute was the manufacture of some of the world's finest porcelain and chinaware. With the war all but won, it constituted a criminal act by the Allies (revenge of a sort for the Luftwaffe's November 1940 firebombing of the British city of Coventry in an attack demonically code-named "Moonlight Sonata" by Reichsmarschall Herman Goering's minions) that approaches every definition of a massive war crime.

The end goal of war is destruction of the enemy's capabilities and in particular his will to resist. By misjudging the willpower of the North Vietnamese leadership to resist the bombings of cities, bridges, and seaports in North Vietnam, together with attrition of its armed forces—and near-decimation after the failures of the Tet Offensive—the triumvirate of Johnson, McNamara, and Westmoreland totally miscalculated and underestimated the enemy's determination to persevere with its conquest of South Vietnam.

In the early stages of America's commitment of its combat elements to Vietnam (1965–1966), the press was for the most part supportive. Popular culture in films and songs (see Chapter 1) was often positive. But by mid-1967 and particularly following the Tet Offensive in the opening months of 1968, the American news media began to smell blood in the water. Like a swarm of sharks, the media began to pick apart the unraveling tale of America's misfortunes in Southeast Asia.

And in truth, there was much for the predators to feed upon. Westmoreland, *Time* magazine's Man of the Year for 1965, was proclaimed in *Time*'s first issue of 1966 as "the sinewy personification of the American fighting man in 1965." Brought home by Lyndon Johnson in April 1967 to revitalize flagging support for the war effort, Westmoreland spoke at New York's Waldorf Astoria hotel to a meeting of the Associated Press Managing Editors—a highly important media assemblage—and described how he was dealing with the enemy: "We will have to grind him down"—justifying the war of attrition he was waging in vain against the NVA.

Before a joint session of Congress on April 29, 1967, Westmoreland opined that the withdrawal of American troop units could begin in two years or less. That is, MACV's mission in Vietnam was likely to be accomplished by 1969, if not sooner. "Given the nature of the enemy," he told the assembled legislators, "it seems to me that the strategy we are following at this time is the proper one, and that it is producing results." Like a conquering hero from the days of imperial Rome, he concluded his speech by doing an about-face and saluting Vice President Hubert H. Humphrey, Speaker of the House John W. McCormack, and then senators and congressmen on both sides of the aisle. (If he held any presidential aspirations, a la Dwight D. Eisenhower, Westy was sure burnishing them that day.)

Westmoreland truly believed what he was preaching. None of it was lies. In his continuing self-deception, he refused to acknowledge that storm clouds were looming on the horizon and that as fast as he could "grind" the enemy down, Ho Chi Minh and General Giap were sending replacements and reinforcements down the Ho Chi Minh Trail through Laos and Cambodia despite U.S. interdiction efforts.

And when the enemy's determined Tet Offensive of 1968 appeared in living color on television sets in America's living rooms (by the end of 1966, all of America's prime-time TV shows were being broadcast in color), and when Cronkite did his own about-face and reversed his support of the war, the American press concluded that they'd been lied to and deceived by LBJ, McNamara, and by *Time* magazine's depiction of the "sinewy personification of the American fighting man."

The American news media, which for the most part had been lazy and complacent in covering the war from the Saigon Bar on the rooftop of the Caravelle Hotel, was shocked, yes shocked, at the turn of events in early 1968. Rather than admit they'd been asleep when they should have been alertly on duty, the media found it easier to place the blame on our nation's overly optimistic military and civilian leadership. McNamara's mounting body count of dead enemy combatants, the press concluded, had been a Wizard of Oz-like deception, while Westmoreland's "light at the end of the tunnel" failed to inform in which direction the train was speeding.

And so the next generation of U.S. newsmen who arrived post-Tet in Vietnam in 1968 and 1969, replacing the old pros who had been with the war pretty much since its beginning, knew which way the wind was blowing back home in NYC and DC. In a steady stream of negativism—beginning with the enemy's massive defeat at Tet that somehow was never adequately reported at the time—a second generation of younger American newsmen and newswomen began arriving in-country and began writing copy and filming stand-ups against backdrops of the war's devastation that would gratify their editors back home. The editors and anchors, eager to atone for having been buffaloed by the Pentagon and Five O'clock Follies that the war was on the verge of being won, went out of their way to balance the scales by running news that was for the most part negative and defeatist, causing the presidents who succeeded Lyndon Johnson—Richard Nixon and Gerald Ford—to extricate our soldiers and Marines as expeditiously as possible.

And so a war that seemed in 1965 to be very winnable, one that Sgt. Barry Sadler could sing about, and John Wayne could find glory in, and which motivated *Time* magazine to laud our military's leadership, didn't quite turn out the way it was intended. And, in the process, it tore apart our nation—along with its armed forces—for the generation to come.

"If I've lost Cronkite, I've lost middle America," the president of the United States reportedly remarked to an aide the evening of February 27, 1968, after viewing a tape of CBS news anchor Walter Cronkite's special report upon returning from a fact-finding visit to Vietnam in the aftermath of the NVA/VC Tet Offensive.

Whether Lyndon B. Johnson's comment was actually uttered or not (he might have said, "If I've lost Cronkite, I've lost the American people," according to press secretary George Christian, who was with him), it still rings metaphorically true. An estimated 20 million Americans watched Cronkite's gloomy reassessment of the Vietnam War in a special one-hour broadcast in prime time—"Report from Vietnam: Who, What, When, Where, Why?"—in which Cronkite told Americans that, in his considered opinion, the war in Vietnam had become a no-win situation and it was time to pull up stakes in Southeast Asia and clear out.

Seven days after the onset of the Tet Offensive at the end of January 1968, Cronkite and his CBS News crew arrived in Saigon. Accompanied by executive producer Ernest Leiser, who had urged Cronkite to make the Vietnam journey, Cronkite spent the next several weeks in Vietnam, beginning with dinner their first night in Vietnam with General Creighton W. Abrams Jr., who, in June 1968, would succeed General William C. Westmoreland as Commander, U.S. Forces Vietnam (COMUSMACV). Abrams, a 1936 West Point classmate of Westmoreland's, was at the time Westmoreland's deputy commander in Vietnam.

Cronkite and Abrams had known each other since World War II, when Abrams—as the hard-charging commander of General George Patton's lead tank battalion, who had broken through the Wehrmacht's encirclement of Bastogne at Christmas 1944—was termed by Patton as his "only peer" for the title of best tank commander in the U.S. Army. Leiser in World War II was a reporter in Europe for the military's *Stars and Stripes* newspaper and was one of the first reporters to reach Berlin when Nazism and its armed forces collapsed in May 1945.

At dinner that night, according to Leiser, with a few libations being shared, Abrams declared firmly that "we cannot win this g-d damned war, and we ought to find a dignified way out."

Returning to CBS headquarters in New York City, Leiser and Cronkite wrote separate memoirs recounting their Vietnam experiences. According to Leiser, he penned a better narrative than the anchorman about what they'd encountered in Vietnam (with particular emphasis on Abrams's comment at dinner). Cronkite, acknowledging this, decided to go on air with Leiser's script, rather than his own. "I wrote every word of it" (i.e., Cronkite's broadcast) Leiser told a colleague as his health was failing in 2002, but "it could not have gone on the air without Walter's approval."

Lyndon Johnson had viewed a recording of Cronkite's special report while in Austin, Texas. Leaning in from his chair, the president watched as Cronkite—judged "the most trusted man in America" in a 1972 opinion poll—spoke bleak, somber words about what he had come to conclude about the Vietnam War:

> *To say that we are closer to victory today is to believe, in the face of evidence, the optimists who have been wrong in the past. To suggest we are on the edge of defeat is to yield to unreasonable pessimism. To say that we are mired in stalemate seems the only realistic, yet unsatisfactory, conclusion. On the off chance that military and civilian analysts are right, in the next few months we must test the enemy's intentions, in case this is indeed his last big gasp before negotiations. But it is increasingly clear to this reporter that the only rational way out then will be to negotiate, not as victors, but as honorable people who lived up to their pledge to defend democracy, and did the best they could.*
>
> *"This is Walter Cronkite. Good night."*

Five weeks after Cronkite's stunning editorial report, it was Lyndon Johnson's turn to address a prime-time 9 p.m. national television audience. Speaking from the Oval Office on March 31, 1968, Johnson recounted the battlefield setbacks sustained by the enemy in its Tet Offensive and urged "peace through negotiations," beginning with his decision to halt virtually all bombing of North Vietnam. He pointed out that South Vietnam was intensifying efforts to exert "control over its own destiny" by increasing the size of its armed forces, beginning to draft nineteen-year-olds into the military, extending tours of duty, etc.

After his speech drifted through the need to raise taxes and the justification for "our stand in Vietnam," Johnson—who everyone anticipated would shortly begin to campaign for re-election come November—concluded his address with these words:

> *With America's sons in the fields far away, with America's future under challenge right here at home, with our hopes and the world's hopes for peace in the balance every day, I*

do not believe that I should devote an hour or a day of my time to any personal partisan causes or to any duties other than the awesome duties of this office—the Presidency of our country.

Accordingly, I shall not seek, and I will not accept, the nomination of my party for another term as your President.

But let men everywhere know, however, that a strong, a confident, and a vigilant America stands ready tonight to seek an honorable peace—and stands ready tonight to defend an honored cause—whatever the price, whatever the burden, whatever the sacrifice that duty may require.

Thank you for listening. Good night and God bless all of you.

And so with words reminiscent of John F. Kennedy's inaugural address seven years earlier ("Let every nation know . . . that we shall pay any price, bear any burden, meet any hardship, oppose any foe, in order to ensure the survival and the success of liberty"), Lyndon Baines Johnson in effect announced that he was abdicating the presidency of the United States that presumably would have been his for another four-year term. Instead, in November 1968, America elected Richard M. Nixon as president and Spiro Agnew as vice president, both of whom resigned in disgrace in 1973 and 1974 during their second terms in office.

LBJ's announcement in his March 31 address that South Vietnam in the past month had begun drafting its nineteen-year-old men into military service, to be followed by conscription of eighteen-year-olds in two months, caused many in the United States to wonder, "Why the heck has it taken so long? We've been drafting our young men for years to serve in Vietnam. Why have so many young Vietnamese been at liberty to joyride their Honda and Vespa motor scooters through the streets of Saigon and Da Nang while American boys have been fighting and dying in their behalf?"

The answers are to be found in the failed strategies and unwise policies by which our nation waged the war in Vietnam, strategies pursued by the misguided leadership triumvirate of Lyndon Johnson, Robert McNamara, and William Westmoreland, among others in the civilian-military chain of command. By failing to strategize that the war was one to be waged primarily by the ARVN and other South Vietnamese armed forces—firmly and resolutely supported by U.S. arms and equipment, air and naval gunfire, helicopter-borne logistical support and firepower, and the constant presence of American advisors—McNamara and Westmoreland ultimately transformed what should have been primarily a South Vietnamese struggle to resist a communist take-over into an ill-fated U.S. effort on behalf of an ally who should have been out front from the beginning in the battle for its own national sovereignty and survival.

"No single factor more definitively illustrates Westmoreland's neglect of the South Vietnamese armed forces than the M-16 rifle, then a new light-weight weapon considered ideally suited for the Vietnam environment," wrote historian Lewis Sorley (West Point graduate, tank battalion executive officer in Vietnam) in his damning 2011 biography, '*Westmoreland: The General Who Lost Vietnam.*'

Chapter 11, "Why Not the ARVN?" addresses in detail the failure of MACV, under Westmoreland's leadership, to prioritize arming and equipping South Vietnamese armed forces with a weapon—the M16 rifle—which would appear to be ideally suited for the small stature of Vietnamese fighting men. But an additional quote from Sorley's study succinctly sums it up:

> *General Frank Besson was at that time (1964–1969) commanding the Army Materiel Command, and he remembered Westmoreland's request for 100,000 M-16 rifles. "I also recommended that we give it to the Vietnamese, the South Vietnamese," recalled Besson, "because I felt we ought to give our allies the best we could. But they said, 'No, we can't give it to the South Vietnamese because it will undoubtedly be captured by the Viet Cong and the North Vietnamese and will be used against us.'" The honest-to-god fact—that is what they said.*
>
> *It was not until March 1967 that an allocation of M-16 rifles for the South Vietnamese was reinstated, the first shipments arriving the following month. "But," said Brigadier General James Lawton Collins Jr., "until 1968 there were only enough to equip the airborne and Marine battalions of the General Reserve."*
>
> *In his debriefing report upon leaving Vietnam in August 1968 General Fred Weyand emphasized the effects. "The long delay in furnishing the ARVN modern weapons and equipment, at least on a par with that furnished the enemy by Russia and China, has been a major contributing factor to ARVN ineffectiveness."*

Elsewhere in his chapter on the M16, Sorley notes:

> *In April 1968 [two months after the end of the Tet Offensive] Time magazine reported that the new Secretary of Defense, Clark Clifford, had announced "a dramatic increase in the U.S. production of the M-16 so as to equip all ARVN units by mid-summer." That was something McNamara had never agreed to and that Westmoreland made only sporadic and at best halfhearted efforts to advocate, further evidence of just how pervasive was his belief that U.S. forces could come in and do the job for the Vietnamese without the necessity of ever equipping them to do it for themselves.*

McNamara, who had been installed as secretary of defense one day after John F. Kennedy's inauguration as president, resigned his post as of February

29, 1968, one month after the Tet Offensive commenced and five days after it was ended. He had overseen the Defense Department for slightly more than seven years—the longest-tenured SecDef ever—under Presidents Kennedy and Johnson. McNamara left the Pentagon to become president of the World Bank.

In addition to the "too little, too late" decision to expedite shipments of the M16A1 rifle to ARVN units in the aftermath of the Tet Offensive, steps had been taken in 1966 and 1967 to help cure the rifle of its demonstrated shortcomings on the battlefield.

The lengthy list of needed M16 product and training improvements identified by the Ichord Committee (Chapter 8) had for the most part been remedied by late 1968, three years into the American war effort in Vietnam.

For example, "Subsequent to the subcommittee's visit to Vietnam (May 1967), the Commanding General, III Marine Amphibious Force (Lt. Gen. Robert E. Cushman Jr.), established an orientation team for the M-16 rifle." The team thereupon visited every Marine unit in Vietnam, recounting problems experienced with the rifle by other Marines and describing necessary corrective actions.

When the committee queried Marine Corps headquarters in Washington, "What, if anything, after the committee's visit, was done to assure that every man using the M-16 rifle has the necessary cleaning equipment, particularly a cleaning rod and chamber and bore brushes?" The committee was told that "the Marines have instituted 'Operation M-16' where cleaning equipment has been airlifted to our forces in Vietnam. Also, it is reported that accelerated procurement of additional quantities of cleaning equipment is underway to cope with the unexpected utilization of equipment being three times the expected rate." In other words, the new rifle that had been touted by Colt and the Army as being virtually maintenance-free in actuality was requiring three times the amount of cleaning equipment that had been anticipated and procured.

DoD didn't fare any better in the Ichord report. In response to the report, McNamara's deputy, Paul Nitze, "on July 31, 1967, issued a memorandum directing a technical evaluation and field survey of the performance of the M-16 rifle." Its purpose: "to determine whether any major deficiencies exist in the weapon, and, if so, to recommend corrective action."

In other words, with American force levels in Vietnam approaching half a million in July 1967, and with many of those soldiers and Marines equipped with a troublesome weapon, perhaps it might be prudent (after a congressional investigation had detected numerous flaws in the manner in which the weapon was rushed into deployment without adequate field testing) to inquire whether the weapon had any "major deficiencies" or not.

In March 1963, six months before the Army re-designated the AR15 as the rifle 5.56mm XM16E1, a joint-service coordinating committee was formed to meet at Rock Island Arsenal in Illinois. Army Col. Harold W. Yount was designated project manager for the AR15/M16 rifle program, and his committee included not only representatives from each of the armed services, but also a DoD presence.

As described by C. J. Chivers in *The Gun,*

> Two of McNamara's aides were given seats on it, along with veto power over all its decisions. This gave the AR-15 a high priority. It also left the program vulnerable to political interference on technical matters and introduced fresh tensions between the defense secretary's office and the ordnance service.
>
> McNamara had already expressed his dissatisfaction with the army's weapons experts . . . The defense secretary wanted to put his stamp on the AR-15 program and place it under his protection. But the top-heavy assignment of political appointees to the committee risked alienating or even removing people with weapons expertise from participation in the AR-15's development. McNamara's whiz kids were smart. But they had almost no experience in either war or weaponry, and were not necessarily an able substitute for those whose careers had been a study of ordnance and guns. One of the government's ballistic experts was appalled at their role. "Their qualifications," he said, "consisted of, and apparently were limited to, advanced academic degrees, supreme confidence in their own intellectual superiority, virtually absolute authority as designated representatives of OSD (Office of the Secretary of Defense), and a degree of arrogance such as I have never seen before or since."

On June 21, 1967, the Ichord Committee had interviewed Eugene Stoner, inventor of the AR15, and gotten his views on what went astray when the rifle was committed to combat, including the improper substitution of ball powder for the prescribed IMR propellant. When the committee reconvened a month later, "several letters from servicemen or their relatives were entered into the record relating to malfunctions of the M-16 rifle in combat in Vietnam, specifically failure to extract a spent cartridge."

After interviewing a Colt executive who "attributed most all of the extraction problems to pitted and bad chambers" resulting from climate conditions in Vietnam and who noted that "both Colt and Weapons Command are doing everything in their power to minimize the cause, or the causes of malfunctions" (lubrication, lack of chrome chamber, and buffer), the committee began its session with Colonel Yount. It should be noted here that blaming "most all" of the extraction problems on pitted and bad chambers was self-serving at best, an apparent attempt by the Colt executive to absolve Colt of any responsibility for the problem. Chairman Ichord did most of the questioning:

> *Ichord: The next witness is Colonel Yount. Colonel Yount, will you please come forward?*
> *Col. Harold W. Yount is a former project manager for rifles. You have been in the weapons command. I thought you were a project manager for the M-16 rifle. What is your current status?*
>
> *Yount: Casual en route on my way to Korea at the present time, sir.*
>
> *Ichord: I see. When did you assume your duties as project manager for the M-16 rifle, Colonel?*
>
> *Yount: March of 1963 until June 1967.*
>
> *Ichord: March of 1963 until June of 1967. Where were you stationed during that time?*
>
> *Yount: At Rock Island Arsenal, Ill., the entire period.*
>
> *Ichord: Would you briefly explain to the committee the extent and nature of your duties?*
>
> *Yount: I was designated as the project manager of the AR-15 rifle back in March of 1963, and I reported to the Commanding General of the Army Materiel Command through the Commanding General of the Weapons Command. I was delegated full line authority by the Commanding General of the Army Materiel Command.*
>
> *In that I was responsible for the overall management of my entire procurement program. And at the present time, or at the time of my leaving the project manager's office, I was responsible not only for the M-16 rifle but also other rifle systems—as well as the accessories, various components, and ammunition peculiar to the rifle systems classified type standard A.*

Yount went on to list his other responsibilities "extracted from (his) charter as project manager." Then, because of the committee's strong focus on problems with the M16's ammunition, Chairman Ichord turned his attention to that aspect of the rifle's problems:

> *Ichord: Of course as a weapons expert, you do realize it makes a lot of difference in the functioning and the cyclic rate of the weapon, depending upon which powder you use, is that correct?*
>
> *Yount: That is correct, sir.*
>
> *Ichord: Were you advised of any proposed change from IMR 4475 to ball propellant? And if so, when?*
>
> *Yount: As I recall, in the latter part of 1963, or early 1964, we received a request from the Air Force to purchase some ammunition for them. On this request they specified*

exclusively ball propellant. This ball propellant was not authorized at the time in our technical data package, and we had to make an exception for the procurement.

Ichord: *They specified?*

Yount: *They specified ball propellant.*

Ichord: *Ball propellant.*

Yount: *The U.S. Air Force would not accept anything else, except ammunition loaded with ball propellant.*

Ichord: *Now, in your position as project manager for the M-16, were you charged with the responsibility of purchasing ammunition, too?*

Yount: *I was, sir.*

Ichord: *For the Air Force, also?*

Yount: *Yes, sir.*

Ichord: *What did you do when you received that information?*

Yount: *This was coordinated through our four services' technical coordinating committee, and we agreed to go ahead and buy this for the Air Force and subsequently have it thoroughly tested and make a determination if we were going to standardize it as part of our technical data package for the ammunition.*

Ichord: *Did you have some reservations about buying it and using it in 5.56 ammunition?*

Yount: *Reservations only to the effect, sir, we didn't have the test experience data and not because we had any reservations it would be unsatisfactory. . . .*

Ichord: *You did know it would speed up the cyclic rate?*

Yount: *We did not. There had never been any indication prior to the M-16 rifle, that this would result in an increase in cyclic rate in a weapon.*

Ichord: *Where was Mr. Stoner at this time, the inventor of the weapon? Were you in contact with him?*

Yount: *Yes, indeed, right from the beginning of the program.*

Ichord: *Did you talk to him about the conversion and the use of ball propellant ammunition in the M-16?*

Yount: *No, not until after it had actually been put into operation.*

Ichord: *Are you telling this committee that you do not feel that the ball propellant has had any adverse effect upon the operation of the M-16 rifle?*

Yount: *I am telling the committee that I had no evidence it has had any adverse effect.*

Ichord: *You have had no evidence, after being project manager from March of 1963 to June of 1967, that the use of ball propellant ammunition is a part of your problem?*

Yount: *It was a part of the problems as far as the cyclic rate is concerned.*

Ichord: *You said that you had never talked to Mr. Stoner, the inventor of the rifle. What would you say if I told you that, if you had checked with him, he would have been greatly opposed to the change from IMR to ball propellants? Would you think that would be a serious mistake, the inventor of the rifle, one who obviously knows more about the rifle than anyone else?*

Yount: *I would agree with him. However, I want to qualify the statement there that this increase in malfunctions would be primarily due, with all the evidence that we had, due to an increase in cyclic rate; we have satisfied this requirement with the new buffer.*

When the committee had interviewed Stoner a month earlier in June 1967, the inventor stated, "The gun was designed only to fire IMR type powder, which is an extruded propellant, which was made at the time by Du Pont." Ichord, after establishing that testing of the M16 at Fort Benning had in fact used only extruded propellant (in fact, it seems that mostly ball propellant was used in the SAWS test), or IMR powder, then queried Stoner:

Ichord: *You seem to be leading into the opinion that the type of powder we are using may have or may be the cause of some of the trouble.*

Committee Member Bray: *Using ball powder, anyhow.*

Stoner: *Well, the ball powder—I am acquainted with that. I was asked about it some years ago by some people in the government, my opinion on what was going to happen when they used it. I will go back a little bit.*

> *When the Army got serious about this and they wanted to standardize the ammunition and get up a technical data package, at the time, through all the tests, and at the beginning of the Air Force adoption of the weapon, the ammunition was a commercial buy from Remington. We didn't have a regular tech data package. But when the Army got into it, then they set up a board to make up a tech data package in the ammunition. They made some changes in the ammunition, and I was asked to look at the ammunition technical data package after it was made, which I did. I told them, or this party, that in my opinion it would be very, very risk—*

Ichord: *Was that ball?*

Stoner: *That was ball propellant, and also—they did two things.*

Ichord: *You recommended against ball propellant?*

Stoner: *The reason I did was they were getting into this thing heavily and the fact that we had years of firing, both in Vietnam and this country, using the IMR propellant, which the weapon was designed to fire in the first place.*

Ichord: *IMR is the—*

Stoner: *That is the extruded propellant. It is called improved military rifle powder, IMR.*

Ichord: *Let me at this time interject, Mr. Stoner.*

Stoner: *Yes, sir.*

Ichord: *Have you been called by the Army or the military into this problem in Vietnam? Have you gone to Vietnam and looked into the problem?*

Stoner: *No, I have not. I haven't been asked. In fact, for the last two years or so, most of the information that you are talking about, about a buffer, I can only speculate what a buffer is doing.*

Ichord: *In the opinion of our experts, the buffer is really not getting at the basis of your problem, or of the problem. As you understand it, you would agree with that conclusion?*

Stoner: Well, if you are talking about extraction problems, the buffer would have nothing to do with it. The only thing is, the buffer, as I understand it, was to cut down the cyclic rate, and the cyclic rate was causing a lot of their problems.

Relating to the ammunition changeover, Stoner was asked: "Are you familiar with the reasons stated by the Army for the changeover from the IMR to the ball powder? Do you have any firsthand or secondhand knowledge of that?"

Stoner: Well, the only—I have a little firsthand knowledge because I was approached after this ammunition inspection was made by a person, I think it is the Secretary of Defense's Office, in looking at the technical data package.

Ichord: When was this?

Stoner: This was at the time, I forget how long it was, but it was at least a couple of years ago. He asked me my opinion on it, and I asked him why they were holding out for the ball propellant and they said, well this was more or less, as I could gather, a policy within the Army. They wanted to have everything ball propellant that they could in small arms.

Mr. Morgan, Ichord Committee counsel: Because of the cost savings or what?

Stoner: Well, I think this was one of their reasons, and the fact that it burned a little cooler and so forth. Like I said before, I didn't advise it because we already had 1,000 weapons in Vietnam that had gone through I thought, very well. These were the weapons that were sent over by ARPA (Advanced Research Projects Agency), you know, prior to the adoption. I'm not sure of these times, but in that area of time.

Morgan: Do you care to identify the individual in the Department of Defense, or the office in the Department of Defense, that asked for your advise [sic] on this?

Stoner: Yes, that was Mr. Frank Vee—I think it is V-E-E and I think he was in the comptroller's office. He had to do with procurement, anyway, on ammunition. And he asked my opinion after the fact. In other words, this was rather an odd meeting. He asked me to meet him and I did, and I looked at the technical data package and he said, what is your opinion, and I said I would advise against it, because—for the reason I just stated. I asked, so what is going to happen and he said, well, they already decided this is the way they are going to go, meaning the committee. I said, so why are you asking me now, and he said, "I would have felt better if you had approved of the package." And I said, well, we both don't feel so good. That was it.

Morgan: Did anyone ever mention to you that the Army might have a large surplus of World War II, or Korean powder that might be reworked for salvage purposes and they might be able to use the extremely large amount of nitro-cellulose that was available, that could convert to ball powder?

> Stoner: *No, that wasn't mentioned. But I do know this is one of the advantages of this particular propellant, is that you can salvage other propellants and make ball powder out of it. But this wasn't mentioned, no.*

During the course of Colonel Yount's testimony, Chairman Ichord inquired how many times Yount had gone to Vietnam while he was serving as M16 project manager, and was told that Yount had been to Vietnam one time, in November 1966. Ichord asked what the occasion was for Yount's visit at that time and was told:

> Yount: *I had already dispatched a team to Vietnam as a result of their request to assist . . .*
> Ichord: *Why did they request you go to South Vietnam?*
> Yount: *They said they were having an undue rash of malfunctions, and I volunteered at that time to send a team of experts over there to help them ascertain the problems, and put the weapons back into condition, if they would simply request that I do so . . .*
> Ichord: *You were head of the team?*
> Yount: *No, sir. Colonel Underwood of my office was head of the team.*
> Ichord: *That was in—*
> Yount: *He went over in October of 1966.*
> Ichord: *I see. Then you came later?*
> Yount: *Right. He called me on the telephone and told me that he would advise me to come over here and see this for myself, because when he came home he didn't think he would be able to convince me of the conditions, of the various things that we would have to do in order to correct the situation.*

As documented by C. J. Chivers in '*The Gun,*' Lt. Col. Herbert P. Underwood of Yount's M16 project manager's office had written a letter from Vietnam to Yount, dated October 30, 1966. Part of the letter read:

The 173rd (i.e., 173rd Airborne Brigade) uses some kind of field expedience [*sic*], primarily for cleaning the chamber and the bore of the weapons. They either use a piece of commo wire, a shoe lace or a nylon cord which they carry with them. They take a .30 caliber patch, cut it in half, fold it once and loop the string or what ever [*sic*] it is to the center of this patch. Then using oil they pull it through the bore of the weapon starting from the chamber. As they do this, they clean both the chamber and the bore and then dry it off. They also put a little bit of oil in the chamber of the weapon to prevent it from corroding. I try to discourage it, however I am not completely convinced myself that if you leave the chamber completely dry you won't have a problem resulting from corrosion, even if you cleaned your weapon every day.

Commenting on Underwood's letter, Chivers said, "No one, it seemed, was quite sure what to do with this new rifle, even the officers issuing it."

In other words, it proved to be yet another manifestation of the Defense Department's rushing the weapon into production without adequate field-testing, without a tried and tested logistical tail, and without adequate training on the weapon at virtually every level of command.

Shoelaces being employed by paratroopers of the 173rd Airborne to help pull a cleaning patch through an M16 rifle bore recalls Ben Franklin's proverb (Chapter 1) that begins "For the want of a nail the shoe was lost" and ends unhappily with the kingdom being lost.

Two instances of sole-source procurement of the AR15/M16 rifle and its ammunition proved troubling to the Ichord Committee—and with some justification, it appears.

With the establishment of Colonel Yount's project manager's office in March 1963, the Army was also designated as procurement agency for the AR15 rifle and its ammunition. Colt's (as Colt was then known) Firearms Division in Hartford, Connecticut, became sole-source contractor for the new weapon.

As noted by the Ichord Committee, "The 1963 decision by the Army to procure the AR-15 was authorized to equip airborne, assault and the Special Forces. This allegedly was then intended as a one-time-only procurement. A direct bearing on the Army's decision to order the AR-15 was the Secretary of Defense's disapproval of the Army's request to continue to procure the M-14 to replace all of the M-1s." (This relates to the fact that some World War II-era M1 Garand rifles were still in use by reserve components and by some Allied forces.)

The Army began negotiations with Colt's and Fairchild Engine and Airplane Corporation of Hagerstown, Maryland, which had formed an ArmaLite division in 1954 after acquiring the small, privately owned Hollywood, California-based ArmaLite Corporation. Eugene Stoner, a Marine Corps veteran who had a background in aviation ordnance, was brought aboard the new concern, bringing with him his innovative concepts for a new assault rifle that would morph into the AR15/M16. The negotiations included pricing of bayonets, bipods, spare parts, and cleaning gear, and included authorization to procure 28 million rounds of the newly standardized cartridge, ball, 5.56mm, M193.

Eleven modifications to the weapon were made, causing the contract to be amended a number of times. The procurement order was later increased to

201,000 rifles, 5.56mm, XM16E1, as the weapon had been type-classified in September 1963.

So what was thought to be a "one-time-only procurement" of 104,000 AR-15s (85,000 for the Army, 19,000 for the Air Force) turned out to be a $13,300,000 financial bonanza for Colt's, which added 510 new employees at its Hartford plant between May 1966 and April 1967, according to C. J. Chivers.

Firmly in the driver's seat with respect to the military's decision to commit to the black rifle, "Colt's," according to the Ichord Committee, "also stated that it did not intend to propose, as a part of or in conjunction with, the present procurement of 104,000 rifles to sell or license all or any portion of its proprietary rights to the U.S. Government."

The Ichord report called this "unquestionably a direct refusal by Colt's" to the U.S. government's efforts to broaden the M16's manufacturing base. Among other issues, Colt's had been experiencing quality-control problems, debates over ammunition-related concerns, labor union unrest, etc.

"Subsequently," the Ichord Committee reported, Colt's clarified its position on this point on September 30, 1963, when it advised the Army that they had not meant to imply that Colt's would never consider such a sale of licensing, but as previously stated:"

> Colt's will consider licensing other sources of production and providing manufacturing know-how to them at such time as the total requirements for this rifle shall exceed 500,000 units.
>
> A meeting was held in the office of the Assistant Secretary of the Army Ignatius (this is apparently an incorrect reference to Paul R. Ignatius, who served as assistant secretary of defense for installation and logistics, and later as secretary of the Navy), on October 4, 1963, to discuss Colt's refusal to negotiate with the Army for the fiscal year 1964 procurement. A memorandum for the record on the meeting, signed by Lt. Col. Arthur G. Moore, indicated that the request to attempt to procure these rights stemmed from the Assistant Secretary's impression that Department of Defense instructions called for competitive procurement.

The memorandum by Moore read in part, "After some discussion of the problem, and further review of the background, Secretary Ignatius stated it was his opinion we should amend the RFQ (Request for Quote) to delete the requirement regarding 'Technical Data Package' for the fiscal year 1964 procurement and that negotiations should be continued with Colt after the award to obtain proprietary right in the event of a possible future requirement."

In other words, Ignatius seemed to be saying that Colt was in the driver's seat at present, but perhaps conditions might be changed with subsequent rifle purchases.

In addition to Colt's privileged position as sole-source contractor for the AR15/M16, apparently in conflict with DoD guidelines for "competitive procurement," Colt may have held one other high-powered bargaining chip in its hand.

The commanding general of the Army Weapons Command (to whom Colonel Yount reported, along with also reporting to the head of the Army Materiel Command) was Maj. Gen. Nelson M. Lynde Jr. Lynde had testified before the Ichord Committee that "he was responsible for the development, procurement, and field service support of Army weapons," including of course the AR15/M16 rifle system.

Lynde would, upon his retirement from the Army as of March 1, 1964, become an "executive consultant" with Fairchild Whitney, the parent company of Colt Industries, effective August 1, 1964. In his new position in industry with Colt, Lynde would be "accountable to the president (of Colt) for professional and technical guidance to the Corporation and/or its subsidiaries, in planning for new products for the future and in evaluating current product or projects, particularly in the area of military weapons."

The General Accounting Office, acting on behalf of the Ichord Committee, found that Lynde, on October 26, 1964—roughly three months after his employment had commenced at Colt—had sent a letter, signed by Lynde as a retired general, "requesting copies of four classified documents including one entitled 'Comparative Effectiveness Evaluation of the AR-15, M-14.'"

According to the Ichord Committee, Lynde, "when notified of the Assistant Secretary's (Ignatius's) decision on October 4, 1963, stated 'he thought we were in a position where it would be very difficult to negotiate the rights necessary for competitive procurement in the future, but apparently the decision has been made.'"

The Ichord Committee took note of the fact that Lynde had overseen the "negotiations for the first Army procurement of the M-16 rifle and in fact approved the terms of the contract negotiated by his subordinates." The committee, as discussed in Chapter 8, noted without "passing judgment on the legality of General Lynde's activities since becoming associated with the company that produced a rifle contracted for by his immediate command while he was on active duty, that the subcommittee does seriously question the wisdom of such action in view of the suspicion aroused by this type of association."

As for Lynde's post-retirement employment by Colt, the Ichord Committee generously termed it "at least unethical." Lynde, a West Pointer who graduated with the class of 1929, was originally an infantry officer, later transferring to the Ordnance Corps. A member of the Ordnance Corps Hall of Fame since 1980, he died in 1993 at age eighty-eight.

The Ichord Committee, as stated in Chapter 8, was disappointed that the Army and DoD expended "minimum effort" in "attempting to acquire the production rights and technical data package for the purpose of establishing additional sources for the production of the M-16 rifle." The committee also opined that "it appears that Colt's has enjoyed an excessive profit on M-16 production contracts to date."

Such were the hazards of sole-source procurement practices, along with perhaps too-cozy relationships between companies furnishing weapons and equipment for the military and the military and civilian personnel overseeing government contracts.

This brings us to the second major procurement area where the Ichord Committee was skeptical of sole-source procurement procedures: the 5.56mm ammunition for the M16 rifle. (A fuller discussion of the controversy over ball propellant versus IMR [Improved Military Rifle] powder can be found in Chapters 6 and 8, and earlier in this chapter.)

In April 1954—not quite a year after the Korean War had ended—the Army's Chief of Ordnance had directed that all military small arms ammunition should be loaded with ball-type propellant powder, the only supplier of which was Olin Mathieson Chemical Corporation, formed also in 1954 with the merger of Mathieson Chemical Corporation and Olin Corporation.

Aware that IMR propellant was required for its AR15 rifles, the Air Force—with its chief of staff General Curtis LeMay very much a convert of ArmaLite and Colt weaponry (see Chapter 1)—placed an order with the Remington Arms Company on October 8, 1963, for 19 million rounds of IMR 4198 propellant (or any propellant meeting its specifications), which was coordinated with Colonel Yount's project manager's office.

In February 1964, the Army asked the three major U.S. propellant manufacturers—Olin Mathieson, Remington, and Du Pont—to submit "candidate propellants for testing as replacements to the IMR 4475," since in early 1964 one million rounds loaded with IMR 4475 propellant "were the last ball ammunition to be loaded with IMR 4475."

Based on tests, propellants submitted by Du Pont and Olin Mathieson were recommended as "permissible alternatives to IMR 4475 in the loading of 5.56-mm. ball ammunition," the Ichord Committee recorded. But after 50 million rounds loaded with this IMR propellant had been produced, Remington found itself unable to comply with the velocity/pressure requirements.

Accordingly, in February 1965—just a few weeks before the 9th Marine Expeditionary Brigade would arrive in Vietnam on March 8 as the first U.S. combat unit in-country—the Army again requested the propellant manufacturers to submit new candidates for the 5.56mm cartridge. Olin Mathieson was unable to meet the required specifications, Hercules Powder failed the fouling-test requirement and was disqualified, but Du Pont was found to be qualified. However, ammunition samples for the test weren't received at Frankford Arsenal until September 1965, and test results weren't approved until April 1966. "This delayed action (more than a year)," according to the Ichord report, and "indicates to the subcommittee a lack of any sense of urgency on the part of the Army."

The committee also noted that "unless close quality control is maintained in the loading of each lot of cartridges, the chemical composition and performance characteristics can differ. It is inconceivable that the Army would accept as many as 59 million cartridges on the basis of testing only one preproduction lot."

Summing up its dissatisfaction with sole-source procurement, the Ichord report said, "A sole source of production of both the ball propellant and the M-16 have contributed to the delay in product improvement and the corrective action required."

As stated in Chapter 8, word choices made by the Ichord Committee in its final report (goofed, remiss, bias and prejudice, unethical, unbelievable, borders on criminal negligence, etc.) indicate a laxness and total lack of a sense of urgency to equip and supply half-a-million young American men with adequate weaponry, ammunition, and cleaning equipment.

At virtually every level of command—from the White House, through the Pentagon, to Pacific Fleet headquarters in Hawaii, to MACV headquarters at Tan Son Nhut Air Base—the rush to install an imperfect, not-fully-developed, not-ready-for-prime-time weapons system and put it in the hands of America's soldiers and Marines in combat was inexcusable, bordering, as the Ichord Report says, "on criminal negligence" in some instances.

C. J. Chivers, in an October 27, 2010, *Esquire* magazine adaptation of his *The Gun*, sums it up better than anyone else:

The early M16 and its ammunition formed a combination not ready for war. They were a flawed pair emerging from a flawed development history. Prone to malfunction, they were forced into troops' hands through a clash of wills and egos in Robert McNamara's Pentagon. Instead of a thoughtful progression from prototype to general-issue arms, the M16's journey was marked by salesmanship, sham science, cover-ups, chicanery, incompetence, and no small amount of dishonesty by a manufacturer and senior military officers. Its introduction to war was briefly heralded as a triumph of private industry and perceptive management. It swiftly became a monument to the hazards of hubris and the perils of rushing, a study in military management gone awry.

The next chapter looks at the flawed developmental and procurement policies of McNamara's Department of Defense.

10

THE UNCERTAIN TRUMPET

For if the trumpet give an uncertain sound, who shall prepare himself to the battle?

—First Epistle to the Corinthians 14:8

Three weeks into what would become his seven-year tenure in the Pentagon as secretary of defense, Robert S. McNamara made a decision with respect to developing a radical new warplane that would satisfy both Navy and Air Force requirements for a new fighter-bomber. In addition, the SecDef believed, it could also be used by the Army and Marine Corps in the close-support roles they required. In other words, he believed a "one size fits all" warplane could be developed that would be suitable for all four armed services.

The plane would become known as Tactical Fighter Experimental, or TFX, and would emerge as one of McNamara's most pronounced decision-making blunders, rivaling that of his misjudgments on and mismanagement of the AR15/M16 rifle program.

McNamara, who had served in World War II as a lieutenant colonel in the U.S. Army Air Forces in non-flying management posts involving statistical control systems, believed it possible to develop such an all-purpose aircraft, thereby significantly reducing development, procurement, training, and maintenance costs.

In McNamara's self-serving memoir, *In Retrospect: The Tragedy and Lessons of Vietnam*, published in 1995, twenty years after the fall of South Vietnam, he recounts how he became secretary of defense. Seven weeks into his new job as president of Ford Motor Company in Dearborn, Michigan, McNamara received a phone call from Robert Kennedy, brother of the president-elect, who was slated to become attorney general in the new administration.

Bobby came quickly to the point: "The president-elect would be grateful if you would meet with our brother-in-law, Sargent Shriver." Shriver, who had married Eunice Kennedy (sister of the Kennedy brothers) in 1953 and would later play key roles in the founding of the Peace Corps, Job Corps, and Head Start, as well as running unsuccessfully for vice president in the 1972 presidential election won by the subsequently-to-be disgraced Richard Nixon and Spiro Agnew, was in McNamara's office at Ford at four o'clock that afternoon.

"The president-elect," said Shriver, "has instructed me to offer you the position of secretary of the treasury."

As McNamara remembers the meeting in his memoir—written thirty-five years after the fact—he was astonished at the offer. "You're out of your mind," he told Shriver. "I'm not qualified for that."

> Shriver's response: "If you hold to that position, I am authorized to say Jack Kennedy wishes you to serve as secretary of defense."
> McNamara: "This is absurd. I'm not qualified."
> Shriver: "Well, the president-elect at least hopes you will give him the courtesy of agreeing to meet him tomorrow in Washington."
> McNamara: "I could not say no."

The next day, Kennedy and McNamara held their meeting at the Kennedy residence on N Street in Georgetown.

As noted in Chapter 1, according to *The New York Times*, McNamara initially declined the SecDef post, claiming that he "could barely tell a nuclear warhead from a station wagon when he arrived in Washington." McNamara's memoir tells how Kennedy responded by pointing out that there "were no schools for defense secretaries, as far as he knew, and no schools for presidents either."

Despite McNamara's protestations, Kennedy went ahead and picked him for the defense post. For the next seven years, McNamara and his underlings ran the Pentagon like field marshals of the Napoleonic era.

It's interesting to speculate, years after McNamara's death in 2009 at age ninety-three, how history might have been altered had McNamara accepted Kennedy's initial offer of the treasury secretary's post. Clearly, given McNamara's background and experience, the management of money fell solidly within his purview, while the administration of human resources, the conduct of military strategy, and decisions on key weaponry procurement were probably not well suited for a man who was frank in acknowledging his limited knowledge of defense matters.

Had McNamara, for example, spent the next seven years ensconced in the Treasury Building at 1500 Pennsylvania Avenue, just down the street from the White House, instead of micromanaging the Defense Department from the Pentagon on the far side of the Potomac River, who can say how world events—including the unfolding tragedy taking place in Vietnam—might have turned out differently?

John Kennedy and Robert McNamara both assumed their new duties and responsibilities the third week of January in 1961 with a shared belief that the leaders of the American military establishment had gotten out of control and that civilian control of the military needed to be reestablished without delay.

Undeterred by his inexperience in matters affecting the military and its weaponry, McNamara took over the controls at the Pentagon. It's been said that a basic reason for McNamara's poor decisions in the TFX/F-111 and AR15/M16 programs wasn't so much his lack of military knowledge but rather his persistent failures to listen to the views of people who had that knowledge, while still retaining his final decision-making authority.

Fully confident in their ability to render sound judgments and decisions, McNamara and his assemblage of whiz kids began promptly, early in 1961, to focus on the daunting task of imposing their collective willpower on the unenlightened generals and admirals who led America's armed forces.

Since both the Navy and Air Force were clamoring for a new, improved fighter-bomber, why not combine the requirements, the whiz kids reasoned, into one super-efficient airframe? Given the forward-thinking now being introduced into the Pentagon's corridors, it was more than conceivable that a properly configured new warplane might also satisfy the need for a new close-support plane desired by the Army and Marine Corps. Simple logic, of a sort not practiced by the antiquated generals and admirals used to having their way in the Pentagon, could surely design and develop such an airplane.

And so planning for the Tactical Fighter Experimental—or TFX—commenced in 1961. The result, six years later, was the F-111 airplane, built by General Dynamics Corporation in Fort Worth, Texas, in a head-to-head competition that virtually everyone except McNamara thought had been won by the Boeing Company of Seattle.

Aviation expert Joe Baugher (his website boasts facetiously that he has "written and published an enormous amount of aircraft articles") summed up the development of the TFX/F-111 this way:

> The General Dynamics F-111 is one of the most controversial aircraft that ever flew. Perhaps no other aircraft before or since has been so bitterly criticized in the media. It suffered a protracted development cycle in which numerous serious problems had to be identified and repaired, and cost overruns came to be a serious concern. Of the several thousand that had originally been planned, only 562 flightworthy examples of seven different variants were completed. The F-111 was the subject of protracted and bitter debates within the Congress, with opponents denouncing the aircraft as a "flying Edsel" that was more dangerous to the U.S. than it was to any potential enemy.

In McNamara's memoir, *In Retrospect*, published in 1995, twenty years after the war in Vietnam had ended, he provides his rationale and explanations for what he terms "The Tragedy and Lessons of Vietnam." Here's how, in the book's preface, he explains his lengthy silence about the war by saying, "I hesitated for fear that I might appear self-serving, defensive or vindictive, which I wished to avoid at all costs. Perhaps I hesitated also because it is hard to face one's mistakes. But something changed my attitude and willingness to speak. I am responding not to a desire to get out my personal story but rather to a wish to put before the American people why their government and its leaders behaved as they did and what we may learn from that experience."

In his next paragraph McNamara asks rhetorically, "How did this group— 'the best and the brightest,' as we eventually came to be known—get it wrong on Vietnam?" (If you'll glance back to the final pages of Chapter 1 of this book, pretty much the same question was raised.)

Later in his preface, McNamara goes on to say: "We of the Kennedy and Johnson administrations who participated in the decisions on Vietnam acted according to what we thought were the principles and traditions of this nation. We made our decisions in light of those values.

"Yet we were wrong, terribly wrong. We owe it to future generations to explain why."

McNamara was seventy-nine years old when his book, written with Brian VanDeMark (at the time a professor of history at the U.S. Naval Academy), was published. Whether or not the memoir (which became a #1 nonfiction bestseller) was "self-serving, defensive or vindictive" is for others to evaluate. In the passages quoted above, the editorial "we" is used far more than the singular pronoun "I" to account for the "wrong, terribly wrong" decisions that were made. And when McNamara died in 2009 at age ninety-three, it's doubtful if he was prepared even then to confront his maker with a frank and candid mea culpa.

As an instance, when McNamara describes the body-count syndrome employed by his Pentagon analysts (Chapter 1), someone else gets fingered for coming up with that unit of measurement: "The body count was a measurement of the adversary's manpower losses: we undertook it because one of Westy's objectives was to reach a so-called crossover point, at which Vietcong and North Vietnamese casualties would be greater than they could sustain."

So in McNamara's considered judgment, Westmoreland bore major responsibility for creating the fiction of inflated enemy body-counts as a measure of progress being made in Vietnam. In actuality, as shown in Lewis Sorley's *Westmoreland: The General Who Lost Vietnam*, Westmoreland consistently spoke out of both sides of his mouth when addressing body counting, at times acknowledging that the statistics were inflated, while on other occasions defending the practice of body-count reporting as a useful statistic.

Sorley cites a study conducted by Brig. Gen. Douglas Kinnard, chief of the operations analysis branch in Westmoreland's J-3 (joint operations directorate). Kinnard's survey showed that 61 percent of Army generals who served in Vietnam under Westmoreland "thought that body count was 'often inflated,'" eliciting comments such as "They were greatly exaggerated by many units primarily because of the incredible interest shown by people like McNamara and Westmoreland."

It's more than likely that Westmoreland's defense of body-count reporting (when he chose to speak in its favor, as contrasted when he spoke against it) was in deference to McNamara's bevy of systems analysts working in the Pentagon under assistant defense secretary Dr. Alain Enthoven.

A review in *Commentary* magazine of McNamara's memoir took a particularly harsh view of body counting. "This macabre accounting protocol," Gabriel Schoenfeld wrote, "fell victim to the most basic flaw of systems analysis: garbage in garbage out." "Ah *les statistiques*," a South Vietnamese officer once said of McNamara, "your Secretary of Defense loves statistics. We Vietnamese can give him all he wants. If you want them to go up, they will go up. If you want them to go down, they will go down." As McNamara himself admits, the data reported back from the battle front as often as not were erroneous, and Washington learned only what it wanted to hear.

McNamara's litanies of mea culpas in his memoir (as posted by *Commentary* magazine) runs a gamut of "we's": "we lacked experience dealing with crises," "we knew very little about the region," "we failed to analyze our assumptions critically," "the foundations of our decision-making were gravely flawed," and "it is very hard to recapture the innocence and confidence with which we approached Vietnam." "We both overestimated the effect of South Vietnam's loss on the security of the West and failed to adhere to the fundamental principle that, in the final analysis, if the South Vietnamese were to be saved, they had to win the war themselves."

For Robert McNamara, then, the decision-making failures he chose to articulate twenty years after the fact originated with a nebulous group of military and civilian officials (the "we") who badly mismanaged virtually all aspects of the eight years (1965–1973) that U.S. armed forces were the primary participants in the fight in South Vietnam against the army of North Vietnam and Viet Cong.

The word "I" in McNamara's recollections appears largely in strategic discussions taking place in the White House and Pentagon, where he was usually at loggerheads with the deeply entrenched military brass. "We," however, becomes his operative pronoun when fault-finding is being allotted.

And—incredibly—there's not a single mention in McNamara's 414-page memoir of either of two very wrong-headed weapons-system decisions that McNamara personally made, involving the TFX/F-111 airplane and M16 rifle. Neither project rates as much as a single sentence in *In Retrospect*, although in congressional testimony in March 1963 McNamara could point with pride to the "use of often arbitrary and wasteful rule-of-thumb measures" in Pentagon procurement: "Let me give you a specific example: in the case of the M-88 tank recovery vehicle, we found that the substitution of a fully adequate transit pipeline factor of 55 days for the previously used arbitrary factor of 120 days enabled us to realize savings of $12.5 million on just this one item."

So while the FTX/F111 program was already in splinters, and with the AR15/XM16E1 debacle still largely ahead of him, McNamara could point with pride to the vast cost savings and efficiencies being realized through his prudent oversight of the Defense Department.

Perhaps it's ironic that McNamara—as a micromanager—was significantly involved in the development and procurement of both the F-111 and M16 weapon systems, when at the same time he was failing to exert adequate controls over our nation's involvement and strategy in Vietnam, which was his primary and ultimate responsibility as secretary of defense.

Do common threads exist in the fault-laden rush to judgment in both instances, and what lessons can be learned from the wasteful expenditures of lives and dollars in the development of both weapons before they were ready for prime time?

Three weeks into his tenure as defense secretary, the man who in a semi-jocular manner reportedly had told President-elect Kennedy that he "could barely tell a nuclear warhead from a station wagon" had already concluded that a multiservice attack bomber could be developed that would meet the needs of the four armed services.

From December 19, 1960, when McNamara was offered the SecDef post by Kennedy, through his swearing in to that post on January 21, 1961 (one day after Kennedy's inauguration), to February 14, 1961, when McNamara ordered the armed services to commence development of such a warplane, he apparently had learned a great deal in less than two months about what differentiates a nuclear warhead from a fully loaded six-passenger 1960 Ford Country Squire Station Wagon retailing for $2,752. (The cost of each TFX/F-111 would come in at $15,873,748—$102.6 million per plane in current dollars—for the 547 airplanes that were actually produced, a total expenditure of $8.672 billion [$56.3 billion today] to complete the program, according to figures provided by the comptroller general of the United States to an investigating Senate subcommittee in 1970.)

Early in the 1960s, well before Kennedy's election to the presidency and McNamara's appointment as SecDef—well before many in the American public had ever heard of a nation in Southeast Asia called the Republic of Vietnam—the U.S. Air Force and Navy had each identified legitimate needs for new airplanes to replace aging veterans and keep pace with threats arising from new surface-to-air missiles and air-to-air missiles launched from Soviet bombers.

Robert McNamara, with three weeks of Pentagon experience behind him, perceived that there were a number of areas of commonality in proposals submitted by the two armed services: both would carry two-man crews, both would employ swing wings for low-speed flight operations, and both would be roughly the same size. As an added bonus, it seemed only logical that a warplane could be developed which would also satisfy Army and Marine Corps requirements for a close-support plane to assist ground-combat units in contact with an enemy.

Ergo, on Valentine's Day 1961, McNamara directed that a study be conducted to see if a single aircraft could fulfill both the Air Force and Navy mission requirements, as well as the close-support role needed by the Army and Marines. He announced that all four services would thereupon participate in a Joint Services Acquisition Program, using the Air Force's design criteria as the basis for planning and development.

The study's results in May 1961 quickly determined that the close-support role was incompatible with Air Force and Navy needs. That requirement was spun off into a separate program that resulted in the development of the highly successful Vought A-7 Corsair II.

But since the study confirmed that it was theoretically practical to combine the strike role sought by the Air Force with the Navy's fleet interceptor requirement, McNamara found confirmation in his basic assumption that a jointly acquired airplane was feasible. Accordingly, on June 7, 1961, he ordered development of the Tactical Fighter Experimental, or TFX, with the Air Force as program manager. With slightly different versions—an F-111A for the Air Force and F-111B for the sea service—both requirements could be satisfied. Ignoring a request by Navy secretary John Connally (later to be wounded in the November 1963 assassination of President Kennedy while serving as Texas governor) that the Navy play a central role in the TFX development because of aircraft-carrier constraints, McNamara gave the Air Force secretary the key role, but directed that the two services work closely together.

Predictably, the Air Force and Navy service chiefs took issue with McNamara's fiat, since both services felt that their mission requirements were being compromised. Gen. Curtis LeMay, who became Air Force chief of staff on June 30, 1961, argued forcefully that the TFX should have the characteristics of a bona fide bomber, with less emphasis on its strike-fighter capabilities. (LeMay's unilateral decision in May 1962 to procure 8,500 AR15s for the Air Force had helped tilt the scales in favor of purchasing the AR15/M16 rifle.)

Admiral George W. Anderson Jr., chief of naval operations who had directed the successful blockade of Cuba during the 1962 missile crisis, had long-standing disagreements with McNamara, and was forced into early retirement by the SecDef. To minimize and cover up the true nature of Anderson's premature departure from the CNO post, Kennedy appointed him ambassador to Portugal.

A request for proposals, or RFP, for the TFX was announced in September 1961, with development of the aircraft to begin four years later. Nine aircraft manufacturers submitted proposals, from which Boeing and General Dynamics were chosen as finalists. Boeing's design concept was preferred by both the Air Force and Navy, which was also favored by the Selection Review Board. Boeing's proposal prevailed in the first three of four separate competitions between the two companies; in the fourth, the General Dynamics bid was moved up to an "also qualified" role.

According to a master's degree thesis paper written by Air Force Maj. Brian L. Reece at Fort Leavenworth, Kansas, in October 2011, "All boards from the Evaluation Group up to General LeMay and Admiral Anderson unanimously agreed that the Boeing design better met their needs. Not only was it the superior design to each of the services, it was also cheaper."

"On 24 November (1961)," Maj. Reece's paper continued, "the Department of Defense made a public announcement that the General Dynamics version was selected and that they would develop 22 prototype F–111's for a cost of $439 million. The Air Force was forced to accept an aircraft they felt was inferior. They also felt forced to accept a lighter, slower, smaller and generally less versatile aircraft in order to appease the Navy and Secretary McNamara. General LeMay and all of the other Air Force generals were crushed by the decision, but production was to begin immediately."

McNamara's explanation for his decision, in his March 1963 testimony before a Senate Subcommittee on Defense Procurement, went like this: "My examination of the facts, in consultation with my advisers, convinced me that, as compared with the Boeing proposal, the General Dynamics proposal was substantially closer to a single design, requiring only relatively minor modifications to adapt it to the different requirements of the Navy and the Air Force, and that it embodied a more realistic approach to the cost problem. Accordingly, I decided to select General Dynamics as the development company, since I concluded that it was best qualified to design the most effective airplane that could be produced at the least cost, in the least time, to meet our military requirements."

So even though he was still stubbornly hewing to his belief that a "single design," requiring "only relatively minor modifications" was still feasible, McNamara steadfastly refused to listen to the mounting evidence that a single design was impractical and that the TFX was too large and too heavy for aircraft–carrier operations. Four separate review panels, along with the uniformed leaders of the Air Force and Navy, had endorsed Boeing's bid; McNamara couldn't bring himself to trust the evidence being presented to him.

His unshakeable belief in a "single design" that would result in economies of development, production, training costs, and maintenance caused him to ignore and distrust the advice of generals and admirals who had spent perhaps thirty years of their lives gaining expertise and experience in how to prepare for and conduct armed conflicts. By choosing to disregard what they were telling him because he judged them to be inflexible and parochial, McNamara squandered years and billions of dollars in a vainglorious effort at self-justification.

And yet, as aviation expert Joe Baugher stated in his website (last revised September 2015), "After a prolonged gestation period in which many, many problems had to be identified and fixed, the F-111 turned out to be one of the most effective all-weather interdiction aircraft in the world." That comment is somewhat reminiscent of one made about the M16 by Christopher Bartocci in his February 2006 article, "The M16 in Vietnam": "With the development of this rifle in full swing after the (Ichord) hearings, troops who entered into service in late 1968 encountered little trouble and the weapon went on to become one of the most successful small arms the world has ever known."

So if the F-111 was destined to become one of the best "all-weather interdiction aircraft in the world," and if the M16 rifle was fated "to become one of the most successful small arms the world has ever known," how was it possible for McNamara's Pentagon to make so many premature, judgmental, and untested decisions about these weapons systems that handicapped America's armed forces in combat and caused the needless expenditures of lives and dollars, along with loss of confidence that our nation's leadership knew what it was doing?

To iterate some of McNamara's own words in his memoir written twenty years after he and perhaps a dozen others—LBJ, Westmoreland, Enthoven, Hitch, etc.—had caused the loss of the Vietnam War, in retrospect he was wrong, terribly wrong.

The first flight of the Air Force's F-111A took place on December 21, 1964, at the main General Dynamics plant in Fort Worth, Texas. Problems were encountered with the airplane's weight, reliability, twin Pratt & Whitney engines, and engine inlets. The Navy's version, the F-111B, fared even worse a few months later, leading to reports that the plane was very much overweight for aircraft carrier operations and was on the whole unsatisfactory for the Navy's requirements. Additionally, once fixes were attempted, the F-111B's compatibility with the Air Force version shrank from 80 percent to 30 percent. The F-111B was never placed in production, and the total cost for the "abandoned Navy F-111B" amounted to $523 million, according to the comptroller general.

There may have been some political considerations as well in the government's decision to award the TFX/F-111 contract to the General Dynamics Corporation, which was to build the airplane at its Fort Worth plant. First, the company was reportedly close to bankruptcy at the time, according to a *Fortune* magazine article which claimed that "unless it gets the contract for the joint Navy-Air Force fighter (TFX) . . . the company was down the road to receivership."

Next, John Kennedy had appointed his vice president, Lyndon Johnson, a longtime U.S. senator from Texas, as chairman of his National Aeronautics Space Council, giving Johnson a key voice in aerospace matters and decision-making. Also favoring General Dynamics, the company's president, Frank Pace, had served as secretary of the Army during the Korean War era (1950–1953).

McNamara's deputy secretary of defense, Roswell Gilpatric, had been chief counsel for General Dynamics before moving to McNamara's Pentagon. Navy secretary John Connally was, like Johnson, a native Texan, and, as mentioned earlier, was riding with Kennedy as Texas governor when both men were shot in Dallas in November 1963.

When Connally left the Pentagon in 1962 to campaign for the governorship of Texas, his replacement as secretary of the Navy was Fred Korth, a Texan from Fort Worth (where General Dynamics had its main plant). Korth's appointment came about largely because Lyndon Johnson had lobbied President Kennedy to appoint Korth to the post. Korth had served as vice president of the Continental National Bank of Fort Worth, which had loaned considerable sums to General Dynamics in the late 1950s and early 1960s during its financial difficulties. Korth resigned the Navy secretary's post in October 1963, after less than two years in the job. It had been reported in the press that Continental National Bank had been the principal source of funding for the General Dynamics plant in Fort Worth. As a consequence, Korth was forced to resign because of an apparent conflict of interest.

To conclude that General Dynamics had considerable leverage working in its behalf in the TFX competition against the Boeing Company and that Boeing faced a stacked flight deck might be a credible assumption.

In Air Force Major Reece's master's thesis, this assumption looms large. Reece says, "McNamara's decision could have been predicted. He was entirely focused and biased towards his experience with the Ford Motor Company and as an analyst of Air Force efficiency in World War II. As a lieutenant colonel he had been bullied by General LeMay, a man who was now his subordinate. He was focused on efficiency and cost savings. But most importantly, he needed to teach the services a lesson on who would make the final decision. What better avenue for making this point than the TFX, where the final decision was essentially subjective. Then the service chiefs made their recommendation, and McNamara called into question their ability to make wise choices."

(Reece's statement about bullying by LeMay derives from William W. Kaufmann's 1964 work, *The McNamara Strategy*, which is for the most part supportive of McNamara's decisions as secretary of defense. It isn't clear from either author what the circumstances were in the alleged bullying.)

In an attempt to explain Secretary McNamara's selection of General Dynamics as prime contractor, Comptroller General Elmer B. Staats testified as follows in 1970 before an investigating Senate subcommittee:

> Selection of the prime contractor for the F–111 aircraft was based on system analysis and wind tunnel testing of models rather than on actual production of hardware; that is, the competing contractors built no substantive hardware. This 'paper competition' appears to have contributed to unrealistic cost estimates by both the contractors and Air Force. This is particularly true for those system features and subsystems which involved critical unknown factors and for which there was no visible product on which to base estimated costs.

It isn't clear why Comptroller General Staats fingered the Air Force for "unrealistic cost estimates," since the Air Force had to be dragged kicking and screaming into the joint-service program. As stated by Military Analysis Network about the FTX program's failures, "This was less the fault of General Dynamics than of the civilian planners in the Pentagon whose 'cost effective' inclinations ironically produced the major aeronautical fiasco of the 1960s and a costly one at that."

Introduced into the conflict in Vietnam in 1968, a squadron of six Air Force F–111As sustained three crashes in its first fifty-five missions, all classified as accidents resulting from defective wing stabilizers. The airplane was withdrawn from combat and the flaw was remedied at a cost of $100 million. The Navy's F–111B experienced problems in its trials before the program was terminated in 1971; three test planes were lost in accidents, resulting in the deaths of four crew members. Later, however, the F–111A operated very successfully in the Desert Storm campaign, along with missions in Libya and Iraq.

As stated by GlobalSecurity.org, "Ultimately, the Air Force fielded the TFX as different variants of the F–111 at five times the planned unit cost per airframe. The aircraft never developed all the performance capabilities proposed in the original program. The problems with the TFX can be directly attributed to the restrictions and requirements imposed by the common development program."

Ray Panko, writing for the Pearl Harbor-based Pacific Aviation Museum in October 2015, said of the F–111A:

> Unfortunately, this wonderful machine had a terrible childhood filled with bad publicity. It was born in one of the most political and inept procurement debacles ever. The papers called it McNamara's folly. Costs skyrocketed out of control and the Navy version ended in expensive failure. Postmortems of the

debacle also revealed that the wing box was defectively weak and that the inlet and engine were badly matched. NASA had to step in to solve the inlet problem. Fixing the wing boxes and other structural faults cost $100 million. Although the F-111 eventually became an excellent aircraft, its initial publicity gave it an enduring bad reputation.

To what extent does the decision-making process that took place in Robert McNamara's Pentagon involving the TFX/F-111 aircraft provide insights into the flawed commitment of the AR15/XM16E1 rifle into combat in Vietnam?

The report of the Ichord Committee, as detailed in Chapters 8 and 9, is once again very instructive. First, let's take a look at the committee's final, summary recommendation, wrapping up its investigations into the M16's problems in Vietnam: "It is recommended that proper action be taken by the Secretary of Defense and the Secretary of the Army to insure that the design, contracting, procurement, manufacture, development, supply, and testing of future weapons not suffer the same fate (as the M16 rifle)."

Now let's compare that finding in 1967 with the testimony of Comptroller General Elmer B. Staats before a Senate subcommittee investigating the TFX/F-111 program in 1970: "Program costs were undoubtedly increased by an effort to procure an aircraft with a high degree of commonality to serve the needs of the Air Force and the Navy. While the Department of Defense believed that the development and production of a common aircraft could save as much as a billion dollars, I am of the opinion that the effort contributed to increased costs and to delays in development of an operational aircraft for both services."

So in much the same way that the AR15/XM16E1 was rushed into combat in Vietnam without adequate field testing, without adequate training of troops who'd be using it in combat, without provision for necessary cleaning and maintenance equipment, and without full knowledge of the consequences of using improper ammunition in the weapon, the TFX planners relied upon "system analysis" and "wind tunnel testing" rather than using real-world, actual "substantive hardware."

Both the rifle and airplane programs operated under a mantra of concurrency (i.e., speeding things along via concurrent, simultaneous actions) imposed by McNamara and his Pentagon staffers in efforts to shorten their development cycles and conserve dollars. Yet there was a quip making the rounds of the Pentagon in those days that went like this: "Concurrency is when you build it before it's designed and deploy it before it's built." There's a great deal of truth in that assertion with respect to the F-111 and M16 programs.

Because of the distrust and suspicion with which McNamara and his close circle of "whiz kids" viewed the military brass, their inclination in too many instances was to disregard the advice they'd been given by career officers. Air Force chief of staff Gen. Curtis LeMay, for example, despite aiding and abetting McNamara's preference for the AR15 by his coziness with Colt's leadership at the July 4th watermelon shootout (Chapter 1) and premature commitment by the Air Force to procure 8,500 of the still-untested rifles, was frequently feuding with McNamara and his Pentagon disciples over weapons such as the Skybolt missile and B-70 bomber, not to mention his antipathy to the joint-service TFX that would satisfy no one except McNamara himself.

Appearing on the *CBS Reports* documentary news program in September 1963, McNamara had this to say about his differences of opinion with the Air Force chief of staff and chief of naval operations:

"I think there are differences of opinion and I think these are to be expected, frankly, because in that particular instance (the TFX program) General LeMay and Admiral Anderson were looking at the problem from a somewhat narrower point of view than I was, and I think this was appropriate; that's their job. They are my military advisers, they're not my technical advisers, they're not my financial advisers. They are looking at the problem from the point of view of their individual service, and this leads to a difference in conclusion, a difference of views, and forceful presentation of views, I think, tends to shed light on the truth and this is what I am seeking."

It's difficult to overlook McNamara's arrogance in this statement, along with his apparent contempt for the narrow, limited vision of his most senior military advisors. Bear in mind that LeMay and Anderson were backed up in their Pentagon offices by hundreds of experienced—in many cases combat-experienced officers and noncommissioned officers—who provided informed input into virtually all important decisions.

To imply, as McNamara did, that he possessed a worldview far more encompassing than that of his generals and admirals—with their perceived lack of technical and financial expertise in decisions about military hardware—is fallacious. It was McNamara himself, with less than three years on the job as defense secretary at the time of his observation on *CBS Reports*, who lacked experience and who substituted what he felt was his superior vision and judgment in place of his flag officers' advice and recommendations.

When all was said and done with respect to the M16 rifle and F-111A airplane, McNamara's hubris in both instances resulted in lost time when these weapon systems might have been functioning effectively at earlier dates in the emerging war in Vietnam. Dollars were spent unproductively repairing developmental oversights that should have been detected through more rigorous testing and—in the case of the XM16E1 rifle—resulting in an untold number of American casualties who were victimized by misfiring XM16E1s and incompletely upgraded M16A1 rifles.

Not that the armed services were blameless in the blunders associated with the development of a revolutionary new rifle and a radical new airframe concept. In its final report (Chapter 9), the Ichord Committee investigating the development of the AR15/XM16E1 was extremely critical of the Army's mismanagement of the program, recommending that "the Army system of development, production, and introduction of a new weapon into the inventory should be thoroughly reviewed to determine if the rifle program is typical of the manner in which the Army operates. The manner in which the Army rifle program has been managed is unbelievable."

And, as Comptroller General Staats told the Senate subcommittee on investigations in 1970, "the concurrent production and development (of the TFX), coupled with a large number of changes throughout the process have been major contributing factors to the large cost growth and delayed delivery of the F-111 weapon system."

While it's possible that the urgency with which McNamara and his subordinates were pushing forward with both the XM16E1 and TFX developmental processes—committing both to combat roles without adequate testing under field conditions—played a role in the disastrous introductions of both weapon systems, it's also very likely that infighting and conflicts of interests were present in the development and acquisition of both.

Concerns about the awarding of the TFX/F-111 prime contractor's role to General Dynamics Corporation were discussed earlier in this chapter. In the case of the XM16E1 rifle, as pointed out in Chapters 8 and 9, the Ichord Committee determined:

- "The rifle project manager doesn't appear to have control over ammunition. Yet, the weapon system consists of both the rifle and ammunition. It is possible that internal policies and jealousies between the Army Weapons Command and the Army Munitions Command are roadblocks to the successful management of new weapons systems."
- "That it was at least unethical for Major General Lynde to accept employment with the producer of the M-16 rifle upon his retirement from the Army. General Lynde was commanding general of the Army Weapons Command throughout the negotiations for the first Army

procurement of the M-16 rifle and in fact approved the terms of the contract negotiated by his subordinates."

- "That minimum effort was expended by the Army and the Department of Defense in attempting to acquire the production rights and technical data package for the purpose of establishing additional sources for production of the M-16 rifle."

- "That based on information and records made available by the contractor and the Army, it appears that Colt's has enjoyed an excessive profit on M-16 production contracts to date . . . *'It is recommended that the General Accounting Office conduct a complete audit of Colt's military contracts to determine actual profit rates experienced, the adequacy of their accounting system and whether provisions of Public Law 87–653 were circumvented.'"*

In the final paragraph of its report, the Ichord Committee took aim at one of Secretary McNamara's cost-saving and efficiency measures: "The subcommittee recommends that the Secretary of Defense and the Secretary of the Army make adequate studies to determine if the abolishment by the Secretary of Defense of the Office of the Chief of Ordnance (which was accomplished along with the abolishment of other chiefs of various Army services in 1962) could have been partly responsible for the failure of proper control and supervision in the matter of the M-16."

One of the most profound utterances by former President and General of the Army Dwight D. Eisenhower goes: "The search for a scapegoat is the easiest of all hunting expeditions." A scapegoat, of course, derives from the Old Testament Book of Leviticus, where it was incorrectly translated in 1530 to refer to someone or something that gets the blame for others. But in the convoluted development of both the AR15/M16E1 rifle and TFX/F-111 weapon systems, there is certainly plenty of blame to go around.

After all, as a book of the New Testament takes pains to remind us, "If the trumpet give an uncertain sound, who shall prepare himself for the battle?"

The following chapter addresses the issue of why Vietnamization wasn't America's policy from the very beginning of our involvement in Vietnam.

11

WHY NOT THE ARVN?

A s early as 1962, the AR15 had been identified as a suitable weapon for South Vietnamese soldiers who confronted an enemy armed with the Soviet-bloc SKS carbine and AK47 assault rifle.

The XM16E1 was light, capable of fully automatic fire, and employed a 20-round magazine. When functioning properly, it provided firepower equivalent to that of the AK47, with a suitably lethal cartridge. The point could be made that during the 1965–1968 time frame, before the advent of several modifications, the reliability issues of the XM16E1 using the ammunition intended for combat in Vietnam rendered it less effective than either the American M2 carbine or the enemy's AK47.

This reliability issue, however, wasn't a factor in the decision not to prioritize arming the Army of the Republic of Vietnam (ARVN) soldiers with the XM16E1. Then too, getting down to basics, the issue should be how an early issue of the XM16E1 to ARVN and other Vietnamese military forces might have affected the fighting and potentially the outcome of the war. Weapons are used to fight wars, but wars are won or lost by those doing the fighting. Weapons are significantly important but nevertheless play a supporting role.

Lt. Robin Bartlett, a platoon leader with Company A, 1st Battalion, 5th Cavalry, 1st Cavalry Division (Airmobile) in 1968, relates his experience with the XM16E1:

I carried this weapon for a short time as our company conducted search and destroy missions along the DMZ from the Gulf of Tonkin to the Laotian border. I say "a short time" because I experienced all of the issues you [Duryea] enumerate. Specifically, I frequently experienced that the weapon would fail to extract. . . . The only solution was to run a cleaning rod down the barrel to push out the "stuck in chamber" cartridge casing. I always thought that the problem was a swollen cartridge casing that would fail to extract. I spoke with a Cav armorer who told me he thought the problem was in how the bores were chambered. But, of course, the problem may have been in the extractor. This event happened to me on several occasions. I recall that it happened when shooting a "mad minute." It took so long to clear the weapon that I ended up only firing one round. Then I loaded up and tried it a second time with the same result and after firing only one round. I was so concerned about the weapon's malfunctioning that I started carrying pieces of cleaning rod in my pants pocket. The weapon malfunctioned for the last time during an enemy contact where several of my troops were wounded. After that engagement I returned the weapon [XM16E1] to the battalion armorer and drew a regulation M16 [presumably an upgraded M16A1].[1]

In February 1964 Colt had advised the Army that without a new contract by May 1965, it wouldn't be able to keep its production line open. By the summer of 1965, cartridges loaded with IMR propellant were no longer being produced. With the exception of limited remaining stocks of cartridges employing the propellant for which the XM16E1 had been developed, the only ammunition available for testing or shipment to Vietnam was loaded with ball propellant, WC486. There was still a problem with this ammunition exceeding the cyclic rate of 850 rounds per minute, and the Technical Coordinating Committee refused to budge and allow a higher rate of automatic fire.

At that same time, the Army declined to renew a contract for additional XM16E1s. Fortunately, in late May 1965 the Air Force accepted a cyclic rate of fire of 900 rpm (rounds per minute) for its M16s, and ordered 65,358, an order that slipped to 36,682, but was sufficient to keep Colt in the production business.[2]

ARVN soldiers, however, were being issued the World War II–vintage M1 Garand and M2 carbine. The former fired the highly effective .30 caliber (7.62x63mm) cartridge with a muzzle velocity of 2,800 feet per second (fps) and an effective range of 500 yards but was incapable of fully automatic fire. At 11.6 pounds loaded and 24 inches in length, it was unnecessarily heavy and cumbersome for the Vietnamese, who were generally slighter physically than their American counterparts.

The M2 carbine, however, at 5.8 pounds loaded, and 35.6 inches in length, was lighter weight, easier to carry, and could be fired in the full automatic mode, but its .30 caliber (7.62x33mm) cartridge with a muzzle velocity of 1,900 fps was underpowered and had an effective range of only 300 yards. Neither weapon was as effective as the enemy's AK47. That we were entering the era of the assault rifle was just dawning on the American military mind, and thus the M2 carbine was thought to provide a satisfactory automatic rifle capability.

General Westmorland, after departing Vietnam in 1968 when his four-year tour had ended, contended that he had foreseen the desirability of equipping the ARVN with the XM16E1 as early as 1964, but that his deputy, Lt. Gen. John Throckmorton, had recommended against it because of the considerable expense involved. Westmoreland apparently went along with this recommendation at that time.

In the fall of 1965, Westmoreland renewed his request, this time for 170,000 XM16E1s (later reduced to 100,000), and at the time of the request the rifles were intended for issue to South Vietnamese forces. The request was approved by the joint chiefs of staff, but, because of the increased U.S. military buildup, these weapons were redirected to equipping U.S. forces. Secretary of Defense Robert McNamara and Army chief of staff Gen. Harold Johnson had originally planned to use the current supply of M14s for issue to U.S. forces. It took intervention by the chairman of the Senate Armed Services Committee, Richard Russell Jr. of Georgia, to oblige the SecDef and Army chief of staff to accept the reality of the assault rifle era and get the order for 100,000 XM16E1s finally approved in December, but now intended for American use.

The new order of XM16E1s assured the continued viability of Colt's production line until subsequent contracts came on line.[3] The high rate of fire, however, was still a concern, a significant factor in the malfunction problem and one which was intentionally downplayed by project manager Col. Howard Yount in order to meet assigned production schedules.

Priority was given to arming American soldiers and Marines with up-to-date equipment and weapons. American units were being armed with the XM16E1. Colt was the sole contractor, and the build-up of production facilities for the rifle—as well as contracting for adequate 5.56mm ammunition—was a logistical challenge. There would have been additional costs involved in greatly expanding contractual arrangements for XM16E1s. Only Colt was licensed to produce them. Had the Defense Department considered it a priority, America was certainly capable of coming up with weapons and ammunition in sufficient quantities for our forces, along with our Korean allies and ARVN forces.

What was missing was an adequate perception of the need. The hard fighting in the Ia Drang Valley in November 1965 was a wake-up call. In December of that year, Westmoreland decided that the XM16E1 was essential for the Vietnamese as well as for U.S. forces.[4] In March of 1967, the first allocation of XM16E1 rifles for the Vietnamese was made in response to requests from the Vietnamese government. The new rifles began arriving a month later, but there were only enough to equip Vietnamese airborne and Marine battalions as well as reserve forces.[5] When the enemy's Tet Offensive launched ten months later on January 30, 1968, it brought the matter to a head.

ARVN Lt. Gen. Dong Van Khuyen, in a 1976 monograph, commented that weapons modernization for the South Vietnamese military had become urgent as far back as 1964, when it was acknowledged that the NVA and Viet Cong were armed with superior weapons. These included the AK47 automatic rifle which, he further noted, proved more effective than the small arms provided by America and which were in use by ARVN forces. He noted that although the XM16E1 had been approved for issue to the ARVN, there were just enough for the airborne and Marine units of the general reserve. "So, during the enemy Tet offensive of 1968," his monograph read, "the crisp, rattling sounds of AK47s echoing in Saigon and some other cities seemed to make a mockery of the weaker, single shots of Garands and carbines fired by stupefied friendly troops."[6]

In the spring of 1968, the new secretary of defense, Clark Clifford, ordered a sufficient increase in M16A1 production to equip all ARVN as well as U.S. units, something that his predecessor, Robert McNamara, hadn't supported.[7] The Vietnamese went into high gear to distribute the new rifles as they were delivered to Vietnam in the spring and summer of 1968. The ARVN and their U.S. advisors conducted special training on the weapon. Technical manuals and maintenance instruction cards were translated into Vietnamese. Basic loads of 5.56mm ammunition were distributed to Vietnamese units.[8]

By January 1969, increased emphasis on ARVN development by Gen. Creighton Abrams, who had assumed command of MACV upon Westmoreland's rotation home in June 1968, along with the redirection of materiél assets, had begun to improve the effectiveness of the Vietnamese military. Secretary of Defense Melvin Laird coined the catchy term "Vietnamization," and President Richard Nixon adopted the name to indicate that the war in Vietnam was belatedly transitioning to the Vietnamese people.

Vietnamization was a two-part program. First, improve the training and capability of the South Vietnamese military so that American forces could return to an advisory mode. U.S. combat forces would withdraw as the Vietnamese assumed the major combat role. The ARVN would do the heavy fighting and establish security in cities, towns, and countryside. America would continue to provide tactical and strategic air support, but the Vietnamese would be trained to fly helicopters in support of ground operations. (With the required English language training this entailed, it would take two years to train Vietnamese pilots; time we didn't have.) Second, maintain the security with Regional Forces (RF) and Popular Forces (PF) and improve the management and economy of the rural population in areas secured, and to be secured, by major ARVN military operations. In other words, what we call "nation building."

In revolutionary warfare, the reality of a "liberated area" is doubtful. A general rule of thumb in this kind of struggle is that the insurgents or revolutionaries will avoid confrontation with stronger military forces but will continue to communicate and interact with the population, even in nominally secure areas. They organize the inhabitants of hamlets and villages into social and economic groups, reinforcing their authority at night when governmental security is lax and often absent. Thus, revolutionaries generally retain the initiative, a prized military principle. When MACV claimed to have the initiative in South Vietnam, it was avoiding reality.

This was a serious failure of perception and a misunderstanding of what constitutes the initiative in a revolutionary war environment. To insist upon having the initiative in such circumstances is to pander to expectations and as such is a professional character flaw. This is the same character deficiency that moves commanders to report the news they believe will least damage their careers. Any suggestion of a cover-up of any type—human-rights violations, enemy strength and casualty figures, enemy morale—is an immediate indicator that a little more forceful command guidance is called for. There were too many troubling instances of this in Vietnam.

Note that the legal ground rules for combat such as the Geneva Conventions are merely a codification of ethical principles. Americans tend to be very focused on law but too often fail to see the forest for the trees. Issues of ethical conduct weren't adequately addressed in all-too-many American combat units in Vietnam. The training military personnel received on the Geneva Conventions and in-country orientation on the rules of engagement governing combat operations was considered adequate. This was simply not the case.

American military personnel are basically inclined to conduct themselves in a manner of which we all may be proud. However, under the extreme pressure of fighting a dangerous war under very primitive conditions, patterns of behavior change. Americans unfortunate enough to be captured in Vietnam were usually executed by the enemy. When a platoon was overrun—a rarity— wounded men were stripped of clothing, boots, and weapons, and bayonetted or shot. The understandable tendency, if unchecked, was for American soldiers to treat enemy prisoners in an equally harsh manner. Lacking specific command attention, bad things will take place, such as abuses by Col. David Hackworth's platoon-sized Tiger Force, organized in November 1965 to "outguerrilla the guerrillas" and which committed atrocities on a scale equivalent to the enemy.

When prisoners are abused and sometimes made to "disappear," the fault lies almost exclusively with failures of leadership. For every young soldier involved in some atrocity there is a chain of failure reaching up into senior leadership. Specifically, every soldier must be personally advised of the types of conduct that won't be tolerated. It is the responsibility of all officers and noncommissioned officers to make certain that the rules are understood and complied with. It is the direct responsibility of commanding officers, particularly those most senior, to follow through by personally confirming that every man with a rifle has been informed of the prescribed rules of behavior and engagement. This means visits to units in the field by battalion, brigade, and division commanders to talk with the men and ensure that standards of conduct are clear and that the chain of command is working. Rape, pillage, and murder—extremes of unethical conduct—are never acceptable. The March 1968 massacres at My Lai by an Americal Division rifle platoon under the command of Lt. William Calley Jr. were reprehensible and discredited the work being done in Vietnam at that time by half a million other American servicemen.

Acceptance and tolerance of any form of such conduct undermines the chain of command, undercuts the ability of leaders to lead, and directly contributes to psychological problems when troops return home. There is such a thing as moral superiority, and it is earned with good leadership and proper conduct in the management of violence.

Americans are proficient at organizational planning and material support for nation building despite our ingrained reluctance to take responsibility for such time-consuming and expensive initiatives. There are two interrelated challenges: keeping the enemy away from the population, a very difficult mission; and elimination of the corruption that undermines every attempt to establish confidence in and support for governmental authority and administration. However, we are seldom up to committing the political capital necessary to eliminate or seriously reduce corruption, which very seriously undermines our effectiveness. The very people upon whom we depend for implementation of our developmental plans often have their hands in the cash register. Lacking a firm lock on corruption, security is all but impossible to achieve. The people remain indifferent to the government or become openly supportive of the insurgents.

Given the American public's growing disenchantment with the progress and conduct of the Vietnam War, particularly after the unanticipated intensity of the North Vietnamese/Viet Cong Tet Offensive in the opening months of 1968, our government belatedly came to the realization that ongoing U.S. military and logistical support would be required, but that the South Vietnamese would have to do the bulk of the heavy lifting if the war was to be satisfactorily concluded.

With the end of the U.S. buildup, MACV could support a series of improvement and modernization programs.[9] There was a reprioritization of all training and material resources that now addressed the needs of ARVN, together with Regional and Popular Forces. Had our nation adequately resourced both American and Vietnamese forces from the war's outset, it would ultimately have proven to be less expensive in lives and dollars and would have offered a better chance of success.

On the other hand, shortcomings in other areas such as conceptual planning, training of our military personnel, truthfulness with the American public in outlining our strategic goals in Southeast Asia, and insufficient American resolve to stay the course would ultimately have led—in all probability—to the same doomed outcome.

Ultimate political success depends upon more than battlefield success. A battlefield win may be a political loss, as in the case of Tet, for the United States and South Vietnam. A loss in the fight may be a political victory. Tet again for the North Vietnamese. This is a primary consideration in revolutionary warfare.

A battlefield win depends upon more than the type of rifle carried by either side. As always, the key to military and ultimately political success depends upon leadership. Maj. Gen. Richard M. Lee, deputy senior advisor in II Corps Tactical Zone in 1966–1967, stated the situation clearly.

> The problem was not a lack of knowledge or training facilities to do the job expertly, but a disinclination of many ARVN officers to take the time and effort to train their troops carefully and thoroughly. The Vietnamese had been intermittently at war since World War II with only an occasional respite; many ARVN officers looked at the war as a long pull rather than on a one-year basis, as we Americans tended to see our personal contributions. They tended to take the weekends off. They were not inclined to go in for the intensive training methods that the U.S. forces were accustomed to at that time.[10]

Additional observations were that many physicians in Vietnamese military hospitals took weekends off. ARVN officers often hesitated or failed to follow orders they believed would put their soldiers at risk, even when the risk was perceptibly minimal. It's also common in underdeveloped militaries for officers to avoid issuing orders they believe their soldiers may refuse to obey. The truly aggressive Vietnamese officers and noncommissioned officers, the ones whose aggressive spirit appealed to their American advisors, tended to get killed. They went into battle with grace and spirit, but they were not invulnerable and the constant frontline exposure all-too-often caught up with them.

In 1965, the choice of which rifle was to be issued to the Vietnamese military—ARVN, RF, and PF—was an important but relatively minor component of any plan for South Vietnamese military success. Simply supplying XM16E1 rifles and its follow-on M16A1 to the Vietnamese would have been an intelligent move but wouldn't have affected the war's eventual outcome very greatly without a consequent major change in America's type of commitment and its duration.

Vietnamization was the restructuring of prioritization that addressed the nature of the struggle, but it took place belatedly and without a simultaneous commitment to see the struggle in the Republic of Vietnam result in a successful military and political conclusion. The Tet Offensive undermined any public confidence in the United States in the real military progress that was in the making. American political support was fading when it was needed most urgently.

This was largely a failure of the American military and civilian leadership in the White House, the Pentagon, MACV headquarters, and on the battlefield, resulting in inadequate intelligence about the enemy, together with a continuing failure to appreciate his commitment and overly optimistic assessments of the situation. McNamara's emphasis on enemy body counts as a measure of battlefield progress led to inflated reports from field commanders, inaccurate reporting by many members of the news media, and ultimately to a loss of support for the war in all-too-many American living rooms. The North Vietnamese, with more at stake than Americans, benefitted from a correspondingly greater political resolve. The South Vietnamese military commitment, with everything at stake, lacked the leadership and determination to indoctrinate, motivate, and lead their troops.

One wonders in retrospect why Vietnamization wasn't America's policy from the very outset of the war. The answer is plain enough. In the early 1960s we were still dealing with our World War II experience (1941–1945) and the more recent limited war in Korea (1950–1953). We were just beginning to think about limited war and low-intensity conflict and how it related to our national interests, how we could protect those interests while limiting cost and risk. Our failure to appreciate the planning and commitment essential in any counterinsurgency or counterrevolutionary role was a serious philosophical deficiency. The Chinese Communist Revolution should have alerted us to what we might expect. The failed French experience in Indochina was another lesson we all but ignored.

We confronted an enemy in Vietnam whose military philosophy had its roots in Sun Tzu, whose leaders, Ho Chi Minh and Vo Nguyen Giap, were far advanced in their understanding of the strategy, operational art, and tactics that would ultimately succeed in Vietnam. They focused their talent and energy on winning. To be sure, they had their differences of opinion. Giap was the more aggressive, but together their leadership was far superior to that of the South Vietnamese, many of whose civilian and military leaders were very corrupt, and who jockeyed for position and power. This undermined the effort of improving the Vietnamese military and restoring order to governing the countryside.

America entered the conflict in Vietnam with the best of intentions, but with its leaders focused on conventional wars of the recent past and forgetful of the American experience with past counterinsurgency efforts. The Marines in Vietnam were more perceptive of the need to focus on the population, but General Westmoreland envisioned a war of attrition in the mountains and jungles. This is a viable concept only when one has more stomach for casualties than the enemy. Attrition is a last choice as strategy. The decisive battle was political.

In Vietnam, attrition was a recipe for failure. A generally reliable rule of thumb in a revolutionary environment is that the revolutionaries can and will replace any losses they incur. In revolutionary war, intent—backed by will and spirit with a strong philosophical underpinning—will usually wear down logistical and technical superiority. Popular support is the center of gravity in revolutionary war, and the populace is more responsive to political conviction as expressed by idealistic revolutionaries than to an indifferent military presence by government soldiers, often absent at night when the insurgents are most active.

It's not surprising that General Westmoreland didn't initially emphasize the upgrading, training, and development of the ARVN. He went to Vietnam in January 1964 and became deputy commander of MACV, taking command that June. With his successful professional military experience, it's understandable that he immediately identified the incomparably superior capabilities of

American forces compared with those of the South Vietnamese. He thus began to plan for what he thought would be a reasonably rapid and secure ascendancy over the Viet Cong and NVA, the latter not yet active participants in the fighting. He fixated on equipping his American forces with the latest equipment, downplaying the role of the South Vietnamese and consigning them to what he believed to be an easier role: securing the population in liberated areas.

This role, Westmoreland believed, was equally as important as confronting North Vietnamese regulars in the mountains and jungles. As Viet Cong activity increased, it ultimately became even more important and was the critical element for ultimate success. It was the easier role in terms of violence and risk, but in fact a very difficult one, as even very limited insurgent activity compromises areas often defined as "liberated." The South Vietnamese military and civil administration wasn't indoctrinated, trained, or equipped to successfully establish a satisfactory state of security and development in the countryside.

Once upon a time an almost unlimited amount of force might have been used to achieve a military objective. North Vietnam could have been destroyed and defeated, and Westmoreland could have effectively led such an effort. Our objectives in Vietnam, however, were limited. The force we employed was to be limited. Westmoreland almost certainly had read and had studied Karl Von Clausewitz, who theorized and taught and clearly explained that the force necessary to achieve a political objective corresponds to a certain limit of risk, expense, and pain to achieve that objective. Westmoreland incorrectly underestimated the necessary force. National interests determined acceptable risk, expense, and pain, and limited the time and amount of force he would be allocated. His estimate of the situation was flawed and doomed to failure. He failed to understand revolutionary war, with its deep roots in Chinese history. There is a smooth flow of revolutionary protocol from Sun Tzu through the years to the 20th century and present-day revolutionary practice. Mao Tse-tung, Ho Chi Minh, and Vo Nguyen Giap were all apt students, and the Vietnamese revolutionaries indoctrinated and motivated their soldiers accordingly.

Training and equipping a force is insufficient. Our training of foreign militaries generally ignores indoctrination, a mistake that leads to predictably poor results. Indoctrination in this context doesn't imply any form of coercive "brainwashing," but rather the development of a sense of virtue, courage, and duty that is the basis of all successful military organizations. It is a Spartan quality and at the heart of unit cohesion and the willingness to confront any danger. Without it, commanders, knowing their soldiers, will minimize confronting the enemy, and the troops will break for the rear when the shooting gets serious.

Time is needed to rid the military of corruption and deadweight leaders. A sense of national purpose is essential. We downplay indoctrination in our own military training and focus on discipline and military skills. Traditionally, Americans come to the table already "indoctrinated." In Vietnam, however, only the North adequately indoctrinated its fighters. For the South Vietnamese, it was a work in progress—incomplete and inadequately emphasized by the Americans. Indoctrination takes time. That's why it usually requires a full military generation—as much as fifteen to twenty years—to bring a Third World military organization up to speed. Even then, continuing attention and support are imperative.

Americans can do a satisfactory job of training and equipping those we seek to support; in fact, we did a fair job of it in Vietnam. We left the South Vietnamese, however, with the mission only half accomplished. With the political unwillingness to take the war north of the DMZ and into North Vietnam, we needed several more years and greater efforts on indoctrination to bring the ARVN up to necessary levels of professionalism.

In most Third World militaries, the "Old Guard" corrupts the younger officers being trained. Effective change occurs slowly and begins to take hold as the older senior officers retire or are forced out of the system. Many of them are involved in competitive struggles for power, political squabbling, are often inept, and many are corrupt. This was the situation in Vietnam.

Were William Westmoreland to have appreciated—and he failed to—the type of war he was waging, he would have understood that, given the constraints under which he was obliged to operate, only the South Vietnamese could ultimately win that war. To bring the ARVN up to the level of professional competence to meet and defeat the threat would be a very lengthy process. Such a course of action simply didn't accord with the personality of an aggressive American military leader forged in the epic battles of World War II and later in Korea.

This attitude wasn't unique to Westmoreland. He was an exceptionally competent officer, carefully selected for the task in Vietnam. It was simply a type of war in which very few officers were competent, and almost none at senior levels, with the possible exception of Gen. Creighton Abrams Jr., who supplanted Westmoreland as COMUSMACV in 1968, and Gen. Fred Weyand, who was the final MACV commander. Military professionals who specialized in limited war and counterinsurgency—revolutionary war to be more precise—didn't prosper professionally and failed to rise to the top of their armed services.

Vietnamization was a form of counterinsurgency (or counterrevolutionary) struggle involving all the elements of power: political, economic, military, diplomatic, and informational. Successful counterinsurgencies must include "nation building," but this requires a long-term commitment. The rules for revolutionary struggle are essentially the same for both sides, although governments are held to higher standards of conduct than revolutionaries, thus one more "reason," beyond the ethical, for emphasis on human rights.

In the Vietnamese environment, success depended on the Vietnamese, but the time needed to indoctrinate, reform, and train an inefficient military dependent on an inefficient bureaucracy required more years than our declining will and commitment could furnish. The process of preparing a challenged country for revolutionary struggle must begin as soon as the decision to commit is made. The first order of business is to come to an elemental understanding with whomever we intend to support that our commitment depends upon their putting an end to corruption, irrespective of how uncharacteristic to them and incomprehensible to them this may be. Eliminating corruption, both at the political and military levels, is essential. Failing this, any commitment must be reevaluated. Corruption destroys a military.

The American attitude that it is simply "the way they do things in that part of the world," together with our unwillingness to invest the necessary political capital to clean up the mess, reduces significantly the likelihood of success. Tragically, there was just such an insufficient commitment to reduce and eliminate the corruption endemic to South Vietnam.

When the American military assumed the major fighting burden, the incentive was reduced for South Vietnamese forces to hone their fighting skills. When they did conduct major operations, they depended on Americans to provide much of their support: intelligence, equipment, maintenance, transportation, indirect fire, communications, medical evacuation, and back-up in the event of heavy contact. There were high-quality Vietnamese units with courageous officers and soldiers, but too many fell short of the essential standards for success.

Arming the ARVN with heavy, vintage M1 rifles and minimally adequate M2 carbines was a real downer when they engaged Viet Cong and particularly better-armed NVA regulars. This was just one small but important failure of the larger conceptual shortfall. The failure to immediately upgrade the equipment of the Republic of Vietnam military, including providing the ARVN with the latest and best infantry rifle, was simply a fallout of the failure to understand the nature of the war in Vietnam.

More than just the material assistance the Americans furnished was the moral and political support. The American presence in such circumstances constitutes the backbone of the resistance. Remove it before the rebuild is complete and the force will gamely struggle for a while and then collapse under the weight of its own ineptitude and inefficiency. No amount of training and equipment can offset corruption, lack of motivation, and self-interest. That is the reason the process of upgrading any ineffective foreign military organization is a long-term undertaking which demands sufficient political capital to force institutional change.

In Vietnam, this failed to happen, and the outcome was probably inevitable.

The following two chapters summarize each author's comments on the history of the M16 family of weapons, the introduction of the XM16E1 and the M16A1 into Vietnam, and some of the political issues involved.

12

THE RIFLE, POLITICS, THE AFTERMATH

by Lyman Duryea

Author's Commentary

The M16 represented a new concept of arming the American infantryman and Marine with an individual weapon capable of full automatic fire. Early testing and evaluation of different calibers and employing a squad armed with fully automatic weapons established the superior effectiveness of high-velocity smaller calibers over the standard .30 caliber military round employed by the standard eleven-man infantry squad with two automatic riflemen. In the early 1960s the "assault rifle" concept was still on the horizon in U.S. military thinking, although it was appreciated and implemented as early as the latter years of World War II by the Germans, picked up by the Soviets, and effectively used again by the North Koreans and Chinese in the Korean War, and subsequently by the North Vietnamese Army in Vietnam.

An assault rifle is employed in either the semi-automatic or fully automatic mode according to a given situation. In close quarters and sudden confrontations, fully automatic fire is more effective than hastily aimed semi-automatic fire. For various reasons—tradition, cost, reluctance to introduce a new caliber, availability of standard weapons and ammunition, parts on hand, NATO acceptance (after much pushing) of the 7.62mm cartridge, as well as stubborn in-house support of the M14 rifle, the U.S. military did not participate in the initial design and engineering of a smaller-caliber rifle, to say nothing of an assault rifle. Because of this, the AR15/M16 was developed by outsiders.

The German Sturmgewher (STG) 43 and 44, in 1944, marked the start of a design that would reduce muzzle climb by employing a lower-caliber cartridge and by moving the gas tube over the barrel. Kalashnikov continued that thought. Stoner straightened out the stock to further reduce muzzle climb, and made a much lighter rifle by employing "space-age" materials (plastic and aluminum) to accomplish that reduction, while the Germans and Soviets continued on with steel and wood. Stoner's main design innovation is the direct impingement system, whereas the AK and STG both have pistons. This further reduced the weight of the system and resulted in a rifle that was easier to control in the fully automatic mode.

The initial prototype of what would ultimately be the AR15 was the AR10, a rifle that fired the standard 7.62mm round. It did not take advantage of smaller, higher-velocity cartridges and the even lighter weight that could be achieved. It was, however, a first step on the road to an assault rifle, and a big one. At this point the military, recognizing the viability of the AR10 design and responding to earlier tests of high-velocity, smaller-caliber cartridges nudged Stoner to design a version of the AR10 that would employ the lower-caliber 5.56mm round.

What was missing was the expertise and experience of the military establishment that would have assured, from the beginning, compatibility of weapon and ammunition and other standard military requirements such as chroming the chamber, learned the hard way by corrosion in the South Pacific during WWII. There would have been extensive testing of the 5.56mm cartridge, a new caliber for the U.S. military, to determine velocity and cartridge weight and dimensions consistent with effective range and lethality in conjunction with rifling twist, chamber pressure and tolerances, cartridge case hardness, type of propellant, and other engineering considerations. Such tests as were conducted produced a reliable rifle, the AR15, before the military changed the propellant and before the rifle encountered extended use in the harsh conditions of Vietnam.

The AR15 functioned well with the ammunition for which it had been designed. In early evaluations in Vietnam the AR15 validated its superiority over then-standard U.S. weapons, the M14 and M14E2 (firing the 7.62 x 51mm round) as well as the .30 caliber M1 and M2 carbines (firing the 7.62 x 33mm round). But these evaluations were conducted employing the ammunition for which the rifle had been designed.

Several factors came into play that collectively burdened the infantryman with an individual weapon that consistently malfunctioned. As the AR15 and the 5.56mm or .22 caliber cartridge threatened ascendancy over the M14, the office of the Chief of Ordnance aggressively promoted the M14 and thwarted early focus on the AR15. Those in the military who were looking ahead to what they believed would come on line to replace the reliance on the M14 in the reasonably near future looked to a revolutionary new individual weapon, the Special Purpose Individual Weapon. They considered the AR15, at best, to be an interim weapon, and so failed to address engineering issues. The SPIW would come to naught. A good look at early prototypes should have revealed its limitations. If soldiers or Marines were not impressed by the lightweight XM16E1, the "black rifle," that seemed to some to be a toy compared to the M14, they would have been severely disconcerted by the prototype SPIW.

The services opted to accept ball propellant (the standard military propellant; lots of it on hand; easier, less hazardous, and less expensive to produce) for the 5.56 x 45mm cartridge as an acceptable replacement for the IMR propellant for which the AR15/XM16E1 had been engineered. The Army, responsible for contracting for procurement of both the rifle and its ammunition, carelessly accepted the use of ball propellant following insufficient and inadequate comparative evaluations when ammunition contractors couldn't economically regulate chamber pressure consistent with the required velocity to achieve an effective range of 500 yards when using IMR propellant.

These were problems that would normally have been resolved long before a weapon was standardized and issued to troops in combat. The thinking was to modify the rifle rather than to go back to ammunition that worked. This meant piecemeal modifications that were ongoing even as the XM16E1 was re-standardized as the M16A1, and as it continued to fail soldiers and Marines in the field in its developmental configurations.

Secretary of Defense Robert McNamara, tiring of the Army's slow response to improve and hasten to the front whatever version of the M16 and ammunition was available, pushed for production faster than the military could adequately evaluate and correct functional problems. In this haste, quality control in the M16 production line at Colt was lax, a probable further contributor to problems in the field.

The Army was unexplainably slow in developing a maintenance package that would ultimately include maintenance instructions and 5.56mm cleaning equipment, and even then, there was some inconsistency in what was issued to front-line troops.

The foregoing may be attributed to lack of foresight, haste, frugality, impatience, jealousy, tradition, pride, carelessness, and incompetence, complemented by some ethically gray or at least poorly considered decisions. In short, imperfect people, under cost and schedule pressures attempting to do their jobs. On the plus side, we joined the rest of the professional military world in opting for an assault rifle.

On the dark side, Colt continued to test its weapons, according to military and contract protocols (inadequate though they were), using ammunition employing IMR propellant. They did this with the Army's connivance, both Colt and the Army well aware that rifles coming off the production line would fail to pass acceptance tests if they were tested using ball ammunition loaded with the standard ball propellant. The ammunition available to the troops in Vietnam, with some very limited exceptions, was loaded with ball propellant, the underlying cause of high malfunction rates in the field. Colt and Army decision-makers were thus directly complicit in an unknown number of Americans killed in close combat, one of whom was my first KIA as company commander.

Further complicit in unethical or at least unprofessional behavior were those senior commanders (both Marine and Army) in Vietnam who insisted that the malfunctions were the result of poor weapon maintenance by troops. That was an inexcusable professional lapse, and indicates that commanders were out of touch with their men and the reality of the situation. It delayed resolution of the problem and contributed to additional U.S. casualties.

When inspectors from the Army and from Colt came to Vietnam to investigate the mounting and no longer concealable problems with the XM16E1, they too blamed the poor rifle performance on inadequate troop maintenance. Poor maintenance may have played a role in some cases (how could it not, when 5.56mm cleaning equipment was unavailable?), but the basic problem was the incompatibility of the rifle/ammunition combination. These investigations brought a glimmer of light to the problem, but the general reaction of most (not all) of the inspectors was self-serving. Both the Army and Colt were doing their best to avoid responsibility and blame. Some of the inspectors were well-intentioned and simply unaware of the active connivance to keep production moving in spite of problems. Others surely knew what was going on and hoped to preserve their careers.

The Ichord congressional hearings and investigations finally brought to light the crux of the matter. In Vietnam, the congressional investigating team still encountered some commanders who attempted to mislead them, insisting that the problems arose from poor maintenance. One can only imagine why. No one was held accountable for the engineering and production shortcuts and failures or for the intentional cover-ups.

To sum up the picture of the AR15, the M16, the XM16E1 and the M16A1 in Vietnam, the Air Force welcomed the AR15/M16. The Army and

Marines accepted, with some reluctance, a 5.56mm primary infantry weapon. Early testing demonstrated that some caliber smaller than 7.62mm would be the caliber of the future, and this for reasons of weight and lethality. It complemented design and function when employed in an assault rifle.

We lagged behind more thoughtful and perceptive weapon innovators in Germany and the Soviet Union, pioneers in the assault rifle concept. China, North Korea, and North Vietnam were on board early in the game. When we ultimately concluded that 5.56mm was the way to go, and the assault rifle was the best configuration, McNamara and his crew ignored known developmental protocols to get the rifle into volume production. That was the way they erroneously perceived their mission. There was no good excuse for taking shortcuts, but the military, again, was largely responsible for the problems by not having either vision (early on) or, when the die was cast, the courage to demand that developmental protocols be followed. Military decision makers who knew better failed to hold the line, and troop welfare and success on the battlefield were at issue.

The birth of a reliably functioning M16 rifle for military use is a case study of institutional conflicts—political, commercial, and military. The military will always confront civilians in power positions who can make or break careers. It is the professional responsibility of military leaders to insist upon a correct course of action where lives are at stake. There were character shortcomings evident in leadership and management, production oversight, and command awareness in the field. Some military professionals had strayed from the straight path on their way to senior leadership and decision-making status. To be fair, some of them were unaware of their own shortcomings as they followed paths of least resistance. There is enough friction in war without an excess of self-interest and careerism. We must hold ourselves to higher standards. We were, and are, and must prepare ourselves to be the experts in the use of force. We have the guideline of "duty," and duty, an unforgiving mistress, does not tolerate quibbling or deceit.

Politicians march to a different drummer and respond to popular pressure. The industrial complex and its many manufacturers and producers of weapons and equipment of all types for the military are focused on profit. Lawyers in all three camps get into niceties that confound good decision making. Production challenges get wrapped up in contract legalities and issues—to the detriment of production and ultimately function in the case of the M16 rifle in its various developmental configurations.

While inviting and exploiting out-of-the box ideas, suggestions, and innovations, the guidelines and leadership in design and development as well as oversight of the production of military hardware should come from those in uniform or with extensive military experience. Politics and careerism are inappropriate in this arena.

I served a second year, August 1968 to August 1969, as a district senior advisor in the Mekong Delta area in the southern part of South Vietnam. The situation in August 1968 wasn't optimistic. The district capital, Phong Dien, had been overrun a few months earlier during the NVA/VC Tet Offensive. During the course of that year, the Vietnamese endured casualties on a daily basis, mostly trip-wired dud 105mm artillery rounds. On one occasion we were in a boat convoy that was ambushed effectively by the Viet Cong, with the RF and PF troopers suffering heavy casualties. For several months the district capital was routinely mortared, several times a week, at any hour of the day or night.

The situation began to change in early 1969. Phong Dien had been selected for special developmental assistance during the Vietnamization program. An ARVN regiment was assigned to the province. The mortar attacks stopped. Within six or seven months the ARVN, RF, and PF troops secured the district and presumably most of the province. With U.S. support, the Vietnamese revitalized the local economy—various developmental projects including markets, fish ponds, flocks of ducks, and other economic initiatives began to flourish. This was remarkable progress.

Had such developmental support continued, and were it country-wide, and had we continued to provide air cover and technical and logistical support, and had we also zeroed in on continuing Vietnamese dysfunctional political issues, corruption in particular, we might have been on the path to success. However, that was not the path taken.

In August 1972 with the Vietnamese doing the heavy lifting, the last U.S. Army combat unit, the 1st Battalion, 7th Cavalry, Bob Orkand's old outfit, left Vietnam. Then, with political trouble at home, we didn't provide the support we'd promised to the South Vietnamese military establishment, which wasn't ready to go it alone. Rebuilding a damaged country with a developing military is a generations-long task. We quit the war, abandoned our allies, and hung some very fine people who depended on us out to dry. I'm still embarrassed.

By 1968 the strains of anti-war sentiment and social conflict in the States were beginning to insinuate themselves into the military. That was no excuse for indiscipline. I relieved several American advisors for cowardice when they refused to accompany RF and PF night ambushes, basically small security outposts that were accustomed to returning early when they tired or became chilled. Plotted on province operational maps as present and in position all night, they in fact were back "home" before midnight. This was surely one of the reasons that the district had been overrun during Tet. When an advisor accompanied these "ambushes," they could be coaxed or coerced into staying in position all night. The risk to this particular mobile advisory team would have been very minimal. After a week of counseling them with little effect, I arrived at their post and ordered them to accompany me and the ambush patrol. They refused. My boss, the province senior advisor, a decent gentleman, would not court-martial them. That was an early indication of the problem—avoidance. It was a continuation of similar problems where the easy path was to avoid rocking the boat.

Following another overseas tour, I returned to the States in 1972. I was assigned to an armored battalion in the 1st Infantry Division at Fort Riley, Kansas. In the division, indiscipline, substance abuse, and racial conflict were everywhere evident. Good leadership was in short supply. Many good officers were dismissed from the service as part of a reduction in force. This particularly affected those helicopter pilots, captains now, who had survived the risk of flying through enemy ground fire but hadn't completed college prior to service. Morale among officers was poor. Many made little effort to maintain discipline or set an example. The division headquarters conducted an active informational program to impress higher headquarters, but little effort to take care of the troops.

The division headquarters covered up racial incidents. Headquarters was bloated. Field grade officers made decisions that should have been made by junior officers. Junction City, adjacent to Fort Riley, maintained racially segregated drinking establishments. These were "private" clubs, and segregation was at the option of the club owner. The division commander should have put the whole city "off limits" until all soldiers were treated equally. Such negligence doesn't go unnoticed by the soldiers. Black soldiers in effect then took over the enlisted club. In those units where the leadership was good, there were very few problems and morale remained high. Contrary to what some imagined, there was nothing wrong with the men. The problem was one of leadership. The laxity that produced the XM16E1 issues ultimately led to a grave weakening of discipline and breakdown of morale. It is always the leaders who are responsible, for better or worse.

American fighting men and women measure up to high standards. Soldiers and Marines, those actually in the fight, move to the sound of the guns. They hold the pass. They, as Spartans before them, are faithful to their laws. There is no room for a careless commitment to war, or any misunderstanding of what war demands. It is the stay-at-homes that decide for war. It is those-who-avoid-service that make go-to-war decisions, who send the young sons and daughters of farmers and truck drivers, ghetto kids and Appalachian youngsters off to become heroes. These young people never fail them. It seems always to be old men who send the young off to battle. These young people are the betters of those who send them into the fray.

13

"WHEN WILL THEY EVER LEARN?"

by Bob Orkand

Author's Commentary

The telephone rang around 2 a.m. at the rooming house in Arlington, Virginia, where I was boarding with three other men while awaiting my wife's decision about relocating from our house in Columbus, Georgia, to Northern Virginia.

A few months earlier, I'd been assigned to the Pentagon after eighteen months in command of an all-volunteer, 1,000-man mechanized infantry battalion at Fort Benning, Georgia—part of the Army's prototype VOLAR (Volunteer Army) unit, the 197th Infantry Brigade.

My boss at OCINFO (Office of the Chief of Information), Colonel Rolf Utegaard, was on the line at that early-morning hour of Wednesday, September 4, 1974. "Bob," he began without preamble, "Abe died a short while ago. I need you to get to the office and make the call-out. Do you need any help?"

Army Chief of Staff General Creighton W. Abrams Jr. had been in and out of Walter Reed (Walter Reed National Military Medical Center) for several months and, anticipating that he wasn't likely to recover, we'd assembled a preliminary press release about his death. I had in "the can," as we termed it, a brief biography of Abe, a statement from defense secretary James R. Schlesinger about the enormous significance of this man to his nation ever since World War II, all preceded by an official notice where I'd filled in the date and hour blanks before beginning my telephone call-out to the major news media.

Later that day, an Army General Order was issued, reading: "The death of General Creighton Williams Abrams, Chief of Staff, United States Army, which occurred on 4 September 1974 at 0035 hours, is announced with deep regret." Our announcement noted that his death resulted from "complications that developed during recovery from surgical removal of his cancerous lung" on June 6. (We might have added, but didn't, that the removal of Abe's cancerous left lung had taken place on the thirtieth anniversary of D-Day.)

And so, just ten days before what would have been his sixtieth birthday, Abe—very likely the U.S. Army's greatest combat leader in World War II as commander of Lt. Gen. George S. Patton's lead tank battalion in the campaigns across Western Europe—became the first Army chief of staff to die in office.

Armed with the file we'd prepared in advance and which had been scrutinized and approved all the way up to Army secretary Howard "Bo" Callaway of Georgia, to whom we in OCINFO reported, I began my media call-out. One at a time, I read the Army's official announcement to late-night/early-morning news desk staffers at *The Washington Post, New York Times*, Associated Press, UPI (United Press International), the major TV networks, and so on. (Some in the media apparently taped me and later in the day an old comrade from Vietnam phoned from California to let me know he'd heard my voice way out west.)

Sometime around 4:15 a.m., as I recall, I finished my call-out and went out to my car to retrieve my shaving kit (razor, toothbrush, hair brush, etc.), which I'd left in the car when I sped in uniform into the OCINFO offices in the Pentagon's E ring. In my haste to begin the call-out, I'd deliberately parked my POV (privately owned vehicle) in a VIP parking space near the Pentagon's privileged Mall Entrance, reserved for high-ranking military and civilian brass who worked in the Pentagon.

As I went to my car to pick up my shaving kit and move my POV to a less prestigious parking space, I couldn't help but notice a small piece of cardboard stuck under one of my windshield wipers. It was in fact a parking ticket, written during the several hours that I'd been hard at work informing the American public that one of the greatest soldiers of this or any generation had died.

I crumpled up the parking ticket, tossed it on the car's floor mat, and—as I carried my shaving kit into the Pentagon through a lesser entrance—decided that I would after all retire from the Army and accept employment with a large newspaper organization known as Knight Newspapers (which later became Knight Ridder, at one time the largest newspaper company in America in terms of daily circulation and which later sold itself to another newspaper organization in 2006 and doesn't exist anymore).

Six weeks later, wearing a business suit newly purchased in the Pentagon's shopping mall, I began work at the *Miami Herald*, Knight Newspapers' flagship daily paper. A parking ticket for letting everyone know that the man of whom George Patton once immodestly said, "I'm supposed to be the best tank commander in the Army, but I have one peer: Abe Abrams. He's the world's champion," had passed into history? Bah!

The illness and subsequent death of General Creighton Abrams had begun in April 1974, when Abe as Army chief of staff was on an inspection visit to Army units in USAEUR (U.S. Army Europe). After its post-Vietnam malaise (as my colleague and co-author Col. Lyman Duryea reports in Chapter 12), the Army under Abrams's leadership was on the rebound, moving slowly but successfully from a draft-based force to an all-volunteer Army, with forward momentum in training, discipline and—most importantly—re-energized leadership at all levels of command because of Creighton Abrams's willpower and persistence.

In France and headed for Turkey, Abe began experiencing chills and exhaustion. It was time to cancel the rest of the trip and head home to Washington, to his devoted wife, Julia, and to the medics at Walter Reed.

As instructed, I issued a press release that the Army's chief of staff had been admitted to Walter Reed with pneumonia. (I'd been designated as the action officer on Abrams's illness in the public information division of OCINFO.) A few days later, Abe returned to duty in the Pentagon, spending part of each day at his desk, and seemingly improving in health. But then he sickened once again, was readmitted to Walter Reed, and I announced a recurrence of his "pneumonia."

But this ploy failed to satisfy Fred Hoffman of the Associated Press, dean of the Pentagon press corps and later a Pentagon spokesman as assistant secretary of defense for public affairs. "What's going on?" he grilled me over the phone, questioning the second bout of "pneumonia." "That's not a normal pneumonia pattern."

My contact at Walter Reed was a very fine civilian PIO (public information officer), Pete Esker, spokesman for the hospital's commander Maj. Gen. Robert Bernstein. I repeated Fred Hoffman's query to Esker. "What's the story, Pete?"

"Look," he replied, "when we treated the pneumonia we found a growth in one of Abe's lungs. But we can't say anything about it."

"Why?" I asked. "Don't the American people have a right to know that the Army chief of staff is undergoing radiation treatment for lung cancer?"

"No," he replied in a firm manner, "because Mrs. Abrams won't admit that Abe has cancer. She's instructed me to withhold the information." Mrs. Abrams, the former Julia Harvey, known as Julie to her many friends and acquaintances, mother of the couple's six sons and daughters, was the no-nonsense leader of the clan. It was said that while Abe wore four stars, Mrs. Abe wore five. There was no way that General Bernstein or anyone in the news-dissemination pipeline was going to buck Julie Abrams.

And so we carried the fiction of Abe's "pneumonia" through the summer months of 1974. There were, of course, other major news stories taking place in the summer of '74 that riveted much of the American public. For example, for the first time in American history a sitting president—Richard Milhous Nixon—was being forced to resign his office rather than face certain impeachment by the House of Representatives and conviction by the Senate.

Which also meant that on August 9, 1974, Richard Nixon would be replaced as president and commander in chief of America's armed forces by Gerald R. Ford, who had never won a national election to any office and instead had only been elected to the House of Representatives for the past twenty-four years by the good people of Michigan's 5th Congressional District in and around Grand Rapids. (See Chapter 9 for additional details.)

And which further meant that on September 8, 1974—one month after Ford's becoming an unelected president, four days after General Abrams's death, two days after Abe's burial in Section 21 of Arlington National Cemetery—Ford would issue a full and unconditional pardon to Richard Nixon in a heroic effort to begin our nation's healing process and bring an end to what he had termed in his inauguration address "our long national nightmare." Ford's pardoning of Nixon profoundly upset many Americans and may very well have cost him election to the presidency in 1976. Instead, former Georgia governor and Annapolis graduate Jimmy Carter was elected as our 39th president and ended up doing grievous harm to America's military capabilities before being voted out of office four years later. ("Be that as it may," Lyman Duryea points out, "I began six and a half years of back-to-back service in Panama, Haïti, and El Salvador in 1979. President Carter's emphasis on human rights saved thousands of Latin American civilians from beatings, torture, and just plain disappearing, never to be accounted for. He was effective in his politically costly but ethical insistence on respect for human rights. Latin American officers tended to detest him. He had the courage to employ significant political capital to preserve life.")

During World War II, while commanding his famed 37th Tank Battalion, Lt. Col. "Abe" Abrams was frequently out on point for Lt. Gen. George Patton's Third U.S. Army. It was Abe and his 37th that helped break through the Wehrmacht's siege of Bastogne, thereby freeing the 101st Airborne Division from the German encirclement of the Belgian village at the Christmas 1944 Battle of the Bulge.

Months earlier, during the 1944 Rhineland campaign, Abe was a mere lieutenant colonel sitting in on a meeting of more senior officers on the western bank of the Moselle River as differing strategies were being debated for attacking into the heart of the Third Reich. Pointing eastward with his ever-present cigar, Abe thereupon proclaimed to superiors and peers alike, "*That* is the shortest way home." In other words, drive directly east toward Berlin. The very next day, Task Force Abe, with Abrams riding in his Sherman tank named Thunderbolt, led the thrust across the Moselle and into the heart of Germany.

Time magazine called Abe's 37th Tank Battalion "a fearsome weapon of destruction" and said of its commander, he "showed the feel and flair of the born combat man."

Abe usually rode in Thunderbolt (numbered sequentially I through VI, all worn out during the war, not one ever shot out from under him) at the head of his tank column, standing in the turret and chewing on a large cigar. As reported by *The New York Times*, "The retreating Germans were said to be fascinated and terrified by Colonel Abrams because they assumed from his name that he was Jewish and that he saw himself as a wrathful Jehovah taking destructive vengeance on the Germans for what they had done to the Jewish people." (In point of fact, Abe was descended from a long line of Massachusetts Methodists and while in Vietnam converted to Roman Catholicism.)

As Pentagon-based deputy chief of operations in 1962, Maj. Gen. Abrams was dispatched that September to Oxford, Mississippi, where a twenty-nine-year-old black Air Force veteran named James Meredith—inspired by civil-rights programs and speeches of President John F. Kennedy—sought to become the first person of color to enroll at Ole Miss.

Mississippi governor Ross Barnett, however, felt otherwise. In a statewide televised address, Barnett pledged that Mississippi "will not surrender to the evil and illegal forces of tyranny . . . no school will be integrated in Mississippi while I am your governor." Later, Barnett termed Meredith's attempt at enrollment "our greatest crisis since the War Between the States."

Backed up by the 79th Engineer Battalion from Fort Campbell, Kentucky—home of the 101st Airborne Division he had helped liberate at Bastogne—and a force of 538 U.S. marshals and Border Patrol agents sent to

Oxford by Attorney General Robert F. Kennedy—Abrams was repeatedly being badgered by the brothers Kennedy, to whom he reported directly, for all-too-frequent on-the-spot telephone reports.

Getting the job of peacefully integrating the university done with tact, diplomacy and a goodly measure of toughness and resolve, Abrams informed the Kennedy boys that if they'd just get off the blooming phone and let him do his job, everything would proceed a wee bit more smoothly.

Properly chastised, the president and attorney general retreated. James Meredith was successfully enrolled at Ole Miss, following which the pattern of our nation's higher education system—in the Deep South and elsewhere—was irrevocably changed for the better.

Creighton Abrams spent a total of five consecutive years at MACV head-quarters in Vietnam, initially serving one year as Westmoreland's deputy COMUSMACV and then assuming command when Westmoreland rotated home three months after Tet '68 to become Army chief of staff.

It's interesting to note that while Westmoreland did his utmost to turn America's involvement in Vietnam into a classic World War II-type confronta-tion between the United States versus a multinational communist alliance, far more nations were allied with us in Vietnam than has generally been perceived. The Army's official *Vietnam Studies: Allied Participation in Vietnam* (May 1974) notes the following in its preface:

> *More than forty nations provided assistance to the Republic of Vietnam in its struggle against North Vietnam. This aid ranged from economic and technical assistance to educa-tional and humanitarian contributions. Hundreds of Free World civilians worked in Viet-nam as doctors, teachers, and technical specialists. Eight nations also provided military assistance. The flags of these Free World countries—the United States, the Republic of Korea, Thailand, Australia, New Zealand, the Philippines, the Republic of China, and Spain—flew alongside the colors of the Republic of Vietnam at the headquarters of the Free World Military Assistance Forces in Saigon. The military contributions of these nations included combat troops, army medical teams, and individual political warfare advisors.*

So even as William Westmoreland was determined to maximize the role of U.S. forces under his command, simultaneously back-benching participa-tion by our allies (such as continually finding reasons to postpone the issuance of M16 rifles to ARVN forces—see Chapter 11), the United States wasn't alone in the struggle to keep South Vietnam free.

South Korea, as an example, committed a total of 313,000 combatants during the war, with no more than 50,000 serving in Vietnam at any given time. The two ROK (Republic of Korea) divisions, such as the feared Capital "Tiger" Division and the 9th "White Horse" Division, along with the 2nd Marine "Blue Dragon" Brigade, took a back seat to no one in their combativeness, going to extremes on more than one occasion and later being investigated for possible atrocities. The NVA and VC were scared to death (quite literally) of engaging in combat with the dreaded ROK soldiers and Marines.

When Lt. Gen. Chae Myung-shin, the first commander of ROK forces in Vietnam (in effect a corps commander), rotated home to Seoul in mid-1967, U.S. Brig. Gen. Robert L. Ashworth, a keen student of history, presented Chae with the obligatory going-home medal for senior officers, noting at the award ceremony, "General Chae, in 5,000 years of Korean history, you are the first commander of Korean forces outside your own country's borders." Chae, an excellent speaker of English, nodded in modest agreement at the significance of the occasion.

In other words, for fifty centuries Korea's military had been forced to fight against aggressors invading its homeland. But now, in the 1960s and 1970s, Korea—with the United States picking up the tab, to be sure—was capable of playing an emerging role on the world stage. Anyone who has purchased a television set, computer, refrigerator, washing machine, or perhaps an automobile in the past half-century is certainly very much aware of the economic powerhouse that's risen along the banks of the Han River in Seoul.

Australia committed more than 60,000 troops to the battle, in increments of 8,000 at a time. The Aussies sent infantry, airborne, special forces personnel, medics, helicopters, as well as a squadron of B-57 Canberra bombers that compiled an enviable flying record in combat operations.

The 3,500 New Zealanders who served in Vietnam manned artillery batteries and functioned as combat engineers. Thailand (one of the "dominos" that Dwight Eisenhower referenced; see chapter 1), which had also sent soldiers to the Korean War, dispatched its Queen's Cobra Battalion to assist in the effort in Vietnam. Taiwan sent transport aircraft and a hush-hush contingent of special forces operatives. The 10,000 Filipino personnel in Vietnam were largely for medical and logistical support. Canada, unable to officially send troops, manufactured uniforms. An estimated one hundred Canadians, fighting as members of U.S. units, were KIA in Vietnam.

Spain, which had sought membership in NATO for a number of years before finally joining the Western Alliance in 1982, sent a small medical team to Vietnam, thereby participating in the mutual defense of an endangered sovereign nation, South Vietnam.

On my first night in Vietnam, billeted overnight at Saigon's Majestic Hotel while my ultimate unit of assignment was being hashed out, I spotted a large, white ship berthed in the Saigon River not far from the hotel. I went over and asked about it. A man in a white uniform, speaking with a German accent, leaned over the ship's railing, pointed to a large red cross I hadn't yet noticed, and said, "We are Helgoland, hospital ship, West Germany." I later learned that the Helgoland carried a complement of ten doctors and thirty nurses, all dedicated to treating wounded Vietnamese civilians from both sides of the conflict, using berths in Saigon and Da Nang. Vietnamese called the Helgoland "the white ship of hope."

So while historians and assorted academics continue to perpetuate the myth that the conflict in Vietnam was a war waged solely by the United States to protect its neocolonial interests in Southeast Asia, the facts are that forty other nations joined with us in some show of support—large or small—to help protect and preserve the independence of South Vietnam. Had Lyndon Johnson, Robert McNamara, and William Westmoreland fought what historian Lewis Sorley called *A Better War* in his perceptive 1999 study, who can judge how the war's ill-fated outcome might have been averted?

Creighton Abrams was fully aware that his West Point classmate (Class of 1936) had botched things in Vietnam badly, as he confided to CBS's Walter Cronkite and his producer Ernest Leiser at an informal post-Tet dinner meeting in 1968 near Saigon (Chapter 9). Abrams was still assigned as Westmoreland's deputy at MACV headquarters, even though the change of command had been slated for some months earlier.

Abrams had arrived in Vietnam in May 1967 with expectations that he would succeed Westmoreland in a matter of weeks. But in fact the delay lasted a full year, with Westmoreland rotating home in June 1968 to become Army chief of staff in ceremonies held July 3 on the Pentagon Mall.

A number of explanations for the delay have been set forth—none conclusive—and include: a perception by some in the American news media that Westmoreland was being penalized for having failed to anticipate the January–February 1968 Tet Offensive; a *Time* magazine report that he was a potential Republican candidate for the presidency in November 1968 and therefore posed a threat to Lyndon Johnson's reelection and was best kept at bay 12,000 miles away; that he was being punished by Secretary McNamara for inefficient use of American troops; because of widely reported differences of opinion between McNamara and Westmoreland, that a change of command in 1967 could have been construed as a "slap" at Westmoreland, said widely circulated columnist Jack Anderson, and therefore had to be delayed until 1968.

No one seems to know for certain why Westmoreland was kept in Vietnam for four-and-a-half years, but there was a sense of relief among many that the time for a change in tactics and overall strategy was long overdue: As Melvin Laird, who served as secretary of defense in Richard Nixon's first term as president put it, Westmoreland had "Americanized" the war. "We had not been giving the Vietnamese the tools to do the job. We had been doing the job for them."

Laird, a highly influential former congressman from Wisconsin who had served as a junior officer on the destroyer USS *Maddox* in the Pacific and who was wounded in action near the end of World War II, had been the Republican Party's point man in persuading scandal-ridden Vice President Spiro Agnew to resign in 1973. Laird also played a key role in the decision to select Gerald Ford as Agnew's replacement, thereby positioning Ford to become president when Nixon resigned in August 1974. Laird was a staunch critic of McNamara's management style and decision-making.

Among the "tools to do the job" that Laird felt the South Vietnamese military had been denied, the M16 rifle ranks at or very near the top of the list. "No single factor more definitively illustrates Westmoreland's neglect of the South Vietnamese armed forces than the M-16 rifle, wrote historian Lewis Sorley in his 2011 study *Westmoreland: The General Who Lost Vietnam.*

Chapter 11, "Why Not the ARVN?" provides important on-the-ground insights into how South Vietnamese fighting forces were hamstrung by their reliance on World War II-era rifles and carbines that were no match for the enemy's AK47 assault rifle.

A month after arriving in Vietnam as Westmoreland's deputy (but anticipating that he'd assume command of MACV in short order, which didn't happen until a year later), Creighton Abrams cabled Army chief of staff Gen. Harold K. Johnson with these observations: "It is quite clear to me," he wrote, "that the U.S. military here and at home have thought largely in terms of U.S. operations and support of U.S. forces." "The ARVN," Abrams added, "are left to the advisors" (i.e., left to fend pretty much for themselves with the inadequate weaponry and equipment they've been issued by their advisors).

"I fully appreciate," Abrams added in his message to Harold Johnson, "that I have been as guilty as anyone," an apparent reference to Abe's tenure as the Army's vice chief of staff before his assignment to MACV, since he'd been in Vietnam only a few weeks. "The result has been that shortages of essential equipment or supplies to an already austere organization (the

ARVN) has [*sic*] not been handled with the urgency and vigor that characterize what we do for U.S. needs. Yet the responsibility we bear to ARVN is clear."

The lack of "urgency and vigor" in arming and equipping the ARVN is most likely Abrams's polite, tactful way of criticizing Westmoreland, his West Point classmate, for the misguided priorities established by Westmoreland in waging the Vietnam War. As noted by Sorley in his book, Westmoreland consistently refused to acknowledge his failures to equip the ARVN, instead making excuses and blaming everyone but himself.

As Sorley writes, "Given Westmoreland's single-minded focus on the main force war and on his personal conduct of it using American units, it apparently never occurred to him that the wiser course of action would have been to give all the good modern gear to the South Vietnamese first, then to U.S. units if there was any left over."

Once Abrams was in the driver's seat as COMUSMACV, beginning June 10, 1968, he was able to re-structure his predecessor's priorities. "Vietnamization" became the order of the day for Abrams, along with the entire Nixon administration in a doomed, belated effort to win back the hearts and minds of the American public.

Given the surprise element of the enemy's Tet Offensive in late January and February 1968, and supported by Walter Cronkite's February 27 "Report from Vietnam" on CBS television viewed by an estimated 20 million Americans, it's small wonder that a phased U.S. withdrawal from the battlefield was inevitable. And finally the RVNAF (Republic of Vietnam Armed Forces) would at last be issued the equipment they should have had all along— including, very importantly, the M16 rifle—and would thereupon be left to their own devices as America turned its back on the fate of the South Vietnamese people and allowed them to be overrun by their enemies from the North.

As explained in Chapter 11, the decision to equip the ARVN with a small-arms weapon that—modified, improved, and firing its specified ammunition—could more than hold its own against the enemy's AK47 came perhaps five years too late.

By 1968 there was no longer any light at the end of the tunnel. And 58,300 of America's finest young men would surrender their lives in a well-intentioned military campaign that was totally consistent with U.S. foreign policy of the post-World War II era, but which suffered from appalling decision-making by the military and civilian leadership that brought about the quagmire that became the war in South Vietnam.

A modern folk song popular in the 1960s sums it up better than many historians. Part of the song goes:

> *Where have all the soldiers gone,*
> *Long time passing,*
> *Where have all the soldiers gone,*
> *Long time ago,*
> *Where have all the soldiers gone,*
> > *Gone to graveyards, everyone.*
> > *When will they ever learn?*
> > *When will they ever learn?*

—From "Where Have All the Flowers Gone?" by Pete Seeger and Joe Hickerson. Recorded in 1961 by The Kingston Trio; in 1962 by Peter, Paul, and Mary; and later by numerous other recording artists

AFTERWORD

The chain of events that brought this book's co-authors together began in Rockford, Illinois, in the early 1960s.

Capt. Robert E. Orkand, having completed the Infantry Officers Career Course at Fort Benning in 1962, was reassigned to Rockford as professor of military science at the two Rockford high schools.

During this period along came Robert S. McNamara. Yes, the same man who ineffectively micromanaged the Vietnam War and other challenges of the Cold War came along in 1963. In one of his short-sighted cost-cutting decisions (see earlier chapters), McNamara decided to eliminate the Junior ROTC programs in high schools nationwide, on grounds that they produced no commissioned officers (as college and university ROTC programs did) and that the officers and NCOs assigned to high schools could be utilized more productively elsewhere. (Vietnam was not yet in McNamara's gunsights, except perhaps for the Green Beret Special Forces advisors quietly being committed to Southeast Asia by President Kennedy.)

The SecDef's Pentagon penny-pinchers took no notice of the fact that by providing discipline and structure to the lives of American sixteen- and seventeen-year-olds, JROTC was helping stimulate patriotism, motivation, and purpose to thousands of teenagers across our fair land, helping to cut down on delinquency, dropouts, and school absenteeism. Accordingly, civic leaders and educators nationwide bombarded their senators and congressmen with protests against McNamara's action, resulting in the ROTC Revitalization Act of 1964, which expanded both senior and junior ROTC programs.

The executive officer of the cadet battalion that year was a medium-height, fair-haired young man with a very military crew cut. His name was Vernon Miller, he was one of the sharpest cadets we had, and because of Vern Miller you're able to read and digest this book.

After Vern graduated from West High and I moved on to assignments first in West Berlin and then to Vietnam, we lost contact with one another. But in early 2017, after my name had appeared in the 1st Cavalry Division newspaper in a listing of people who had renewed their memberships in the 1st Cav Association, a letter arrived in my mail one day in Huntsville, Texas, from an address in Wisconsin. Vern Miller, retired from the VA in Milwaukee, had spotted my name in the yellow newsprint of the Cav newspaper, tracked me down through the Internet, and decided to tell his old PMS that he too had spent time in Vietnam with the famed 1st Cavalry Division (Airmobile).

In phone calls and even a personal visit that Vern made to Huntsville, I told him that I had a commitment from Stackpole Books to publish a book about our problems in Vietnam with the M16 rifle, and that a weapons expert I was hoping to call upon as co-author had recently backed out. Vern had a solution.

Vern had served in Vietnam under Capt. Lyman Duryea in a rifle squad in 1966–1967 with Company C, 2nd Battalion (Airmobile), 7th Cavalry before leaving the Army as a Specialist 4. He then related how Captain Duryea, prior to his two tours of duty in Vietnam, had participated as a test officer at Fort Benning involving comparisons between the M14 and XM16E1 rifles.

The 2/7 Cav, where Miller and Duryea served, was the sister battalion of the one with which I had spent time in 1967–1968, the 1st Battalion (Airmobile), 7th Cavalry. Both battalions, of course, are lineal descendants of the Seventh U.S. Cavalry Regiment that Lt. Col. George Armstrong Custer led into ill-considered hostilities at the Battle of the Little Bighorn in June 1876 in the Montana Territory. The 7th Cavalry, like most of the 1st Cavalry Division (Airmobile), was usually first into the fighting and, in the process, sustained more casualties in Vietnam than any other Army division (see Introduction).

Vern gave me the address in McDaniels, Kentucky, where I could contact his old C.O., Col. (Ret.) Lyman Duryea. And so I did. I explained the book's concept, we exchanged ideas, had face-to-face meetings in Atlanta, Georgia, and in Killeen, Texas (where today's 1st Cavalry Division is headquartered at nearby Fort Hood), and have been in steady contact ever since, exchanging ideas and sharing drafts of the book's chapters. Chan's death just as this book was being finalized came as a shock to all of us who knew, worked with, and admired him.

Many thanks, Vern, for bringing Chan Duryea and me together for this project. And as the greeting goes among 7th Cavalry veterans ever since our famed leader led us into battle in 1876 with drums and bugles playing his favorite Irish dancing tune, "Garry Owen."

Bob Orkand

ACKNOWLEDGMENTS

The views expressed in this book are the authors'. Any errors or omissions are exclusively those of the authors. The technical data is now in the public domain, and the authors have employed information widely available on the Internet and elsewhere. This material includes the results of tests, reports, and investigations. The many published sources are listed in the Bibliography. Some of the opinions cited remain controversial to this day. The authors have attempted to sort through the available information to produce an accurate summation of the political, economic and technical factors that played such a significant role in the evolution of the AR15, the XM16E1, and the M16A1, specifically accounting for shortfalls in professional leadership and management where applicable. These same factors played a role in the conduct and outcome of the Vietnam War itself.

ORKAND'S ACKNOWLEDGMENTS

First and foremost, "Garry Owen" to Vernon Miller, a rifleman in Capt. Lyman Duryea's airmobile infantry company in Vietnam, and an ROTC cadet in Rockford, Illinois, while Capt. Bob Orkand was professor of military science there. Vern was the linkage that brought two retired Army officers together—Orkand in Texas, Duryea in Kentucky—to collaborate on this book.

My brother, Dr. Donald S. Orkand, PhD, founder and CEO of The Orkand Corporation in 1970 and previously vice president of the Management

Systems Division of Operations Research Inc., was an early proponent of operations research/systems analysis and worked with a number of the McNamara "whiz kids" in the Pentagon. He is a co-founder of DC Ventures and Associates, providing counsel to senior management on information technology mergers and acquisitions. His advice and guidance on multiple occasions helped steer me in the right direction as I drafted chapters about decision-making on the M16 rifle and other weapons systems.

My wife, Belinda J. Orkand, an online teacher of sixth-grade math, has a degree in information technology. Every time my mulish old word-processing computer decided to act up on me, Belinda gave it a rap on the nose and somehow persuaded it to get me where I needed to go.

Dr. Erik Villard of the U.S. Army Center of Military History, one of the world's leading experts on the Tet Offensive and author of the 2017 book, Staying the Course, about combat operations in Vietnam in 1967–68, provided a number of M16-in-action photos from his archives.

Two of my close friends and associates here in Huntsville, Texas—John Lindon and Gerald Crabbe—are highly knowledgeable about weaponry and assisted me in my research.

I'm a firm believer in Wikipedia as a reference source, and I send them a few dollars each time they ask me for financial support. Although it's fashionable in some academic circles to belittle the site as unreliable and unsubstantiated, I've never found this to be the case, and it's the quickest and most convenient reference I know of to locate information I'm looking for on a timely basis.

Lastly, I'd be remiss if I failed to acknowledge the role of my partner in this enterprise, Col. (Ret.) Lyman ("Chan") Duryea. What a resource! Chan participated as a test officer at Fort Benning from 1964–1966 when the XM16E1 rifle was being evaluated and later sustained casualties as a company commander in Vietnam when M16s jammed. His knowledge and experience have proven to be invaluable in the development of this book. Chan's death from a virulent form of cancer while production of this book was in its final stages left all of us—family, friends, fellow veterans, West Point classmates, and his co-author—poorer for his loss, richer because we knew him.

DURYEA'S ACKNOWLEDGMENTS

I would like to specifically thank the following 1st Cavalry Division veterans who responded to our request for firsthand experiences with the rifle when in contact with the enemy in Vietnam as well as training experiences and incidents in the States: Robert Towles, David Southall, Paul Stroessner, Dan Brodt, Mike N. Mantegna, Mike J. Handley, Robin Bartlett, Juan C. Gonzales, Bruce E. Croel, Glen H. Sheathelm, Vern Miller, Rob Weeks, Bruce Thatcher, and Joe Muni Jr.

I would like particularly to thank Richard Hockett for his invaluable organizational, editorial, and technical assistance and Patricia Webster for her careful proofreading of the draft.

NOTES

CHAPTER 2

1. Peoples' Army of Vietnam, the North Vietnamese Army, PAVN was the acronym in use by American troops in 1965 and early 1966. It was apparently perceived to be an inappropriate term to describe the North Vietnamese Army and gradually the term "NVA" came into common use.

2. Robert Towles, Delta Company. 2nd Battalion, 7th Cavalry. The action was during the first day of the battle in the Ia Drang Valley. Bob's malfunction problem was the failure to eject, the most frequent malfunction, which necessitated removal of the spent cartridge case from the breech, usually manually or if lucky, by shaking it loose. This malfunction is second in severity only to the failure to extract. Note here that Bob used the forward assist device which some firearms specialists assert as superfluous.

3. Dick Culver, "The Saga of the M16 in Vietnam (Part 1)," (n.d., Internet), 5.

4. Dick Culver, "The Saga of the M16 in Vietnam (Part 2)," (n.d., Internet), 15.

5. Ralph E. Haines, *Report of the M16 Rifle Review Panel: History of the M16 Weapon System* (Washington, DC: Office Chief of Staff, Office of Weapon Systems Analysis, 1968).

6. James Fallows, "M-16: A Bureaucratic Horror Story," *The Atlantic*, June 1981, Internet.

7. Gordon L. Rottman, *The M16* (Oxford, Long Island City: Osprey Publishing Ltd., 2011), 6.

8. Reynel Martinez, *Six Silent Men* (New York: The Random House Publishing Group, 1997), 191.

CHAPTER 3

1. Robert Fisk, "For Patriotism and Profit," *World Press Review*, 48, no. 7 (July 2001).

2. David Southall, First Infantry Division, Vietnam, 1966–1967.

3. Edward C. Ezell and Blake R. Stevens, *The Black Rifle: M16 Retrospective* (Ontario: Collector Grade Publications Incorporated, 1992, 2015), 7.

4. Ezell and Stevens, *The Black Rifle,* 9.

5. Richard Ichord, *Report of the Special Subcommittee on the M16 Rifle Program of the Committee on Armed Services House of Representatives* (Washington, DC: 1967).

6. C. J. Chivers, *The Gun* (New York: Simon and Schuster, 2010), 274.

7. Holcomb B. Noble, "Eugene Stoner, 74, Designer of M-16 Rifle and Other Arms," *New York Times,* April 17, 1997.

8. James Fallows, "M-16: A Bureaucratic Horror Story," *The Atlantic* (June 1981, Internet).

9. Dick Culver, "The Saga of the M16 in Vietnam (Part 2)," (n.d., Internet), 14–16.

10. S. L. A. Marshall, *Vietnam: Three Battles* (New York: Da Capo Press, Inc., 1971), 119.

11. F. Nathaniel, "Jim Sullivan on the M16 in Vietnam (and Commentary by Daniel Watters)," *TFB (The Firearm Blog),* in *Other Gear & Gadgets* section, January 9, 2015.

12. Nathaniel, "Jim Sullivan on the M16," 54.

13. Nathaniel, "Jim Sullivan on the M16," 56.

14. Ezell and Stevens, *The Black Rifle,* 76–77.

15. Ezell and Stevens, *The Black Rifle,* 71–72.

16. Ezell and Stevens, *The Black Rifle,* 74.

17. Ezell and Stevens, *The Black Rifle,* 74.

18. Ezell and Stevens, *The Black Rifle,* 75.

19. Fallows, "M16" (Internet).

20. Ezell and Stevens, *The Black Rifle,* 87.

21. Ezell and Stevens, *The Black Rifle,* 104.

22. Ezell and Stevens, *The Black Rifle,* 97.

23. Ezell and Stevens, *The Black Rifle,* 79.

24. Chivers, *The Gun,* 285.

25. Ezell and Stevens, *The Black Rifle,* 116.

26. O. P. Bruno, Technical Report No. 1; *M16 Rifle System Reliability and Quality Assurance Evaluation* Aberdeen Proving Ground, Maryland: Aberdeen Research and Development Center (1968), 45–50. This report intentionally avoids casting blame, but the negligence is clear.

27. Ezell and Stevens, *The Black Rifle,* 116.

28. Ezell and Stevens, *The Black Rifle,* 125.

29. Fallows, "M16" (Internet), 14–15.

30. Ezell and Stevens, *The Black Rifle,* 219.

31. Ezell and Stevens, *The Black Rifle,* 148.

32. Fallows, "M16" (Internet).

33. Ezell and Stevens, *The Black Rifle,* 197.

CHAPTER 4

1. Paul Stroessner, Alpha Company, 2nd Battalion, 7th Cavalry. Note the question of whether or not the armorer was authorized to advise him of a mechanical problem with his rifle.

2. Earl D. Robert, USATECOM Project No 8-5-0400-04, Small Arms Weapons System (SAWS), USAIB Project No 3110, Final Report of Service Test (Fort Benning: United States Army Infantry Board, 1965).

3. Robert, *USATECOM Project No 8-5-0400-04,* 199–200.

4. Robert, *USATECOM Project No 8-5-0400-04,* 7–8.

5. Robert, *USATECOM Project No 8-5-0400-04*, iv.

6. Lyman C. Duryea, *The Effect of Duplex Ammunition on Small Unit Firepower* (Fort Leavenworth, KS: The U.S. Army Command and General Staff College, 1974).

7. Robert, *USATECOM Project No 8-5-0400-04*, 205.

8. Robert, *USATECOM Project No 8-5-0400-04*, 226.

9. The steps in the current Army Immediate Action Drill for the M16 family of weapons are: 1—Confirm that the selector is set to semi, auto, or burst. 2—Slap upward on the magazine to make sure it is properly seated. 3—Pull the charging handle completely to the rear and hold. 4—Observe for ejection of case or cartridge, and ensure the cartridge or case is ejected and the chamber is clear. 5—Release the charging handle to feed a new round. 6—Tap the forward assist to ensure the bolt is closed. 7—Squeeze the trigger; the weapon should fire.

10. Robert, *USATECOM Project No 8-5-0400-04*, 192.

11. Robert, *USATECOM Project No 8-5-0400-04*, 197.

12. Chivers, *The Gun*, citing a letter from a Marine to his family, May 17, 1967, 315.

13. Chivers, *The Gun*, 201.

CHAPTER 5

1. Mike Handley, Alpha Company, 5th Battalion, 7th Cavalry Regiment, 1st Air Cavalry Division, Vietnam, August 1966–August 1967.

2. Vern Humphrey, Infantry Adviser, Vietnam 1966–1967; AIT Company Commander, Fort Polk, Louisiana, 1967–1968; Company Commander, Vietnam, Alpha Company, 1st Battalion, 61st Infantry 1968–1969.

3. Rear Echelon Mother F . . .

4. Ezell and Stevens, *The Black Rifle*, 215, 226.

5. Ezell and Stevens, *The Black Rifle*, 215, 226.

6. Dick Culver, "The Saga of the M16 in Vietnam (Part 1)": (n.d., Internet), 6.

CHAPTER 6

1. Dan P. Brodt, Long Range Reconnaissance Patrol Team, 1st Battalion, 7th Cavalry, 1st Cavalry Division, Air Mobile (1967–1968).

2. Mike Mantegna, 2nd Battalion, 7th Cavalry, 1st Cavalry Division, Air Mobile (1965–1966).

3. Edward F. Murphy, *The Hill Fights: The First Battle of Khe Sanh* (New York: Random House Publishing Group, 2003), 56.

4. Reynel Martinez, *Six Silent Men* (New York: Random House Publishing Group, 1997), 320.

5. Richard H. Ichord, *Report of the Special Subcommittee on the M16 Rifle Program of the Committee on Armed Services House of Representatives* (Washington, DC: U.S. Government Printing Office, 1967).

6. Mantegna.

7. Mantegna.

8. Dick Culver, "The Saga of the M16 in Vietnam (Part 2): (n.d., Internet), 9.

9. Ichord, *Report of the Special Subcommittee on the M16 Rifle Program*, n.p.

10. Ichord, *Report of the Special Subcommittee on the M16 Rifle Program*, n.p.

11. Earl D. Robert, Ray E. Ball, Benjamin E. Dishman, Lyman C. Duryea, William M. Knauer, Bruce G. LeBeda, *USATECOM Project No 8-5-0400-04, Small Arms Weapons System (SAWS), USAIB Project No 3110, Final Report of Service Test* (Fort Benning: United States Army Infantry Board, 1965).

12. Ezell and Stevens, *The Black Rifle*, 148.

13. Ezell and Stevens, *The Black Rifle*, 265–66.

14. Ezell and Stevens, *The Black Rifle*, 265–66.

15. Joseph E. Smith, *Small Arms of the World*, 10th Revised Edition (Harrisburg: Stackpole Books, 1973), 651.

16. Christopher R. Bartocci, "The M16 in Vietnam," *Small Arms Review*, no. V9N5 (2006).

17. Gordon L. Rottman, *The M16* (Oxford: Osprey Publishing, 2011), 22.

18. O. P. Bruno, *Technical Report No 1: M16 Rifle System Reliability and Quality Assurance Evaluation* (Aberdeen Proving Ground, Maryland: Aberdeen Research and Development Center, 1968), 45.

19. Ezell and Stevens, *The Black Rifle*, 223.

20. Ezell and Stevens, *The Black Rifle*, 226.

21. Ezell and Stevens, *The Black Rifle*, 224.

22. Ezell and Stevens, *The Black Rifle*, 271.

23. Chivers, *The Gun* (citing Thomas L. McNaugher's *The M16 Controversies: Military Organizations and Weapons Acquisition*), 326.

24. Daniel E. Watters, "The Great 5.56mm Propellant Controversy," *LooseRounds*, n.d.: looserounds.com.

CHAPTER 11

1. Robin Bartlett. Alpha Company, 1st Battalion, 5th Cavalry Regiment, 1st Air Cavalry Division, Vietnam, May 1968–November 1968.

2. Stevens and Ezell, *The Black Rifle*, 196.

3. Stevens and Ezell, *The Black Rifle*, 190; 196–97.

4. Lewis Sorley, *Westmoreland: The General Who Lost Vietnam* (New York: Houghton Mifflin Harcourt, 2011), 132–33.

5. James Lawton Collins, *Vietnam Studies: Development and Training of the South Vietnamese Army, 1950–1972* (Washington, DC: Department of the Army, 1975), 101.

6. Dong Van Khuyen, *Indochina Monographs: RVNAF Logistics* (Washington, DC: U.S. Army Center of Military History, 1984), 57.

7. Sorley, *Westmoreland: The General Who Lost Vietnam*, 133.

8. Khuyen, *Indochina Monographs: RVNAF Logistics*, 57.

9. Collins, *Vietnam Studies*, 101.

10. Collins, *Vietnam Studies*, 75.

BIBLIOGRAPHY

Bartlett, Robin. Platoon Leader, Alpha Company, 1st Battalion, 5th Cavalry, 1st Cavalry Division (Airmobile), 1968.

Bartocci, Christopher R. "The M16 in Vietnam." *Small Arms Review*, no. V9N5. February 2006.

Boudreau, William H. *1st Cavalry Division: A Spur Ride Through the 20th Century "From Horses to the Digital Battlefield."* Paducah, Kentucky: Turner Publishing Company, 2002.

Brennan, Mathew. *Brennan's War: Vietnam 1965–1969*. New York: Pocket Books, 1985.

Brodt, Dan P. LRR Team, 1st Battalion, 7th Cavalry, 1st Cavalry Division (Airmobile), Vietnam, 1967–1968.

Bruno, O. P. *Technical Report No 1: M16 Rifle System Reliability and Quality Assurance Evaluation*. Aberdeen Proving Ground, Maryland: Aberdeen Research and Development Center, 1968.

Chivers, C. J. *The Gun*. New York: Simon & Schuster, 2010.

Collins, James Lawton, Jr. *Vietnam Studies: The Development and Training of the South Vietnamese Army, 1950–1972*. Washington, DC: Department of the Army, 1975.

Culver, Dick. "The Saga of the M16 in Vietnam (Part 1)." Internet. (n.d.).

Culver, Dick. "The Saga of the M16 in Vietnam (Part 2)." Internet. (n.d.).

Duryea, Lyman C. *The Effect of Duplex Ammunition on Small Unit Firepower*. Fort Leavenworth, Kansas: U.S. Army Command and General Staff College, 1974.

Ezell, Edward C., and Blake R. Stevens. *The Black Rifle: M16 Retrospective*. Ontario: Collector Grade Publications Incorporated, 1992; 2015.

Fallows, James. "M-16: A Bureaucratic Horror Story." *The Atlantic* (June 1981): Internet.

Fisk, Robert. "For Patriotism and Profit." *World Press Review* 48, no. 7 (July 2001): Internet.

Gwin, Larry. *Baptism: A Vietnam Memoir*. New York: Ivy Books, 1999.

Haines, Ralph E. *Report of the M16 Rifle Review Panel: History of the M16 Weapon System*. Washington, DC: Office Chief of Staff, Office of Weapon Systems Analysis, 1968.

Handley, Mike. Alpha Company, 5th Battalion, 7th Cavalry, 1st Air Cavalry Division, August 1966–August 1967.

Humphrey, Vern. Infantry Adviser, Vietnam, 1966–1967; Advanced Individual Training Company Commander 1967–1968, Fort Polk, Louisiana; Rifle Company Commander, Vietnam, Alpha Company, 1st Battalion, 61st Infantry 1967–1968.

Ichord, Richard H. *Report of the Special Subcommittee on the M16 Rifle Program of the Committee on Armed Services House of Representatives.* Washington DC: U.S. Government Printing Office, 1967.

Kaufmann, William W. *The McNamara Strategy.* New York: Harper and Row, 1964.

Khuyen, Dong Van. *Indochina Monographs: RVNAF Logistics.* Washington, DC: U.S. Army Center of Military History, 1984.

Kinney, Charles M. *Borrowed Time: A Medic's View of the Vietnam War.* Victoria, BC: Trafford Publishing, 2003.

Mantegna, Mike. 2nd Battalion, 7th Cavalry, 1st Cavalry Division (Airmobile), Vietnam, 1965–1966.

Marshall, S. L. A. *Vietnam: Three Battles.* New York: Da Capo Press, Inc., 1971.

Martinez, Reynel. *Six Silent Men.* New York: Random House Publishing Group, 1997.

McMaster, H. R. *Dereliction of Duty.* New York: Harper Perennial, 1998.

McNamara, Robert S. *In Retrospect.* New York: Vintage Books, 1995.

Moore, Harold G., and Joseph L. Galloway. *We Were Soldiers Once . . . and Young.* New York: Random House, 1992.

Moore, Trey. "The XM16E1 Rifle." *LooseRounds* (October 21, 2014): looserounds.com.

Morgan, Martin K. A. "U.S. M16: A Half-Century of America's Combat Rifle," *American Rifleman.* Fairfax, Virginia: The National Rifle Association, July 2012.

Murphy, Edward F. *The Hill Fights.* New York: Random House Publishing Group, 2003.

Nathaniel, F. "Jim Sullivan on the M16 in Vietnam (and Commentary by Daniel Watters)." *TFB (The Firearm Blog), in Other Gear & Gadgets section* (January 9, 2015).

Noble, Holcomb B. "Eugene Stoner, 74, Designer of M-16 Rifle and Other Arms." *New York Times,* April 17, 1997.

Robert, Earl D.; Ray E. Ball; Benjamin E. Dishman; Lyman C. Duryea; William M. Knauer; and Bruce G. LeBeda. *USATECOM Project No 8-5-0400-04, Small Arms Weapons System (SAWS), USAIB Project No 3110, Final Report of Service Test.* Fort Benning: United States Army Infantry Board, 1965.

Rottman, Gordon L. *The M16.* Oxford: Osprey Publishing, Ltd., 2011.

Shea, Dan. "The Interview: James Sullivan Part 1." *Small Arms Review,* no. V11N6. 2008.

Smith, Joseph E. *Small Arms of the World,* 10th ed. Harrisburg: The Stackpole Company, 1973.

Sorley, Lewis. *Thunderbolt, General Creighton Abrams and the Army of His Times.* New York: Simon and Schuster, 1992.

Sorley, Lewis. *Westmoreland: The General Who Lost Vietnam.* New York: Houghton Mifflin Harcourt, 2011.

Southall, David. First Infantry Division, Vietnam, 1966–1967.

Stroessner, Paul. 2nd Battalion, 7th Cavalry, 1st Cavalry Division (Airmobile), Vietnam, July 1966–1967.

Towles, Robert. Delta Company, 2nd Battalion, 7th Cavalry, 1st Cavalry Division (Airmobile), Vietnam, November 17, 1965.

Ward, Geoffrey C. and Ken Burns. *The Vietnam War*. New York: Alfred A. Knopf, 2017.

Waters, Daniel E. "The Great 5.56mm Propellant Controversy," *LooseRounds*. (n.d.): looserounds.com.

Wikipedia. *M16 Rifle*.

INDEX

ABOUT THE AUTHORS

Colonel (U.S. Army, Infantry, Ret.) Lyman "Chan" Duryea passed away on April 17, 2019, while this book was in its final stages of production, the result of a swift, aggressive cancer. He would have observed his eighty-first birthday the following month. He was a test officer with the U.S. Army Infantry Board at Fort Benning, Georgia, from 1964–1966 when the XM16E1 rifle was being evaluated as a possible replacement for the Army's then-standard M14 rifle.

As a newly promoted captain, he wrote reports that analyzed test results and also maintained detailed records on weapon maintenance and malfunctions in a testing environment that simulated tactical conditions in which the XM16E1 and its 5.56mm ammunition would be employed. This included night firing tests, night parachute jumps, evaluation of the 5.56mm tracer round, etc.

"We attempted to construct tactical conditions," said Col. Duryea, "that were representative of how the weapon and ammunition would be employed. I was present and responsible for—I cannot even guess—how many hours on the range or how many millions of rounds were fired."

During his twenty-nine years of active duty, Col. Duryea—a graduate of West Point, the Command and General Staff College, and the Army War College—commanded a rifle company of the 2nd Battalion, 7th Cavalry, 1st Cavalry Division (Airmobile) in 1966–67. On his second Vietnam tour (1968–69), he served as a district senior advisor in the Mekong Delta.

Upon return from his second tour in Vietnam, Col. Duryea, as a French linguist, served with the Congo Military Mission as its plans and programs officer.

His master's degree thesis at the Command and General Staff College compared the M16 rifle with the 7.62mm family of weapons. He has another master of arts degree in modern languages from Middlebury College, completed in Paris, France.

He taught French for three years at West Point, followed by three years on the staff and faculty of the School of the Americas in Panama. He was then posted to Port au Prince, Haïti, as defense and Army attaché, followed by an assignment as defense and an Army attaché in El Salvador during a period of active insurgency.

In his final active-duty assignment, Col. Duryea served on the faculty of the Army War College at Carlisle Barracks, Pennsylvania.

A soldier-scholar, Col. Duryea earned a doctor of philosophy degree in military history from Temple University following retirement from active duty.

Col. Duryea's 2003 translation of a book by French author Jacques-François de Chaunac, *The American Cavalry in Vietnam: "First Cav,"* outlined problems with the M16 rifle in notes accompanying the translated book.

He has been awarded the Combat Infantryman Badge and is both airborne and Ranger qualified. His personal awards include the Silver Star Medal for gallantry in action; Legion of Merit; Bronze Star Medal with "V" device for valor; Bronze Star Medal with oak leaf cluster for meritorious service; Defense Meritorious Service Medal; Meritorious Service Medal with oak leaf cluster; Air Medal with numeral "two"; Presidential Unit Citation, and more.

He lived in retirement in McDaniels, Kentucky, and was an active participant in outdoor sports: skiing, SCUBA, backpacking, and kayaking among others. He maintained a lifelong interest in revolutionary theory, military and classical history, languages, and science.

Bob Orkand, a retired U.S. Army lieutenant colonel of infantry, holds both the Combat Infantryman Badge and Expert Infantryman Badge.

As deputy director of the Weapons Department at the U.S. Army Infantry School in 1971, he led a team of marksmanship and small-arms experts sent from Fort Benning, Georgia, to Fort Lewis, Washington, to investigate why soldiers who had taken infantry basic combat training at Fort Lewis were shooting poorly in Vietnam with their M16 rifles. (The conclusion: faulty and inadequate training.)

Lt. Col. Orkand served in Vietnam in 1967–68 as executive officer and operations officer (simultaneously because of casualties) of the 1st Battalion (Airmobile), 7th Cavalry, a lead unit of the 1st Cavalry Division (Airmobile). The 1st Cav, with 5,444 of its soldiers killed in action and 26,592 wounded in action during the Vietnam War, sustained more casualties than any other U.S. Army unit, since its 428 helicopters enabled it to be airlifted on a moment's notice to battlefield hotspots.

On an earlier assignment in Vietnam, he was spokesman for the U.S. Army Headquarters Area Command in Saigon, which had responsibility for acts of terrorism in and around the South Vietnamese capital.

Drafted into the Army during his senior year at Columbia University, Lt. Col. Orkand was commissioned as an infantry second lieutenant from Officer Candidate School at Fort Benning. During his twenty years of active duty, in addition to Vietnam duty, he also served in Korea as a heavy mortar platoon leader with the 17th Infantry Regiment, and, in a subsequent Korean assignment, was aide-de-camp to the chief of staff of the Eighth U.S. Army in Seoul. At the height of the Cold War, he served on the staff of the U.S. Commander Berlin.

During an assignment as editor of *Infantry* magazine at Fort Benning, he edited and published a book, *A Distant Challenge: The U.S. Infantryman in Vietnam 1967–70.*

Lt. Col. Orkand was assigned as executive officer of the 197th Infantry Brigade at Fort Benning when the 5,000-man brigade was designated as the prototype unit for the Volunteer Army project. He later commanded the brigade's all-volunteer 1,000-man mechanized infantry battalion for eighteen months.

In his final active-duty assignment, he served in Washington DC, as spokesman for the secretary of the Army on the Volunteer Army project and was also the Pentagon spokesman in 1974 on the illness and death of Army Chief of Staff General Creighton W. Abrams.

His awards and decorations include the Combat Infantryman Badge; Expert Infantryman Badge; Bronze Star Medal (two awards); Air Medal; Meritorious Service Medal (three awards); Army Commendation Medal (two awards); Valorous Unit Citation; and more.

After retiring from active duty, he worked in management positions at the *Miami Herald, Detroit Free Press, Columbus* (Georgia) *Ledger-Enquirer,* and was president/publisher of the *Centre Daily Times* in State College, Pennsylvania.

He and his wife, Belinda (an online math teacher), live in Huntsville, Texas, where in recent years he taught English at Huntsville High School. They both meet weekly with offenders in a Huntsville prison as part of the Bridges to Life rehabilitation program.